AFTER THE SMOKE CLEARS

AFTER THE SMOKE CLEARS

The Just War Tradition and Post War Justice

Mark J. Allman & Tobias L. Winright

ORBIS BOOKS
Maryknoll, New York 10545

Founded in 1970, Orbis Books endeavors to publish works that enlighten the mind, nourish the spirit, and challenge the conscience. The publishing arm of the Maryknoll Fathers and Brothers, Orbis seeks to explore the global dimensions of the Christian faith and mission, to invite dialogue with diverse cultures and religious traditions, and to serve the cause of reconciliation and peace. The books published reflect the views of their authors and do not represent the official position of the Maryknoll Society. To learn more about Maryknoll and Orbis Books, please visit our website at www.maryknollsociety.org.

Library of Congress Cataloging-in-Publication Data

Allman, Mark.
    After the smoke clears : the just war tradition and post war justice /
    Mark J. Allman and Tobias L. Winright.
       p. cm.
    Includes bibliographical references and index.
    ISBN 978-1-57075-859-1 (pbk.)
    1. Just war doctrine. 2. Peace-building—Religious aspects—
Catholic Church. I. Winright, Tobias L. II. Title.
BX1795.W37A45 2010
261.8'73—dc22
                                                    2010010777

CONTENTS

PART 2
FOUR *JUS POST BELLUM* CRITERIA

ACKNOWLEDGMENTS

The two of us first met during our graduate school years, even though we did our doctorates in related fields, moral theology and Christian ethics, at two different universities, and our lives have intertwined ever since. We have even applied for the same jobs, and we used to teach at neighboring institutions in northeast Ohio. Our spouses and children have become friends, and we have tag-teamed as presenters in local settings and at national conferences.

This book is one of the fruits of our collaboration over the years. We initially presented the groundwork for this project as a paper, "*Jus Post Bellum*: Extending the Just War Theory," at the Annual Convention of the College Theology Society (CTS), held at the University of Dayton in June 2007. This, in turn, was included in the annual volume (no. 53) of the CTS, *Faith in Public Life*, edited by William J. Collinge and published by Orbis Books (2008). We are grateful to colleagues and friends who asked us some tough questions and who have generously offered their helpful suggestions along the way. In particular, we would like to thank Patrick Lynch, S.J., who convened the Justice and Peace section of the CTS, for his unflinching encouragement to both of us on this project and in our respective professional careers. Although surely busy enough as chairperson of the Department of Religious Studies and Theology at Canisius College, without fail Pat has gone the second mile for each of us and our work. Another colleague at CTS and the Society of Christian Ethics (SCE), J. Milburn Thompson, chairperson of the Department of Theology at Bellarmine University, has also provided us much constructive advice for our work. Of course, we are indebted to our editor at Orbis, Susan Perry, whom we first approached with our proposal for this book. Her enthusiasm for our work, her heroic patience, and her gentle nudging along the way will not be forgotten.

I (Mark Allman) am grateful for the many who have served as my teachers over the years and for those who have supported my education, scholarship, and career. In particular, I want to thank my students who have challenged me and taken an interest in my work; my colleagues at Merrimack College (Christina Condon; Ray Dlugos, OSA; Kevin Dwyer, OSA; Edward Enright, OSA; Warren Kay; Joseph Kelley; Anthony Laramie; Aldebran Longabaugh-Burg; Jacqueline MacLeod; Curtis Martin; Rebecca Norris; Padraic O'Hare; Charles Tontar; and James Wenzel, OSA) who have supported me with their insights and humor; the graduate faculty at Loyola University of Chicago; John C. Haughey, S.J., who mentored me in the field of Christian ethics; and Patti Jung and William French for their continued support and encouragement. I especially want to thank Tobias Winright, my coauthor and collaborator on many projects. Your intelligence, wit, and work ethic are inspiring. I am honored to be your friend.

I am also especially grateful for those who have taught me many of life's most valuable lessons in less formal settings: my mother and father, James and Jean Allman; my siblings (Joanne, Barbara, Karen, and Matthew) and their families; my extended family by marriage (Barbara, Lisa, Alice, Irene, and John) and their families; the "Holy Man," Rev. Joseph Cotugno; and of course my children, Ezekiel and Agnes, who teach me joy, wonder, and patience every day. To Emily, my wife and beloved companion, I dedicate this book. No one writes a book by themselves. Your generosity and support of these efforts is forever appreciated. You and our children are the greatest blessing in my life.

I (Tobias Winright) wish to express my gratitude to a number of people. For introducing me to the just war tradition when I was his undergraduate advisee in political science at the University of South Florida in St. Petersburg, I am thankful to the late Regis A. Factor. In graduate school I was fortunate to be able to study theological ethics, and in particular the morality of war and peace, with several professors, to whom I shall always be indebted: Harmon L. Smith and Stanley Hauerwas at Duke Divinity School, and John Howard Yoder, Richard A. McCormick, S.J., Todd David Whitmore, Jean Porter, Maura A. Ryan, and M.

Cathleen Kaveny at the University of Notre Dame. I especially miss Professor Yoder and Father McCormick, who were very wise and caring. Of course, I am very blessed to have as one of my best friends Mark J. Allman, whose exuberance, wit, and acumen add zest to my life and work. Another close friend for over two decades, Daniel M. Bell Jr., never fails to help me to think harder about the just war tradition and what it entails for Christians.

My undergraduate and graduate students who have taken my "War and Peace in the Christian Tradition" course over the years also have forced me to be honest and to try to do a better job in thinking and teaching about the tough questions and challenges we face today. I would be remiss if I did not mention my gratitude to my department chairperson, J. A. Wayne Hellmann, O.F.M. Conv., for his support for my work, and to St. Louis University for a Provost's Research Leave and a summer Mellon Research Grant, both of which helped me to write some of what is in this book. During the summer of 2009 I also benefited from being a Visiting Research Scholar at the Fondazione Bruno Kessler in Trent, Italy.

Finally, I dedicate this book to my wife, Elizabeth, and to our daughter, Clare, who have put up with my long hours of writing. They are my joy, my inspiration, and my life.

In his play *The Cure at Troy*, the Irish poet Seamus Heaney writes, "History says, Don't hope on this side of the grave. But then, once in a lifetime the longed-for tidal wave of justice can rise up, and hope and history rhyme." I pray that this book contributes in some way to the rhyming of hope and history for those in need of or those seeking to promote post war justice.

INTRODUCTION: JUST WAR AND JUST PEACE

"They led my people astray, saying, 'Peace!' when there was no peace."

—*Ezekiel 13:10*

Destruction, displacement, and death—these were the consequences of war in the prophet Ezekiel's time. As one of the exiles deported by Nebuchadnezzar in 597 B.C.E., Ezekiel predicted the devastation of Jerusalem. Even if their military defenses were successful in the past, Ezekiel admonished the people about their dangerous illusion of security—promoted by false prophets "saying 'Peace!' when there was no peace"—that underpinned their idolatrous way of life marked by vice, unrighteousness, injustice, and oppression. When his dire warning came to pass a decade later, the focus of Ezekiel's message shifted to the hope of Israel's restoration, the New Jerusalem. The plain filled with dry bones will be transformed into a habitat teeming with new life. The dispossessed would return to their land, rebuild their homes, and regain their livelihoods. This era, moreover, was to be characterized by lives devoted to virtue, righteousness, justice, and true peace, or *shalom*.

Destruction, displacement, and death—these evils sadly continue to accompany war, including putatively (i.e., presumed) just wars, in these initial decades of the twenty-first century. "Victory" is declared by presidents and other leaders, yet all too often no just peace is to be found in the wake of today's conflicts—whether in wars between nations, wars within nations, humanitarian interventions in failed states, or asymmetrical wars between nations and terrorist organizations. Ezekiel's vision of dry bones scattered across a plain is now, millennia later, frequently seen in news reports on our televisions and computer monitors. The names for these places peppered with bones in our day include but are not limited to Rwanda, Kosovo, Afghanistan, Iraq, and the Darfur region of Sudan. Reliable electricity, potable water, edible food, sanitary waste facilities, adequate medical care, modern education, and secure streets are often lacking for days, weeks, months, and even years after the shooting is supposed to have stopped. Unexploded cluster bombs litter fields and forests, severing limbs from farmers and killing children who mistake them for toys or soda pop cans. Thousands of people are displaced from their homes, fleeing to refugee camps or other countries, seeking shelter and security. After the smoke clears, the powers that be may declare "mission accomplished" when, as Ezekiel long ago said, there really is no peace.

HARD LESSONS FROM AFGHANISTAN AND IRAQ

Two recent violent conflicts involving the most powerful military in the world—the U.S.-led wars in Afghanistan in 2001 and in Iraq in 2003—stand as cases in point. French journalist Anne Nivat, in her book *The Wake of War: Encounters with the People of Iraq and Afghanistan*, provides a vivid account of what happened on the ground after military victory was declared in each of these countries. Instead of embedding herself with the occupying troops, she spent twelve weeks in each country, in remote villages as well as major cities, dressing like the ordinary people (sometimes wearing a burka), traveling by taxi, and being welcomed into homes for meals and candid conversations. Many persons told her that each invasion has had "long-term consequences that are hard to make sense of."[1] In both countries, people expressed concerns about a number of post war problems, with doubts aired about the real intentions of the United States in the region. Iraqis and Afghans alike worried about the fault lines between regions, ethnic groups, and religious sects. From university professors to merchants, grandmothers to former military commanders, people feared the outbreak of civil war in Iraq and the Taliban regaining a foothold on power in Afghanistan. All agreed about the need for the creation of jobs, the construction of schools and hospitals, the rebuilding of police and security services, and the restoration of electricity and drinkable water. While nearly everyone was grateful to the United States for removing Saddam and the Taliban from power, the view of Tariq al-Etharei, the director of the theater department at Basra University, was fairly representative in either country: He couldn't "understand why the U.S. troops are doing such a poor job of 'conquering hearts.'"[2]

Of course, the soldiers are not primarily at fault for this sad state of affairs. Indeed, the U.S. government clearly did not possess a realistic plan for Iraq following the cessation of its war with Saddam Hussein's government and military. Nor has the U.S. military, until very recently, done much to train soldiers to conduct peacekeeping and policing-style operations. Thus, the rosy picture of being welcomed as liberators and quickly establishing a new friendly government in Iraq soon dissipated. Even though improvements are now to some extent evident, plans and preparations should have been in place at the outset to facilitate such progress rather than through trial and error over an extended period of several bloody years. Unfortunately, while different from Iraq in many respects, the situation has become precarious in Afghanistan. In her book's conclusion, Nivat somberly reports, "The people of Iraq and Afghanistan have difficulty understanding that such is the price of 'liberation.'"[3] Sorely needed were serious plans and preparations to establish post war justice, or a just peace, wherein people—including soldiers among the occupying forces—could safely return to their homes and livelihoods. Instead, Ezekiel's vision of a valley of dry bones still sadly comes to mind.

WHY SHOULD CHRISTIANS CARE?

We write as Christians who are deeply moved and troubled by this absence of a just peace in the aftermath of conflicts such as these in today's world. Although it may not seem like it given these recent examples of war and its perilous aftermath, we believe that God in Jesus Christ two thousand years ago inaugurated a new era of "peace on earth, good will toward all" (Lk 2:14). The

Galilean taught about—and himself embodied and practiced—God's ways of peace, justice, righteousness, healing, and mercy to all people. According to Bible scholar Donald Senior, C.P., all that Jesus said or did "was evidence that the kingdom was beginning to break into the world."[4] To be sure, this must have sounded and looked like it was news too good to be true for an oppressed people whose land was occupied by the legions of the mighty Roman Empire. Ezekiel's vision of dry bones must have come to mind during that time, too. Nevertheless, as Jesus put it, this kingdom "has come near" and is "at hand" (Mk 1:14; Mt 4:17). While not yet completely in hand and fully present, the kingdom of God was and is, as Jesus's teachings and deeds demonstrated, already in our midst and "among" us (Lk 17:21) wherever and whenever God's will—peace, justice, righteousness, healing, and mercy—is being "done on earth as it is in heaven" (Mt 6:10). Put differently, God's kingdom is more a verb, or an activity, that is characterized by *agape*, "a love that finds sheer delight in reconciliation."[5] Love of God and love for neighbor are central to Jesus's teachings and how he summed up the overall thrust of the Torah (Mt 22:34-40; Mk 12:28-34).

We find a penetrating glimpse of God's kingdom when we consider with whom Jesus spent much of his time. That is, he actively sought out the downtrodden, the outcasts, the alienated, and the outsiders. He showed love for the poor, fed the hungry, spoke with women, healed lepers, ate with tax collectors, and even helped some Gentiles. In his parable of the Good Samaritan, moreover, Jesus surprised his listeners when he included enemies within the category of neighbor (Lk 11:25-37). In the Sermon on the Mount, Jesus proclaimed, "Blessed are the peacemakers, for they shall be called children of God" (Mt 5:9); accordingly, Jesus calls his followers to "love your enemies and pray for those who persecute you, so that you may be children of your Father in heaven" (Mt 5:44-45). Just as Christ is God's peace and God's justice, so too are we Christians—through Jesus's gift of the Spirit—to continue to make present, embody, and practice God's peace and justice in a world that is still marked by destruction, displacement, and death.

These conditions are precisely why we are writing this book! Surely those who are injured, suffering, homeless, fearful, hungry, or grieving the deaths of loved ones in the wake of violent conflict—be they Afghans and Iraqis, or American soldiers serving in such places and their families—are the very people whom Jesus would have us love. These people who have suffered immensely through war are in special need of God's peace and justice, of reconciliation and restoration. We Christians must endeavor to foster and promote a just peace after the smoke clears for all those whom violent conflict affects.

All Christians are called to be peace-builders and to support efforts to prevent war from happening in the first place. Indeed, in their benchmark pastoral letter from 1983, *The Challenge of Peace: God's Promise and Our Response*, the U.S. Catholic bishops wrote, "Peacemaking is not an optional commitment. It is a requirement of our faith. We are called to be peacemakers, not by some movement of the moment, but by our Lord Jesus."[6] Put differently, peacemaking is a nonnegotiable and constitutive component of Christian discipleship. Individually, each and every Christian, by their baptism into the body of Christ, is supposed to be a maker of peace. At the same time, as a body of people, a community, the Christian church has, as the bishops note, a "proper, necessary, and distinctive part to play" in peacemaking.

Not only is this commitment anchored in our baptism, but the calling to build peace is also evident in our worship of God in the celebration of the Eucharist.[7] For example, after everyone recites the Lord's Prayer, the presider adds, "Deliver us, Lord, from every evil, and grant us peace in our day." Then he says, "The peace of the Lord be with you always," and the congregation responds, "And also with you." This is followed with everyone exchanging with each other a sign of peace, which is not merely a greeting. Indeed, the United States Catholic bishops "encourage every Catholic to make the sign of peace at Mass an authentic sign of our reconciliation with God and with one another. This sign of peace is also a visible expression of our commitment to work for peace as a Christian community."[8] After this gesture of peace and before receiving the Eucharist, the assembly sings the *Agnus Dei*, praying that the Lamb of God, who takes away the sins of the world, will "grant us peace." That word keeps coming up.

However, as the Second Vatican Council, in the document *Gaudium et Spes*, notes, "Peace is not merely the absence of war."[9] Rather, drawing on Isaiah 32:7, the council fathers say that peace is "an enterprise of justice," which is "never attained once and for all, but must be built up ceaselessly." Hence, we pray for an end to war. But when war does happen, our task is not done; all that we do during war must be directed toward a just peace. Nor does our duty to build that just peace subside when the shooting stops.

CALLED TO BE PEACEMAKERS: PACIFISM AND JUST WAR

Of course, even though all Christians are called to be God's instruments for peace in this world, disagreement exists among them as to how to go about doing so. On the one hand, many Christians are pacifists who view all war as immoral and always unjust. They instead seek to make peace using only nonviolent means and methods. This moral viewpoint is valid and laudable for Christians, including Catholics, as emphasized in *Gaudium et Spes* and by the U.S. Catholic bishops in *The Challenge of Peace*.[10] On the other hand, many Christians believe that some (not all!) wars are justified—a view associated with the just war tradition. With antecedents in ancient Greek and Roman natural law philosophy, just war reasoning and principles were grafted into Christian theology, beginning with St. Ambrose in the fourth century C.E., and developed through the centuries via an ongoing interplay between secular and religious sources, becoming the gold standard in the Catholic as well as other religious and ethical traditions for morally evaluating warfare.[11] Whereas the concept is often referred to as just war theory, here we wish to emphasize that it is a living, developing tradition, and our focus is on a particularly Christian version of just war theory. Both of these Christian approaches to the morality of war—pacifism and just war—are supposed to be directed toward a just peace even though they disagree with regard to the permissibility of the use of lethal force.

This shared aim of seeking a just peace is evident in a fairly recent joint venture that has broken new ground, known as just peacemaking. Under the leadership of the North American Baptist

Glen Stassen, who teaches Christian ethics at Fuller Theological Seminary, twenty-three scholars, consisting of pacifists as well as just war theorists who alike worry about pacifism's temptation to passivity and withdrawal, and about just war theory's lack of robust teeth with regard to right intention and last resort, have identified ten proactive practices that have been empirically shown as realistic ways for effectively preventing wars.[12] Just peacemaking focuses on addressing, through establishing practices of justice, the root causes of conflict. As Pope Paul VI put it nearly four decades ago, "If you want peace, work for justice."[13] Stated differently, there ought to be *jus ante bellum*, justice prior to war, which hopefully would minimize the likelihood of many wars from ever erupting in the first place. (Stassen and his colleagues admit, though, that there are no guarantees that these practices will eliminate wars altogether.) Among these practices are nonviolent direct action, cooperative conflict resolution, advancing democracy and human rights, fostering just and sustainable economic development, strengthening the United Nations and other international efforts and institutions, and more. Indeed, just peacemaking serves as an excellent example of how pacifists and just war theorists can stop attacking one another and instead work together to offer a compelling alternative to, as the Mennonite pacifist theologian John Howard Yoder once put it, "the realists, crusaders, and rambos on their 'right' who in fact are shooting up the world."[14]

Still, while pacifists and just war proponents can agree on just peacemaking practices that will diminish the likelihood of violent conflict breaking out, disagreement lingers between them about whether lethal force is ever justified. In his contribution to the just peacemaking project, Michael Joseph Smith, a professor of government and foreign affairs at the University of Virginia, calls for strengthening the United Nations by developing "the capacity to identify, prevent, and, if necessary, intervene in conflicts within and between states that threaten basic human rights," such as in Rwanda or the Darfur region of Sudan.[15] Whereas those contributors coming from a just war perspective view forceful military intervention as justified in these cases where just peacemaking practices fail to prevent the outbreak of conflict, pacifist contributors remain reluctant to do so. A similar fault line is evident in recent discussions involving Christian pacifists and other Christians who hold more of a just war perspective in connection with an emerging norm that the United Nations and the World Council of Churches refer to as a "responsibility to protect" (R2P), which is primarily preventive in orientation, but allows for forceful interventions where genocide, for example, is occurring.[16] While these ongoing differences should not be glossed over, note that pacifist and just war Christians are both called to work actively for a just peace, not only before war erupts, or during war, but also, we believe, after the shooting stops.

BEING HONEST ABOUT JUST WAR THINKING

We (Allman and Winright) regard ourselves as a part of this long and ongoing stream of ethical thought about war and peace. We write this book with the Christian just war tradition, in particular, as our primary focus and point of departure. That is, we believe that, sadly, under certain conditions when just peacemaking practices have failed (or there is not time to attempt them), the use of force, including lethal force, is justified—namely, when there is no other way to defend innocent-neighbor lives from enemy-neighbor aggressors. That does not mean that we believe war is inevitable or that it simply breaks out like a disease or a wildfire. War is, in our view, unfortunately, something that happens due to the lingering presence of sin in this transitional time between Christ's resurrection and the consummation of the reign of God with Christ's return. Nevertheless, war is also a human activity that involves decisions and choices. A moral framework ought to govern and evaluate war. The version of just war theory we espouse takes seriously all of the obligations of its criteria, not in some minimal or negative checklist sense but rather along the lines of a discipline that involves commitments, duties, and virtues as well as categories, criteria, and principles.[17] In short, love for the enemy neighbor, along with their families and fellow citizens, is not to be suspended or set aside either during or after a war. The criteria of the just war tradition were developed in order to respect the enemy neighbor's dignity; as such, the goal of a just war is supposed to be a just peace, both for the nation wronged and for the people of the nation that did wrong in the first place.

That we write from a just war perspective does not mean that we regard all wars, including the recent ones in Afghanistan and Iraq, to be just. Indeed we see the terrorist attacks on September 11, 2001, more as criminal acts of mass murder rather than as acts of war. More specifically, the atrocities committed by al Qaeda, though indeed politically motivated, should be viewed as occupying a space somewhere closer to crime than war.[18] Accordingly, a combined intelligence and law enforcement effort, in concert with partners around the world, might have been a more appropriate response. In fact, precisely such an approach has proven to be more effective in identifying and stopping terrorists.[19] This intelligence and law enforcement model, though, still may involve the use of force, including lethal force, which is governed by criteria analogous to those of the just war tradition. In connection with Iraq, moreover, we both raised questions— before, during, and now "after"—about the justice of this war on the part of the United States and its allies.[20]

The Bush administration pitched the wars in Afghanistan and Iraq to the American people and to the world as just wars.[21] However, in the months before the invasion of Iraq, many— perhaps even most—Christian ethicists and theologians actually criticized, on just war grounds, the United States' plans for preemptive war.[22] Similar scrutiny also continued during the actual fighting of these wars. Yet, after victory was declared, a just peace—which is supposed to be the goal of a just war—has remained elusive. And while we suspect many theologians and ethicists are concerned about what has been happening in the wake of war in Afghanistan, Iraq, and all too many other post conflict places around the world, they have had no framework or list of moral criteria to which they can appeal for gauging and evaluating efforts to establish a just peace.

JUS ANTE BELLUM, JUS AD BELLUM, JUS IN BELLO, JUS POST BELLUM

Over time, the just war tradition has come to consist of several criteria—though the lists vary depending on the source—to be used to evaluate morally *when* and *how* a nation may embark upon and conduct a war justly. A war is considered just if these criteria are adhered to and satisfied. Although classical just war thinkers did not explicitly do so, modern articulations of just war theory divide the criteria into two primary categories, referred to by their Latin names: *jus ad bellum* and *jus in bello*. The *jus ad bellum* category consists of criteria that must be met in order for a nation to be justified to embark upon war; the *jus in bello* category includes criteria concerning just conduct during the war. In *The Challenge of Peace*, the U.S. Catholic bishops include under *jus ad bellum* the criteria of just cause, right intention, legitimate authority, probability of success, last resort, comparative justice, and proportionality. Encompassed under *jus in bello* are two criteria: discrimination (or noncombatant immunity) and proportionate force.[23] Taken together, these criteria are meant to ensure justice when entering into war and justice in the way that the war is conducted.

Missing from this equation, however, is not only consideration of the aforementioned just peacemaking practices that ought to be implemented for *jus ante bellum*, but also comparable attention to and criteria for justice in the wake of war.[24] This neglected dimension is now beginning to garner the attention of church leaders. For example, in "Toward a Responsible Transition in Iraq," a statement released on January 12, 2006, Bishop Thomas G. Wenski, who was chairman of the U.S. Bishops' Committee on International Policy, wrote, "It is important for all to recognize that addressing questions regarding the decisions that led us to war, and about the conduct of war and its aftermath, is both necessary and patriotic."[25] Similarly, in their 2007 document *Forming Consciences for Faithful Citizenship*, the bishops call on nations to find ways to prevent conflicts, to resolve them by peaceful means, "and to promote reconstruction and reconciliation in the wake of conflicts."[26] Yet while criteria already exist for addressing questions about the decisions leading to and the conduct during war, no criteria exist concerning its aftermath. Where does one turn for moral principles and practices of a "responsible transition" from war to a just peace in places such as Iraq? In short, what about *jus post bellum*?

While the just peacemaking effort—which has the support of

many just war theorists, including us—has begun to address the period prior to conflict, in our view the just war tradition needs to be longitudinally extended to include also *jus post bellum*. In light of the post war situations like those in Iraq and Afghanistan, we find it even harder to regard these wars as just wars—even assuming (which we don't) they met the criteria of the *jus ad bellum* and *jus in bello* categories. On the flip side, if a war is unjust because the *jus ad bellum* or the *jus in bello* criteria were not satisfied, then the duty to establish post war justice is all the more imperative, even though it won't retrospectively make it a just war.

We do not mean to suggest, though, that the just war tradition has been completely blind to post war ethics. For centuries, military strategists have talked about exit strategies. Some ancient religious examples of just war thought prohibited poisoning wells, salting fields, and cutting down fruit and olive trees because such actions extend the effects of war well beyond the period of active combat. Others such as Cicero, Augustine, Vitoria, Suarez, and Kant also addressed post war ethics, but mostly in passing and not with the same degree of systematic detail that the *jus ad bellum* and *jus in bello* categories enjoy. Moreover, some *post bellum* considerations are implied in the criteria of the *jus ad bellum* and *jus in bello* categories. After all, as the U.S. Catholic bishops point out, the *jus ad bellum* criterion of right intention requires that war can be intended legitimately only for the reasons established as just cause, namely, in the face of a real and present danger, "to protect innocent life, to preserve conditions necessary for decent human existence, and to secure basic human rights."[27] Throughout the conflict, right intention furthermore entails the "pursuit of peace and reconciliation, including avoiding unnecessarily destructive acts or imposing unreasonable conditions" upon the enemy.[28] In a nutshell, just war should aim at establishing a just peace, or what St. Augustine referred to as the *tranquillitas ordinis*. Thus, some thought about post war justice is indeed already implicitly built into *jus ad bellum* and *jus in bello* criteria.

Post war ethics are a natural extension of, and share some commonalities with, the *jus ad bellum* and *jus in bello* categories. However, as international relations scholar Serena K. Sharma has observed, too often these have been viewed as "logically separate and self-contained categories," so the focus has remained on justice immediately before and during war.[29] We believe that all of the criteria are interrelated and interlocking, so that the categories *jus ad bellum* and *jus in bello* are basically shorthand devices that are actually meant to reinforce the way in which the objective of a just peace should not be "merely an afterthought of war," but instead "a guiding principle, present at the initiation of hostilities and continuing throughout all respective phases of war."[30] We are not proposing merely some appendix to just war theory. Rather, adding a *jus post bellum* category will hopefully make more explicit the just war tradition's solicitude for a just peace throughout the conflict as well as in the wake of war.

We are not the first to call for the development of an explicit just war category of *jus post bellum* criteria in recent years. Little more than a decade ago, in a very brief article appearing in *The Christian Century* magazine, theologian Michael Schuck pointed out this lacuna in the just war tradition.[31] Since then, mostly philosophers, political theorists, international law scholars, and military scientists have treated this neglected dimension of just war, while bishops and theologians have largely been silent on the issue. Still, the novel work that has been done in these other disciplines remains underdeveloped at this juncture. Moreover, much of that effort, though certainly not all of it, offers a restricted or minimal account of the requirements of post war justice. Drawing upon this nascent literature on post war ethics, we seek in this book to offer a systematic, more theological account of *post bellum* ethics, with deeper moral foundations than what has been proposed so far.

We propose four *jus post bellum* criteria or components that complement the *jus ad bellum* and *jus in bello* categories of just war: just cause, reconciliation, punishment, and restoration. These four facets of *jus post bellum* mutually should reinforce one another and the overarching commitment to follow through in a way that is congruent with right intent, to restore a just peace. A quick, important caveat, however, is in order at this point. While we are proposing a category and criteria that we hope will be widely accepted as the tradition continues to develop, we acknowledge that room for disagreement will remain with regard to their specific application. On the question of how to relate principles to concrete issues, we follow the U.S. Catholic bishops who admit in *The Challenge of Peace* that "many concrete questions concerning the arms race, contemporary warfare, weapons systems, and negotiating strategies" do not "carry the same moral authority as [their] statement of universal moral principles and formal Church teachings."[32] As Catholic social ethicist Charles E. Curran notes in connection with this moral methodology, differences of judgment and opinion are permitted regarding applications of principles in issues that "by their very nature are so complex and specific that one cannot achieve a certitude that excludes the possibility of error."[33] Still, in our view, a formal and systematic set of *jus post bellum* criteria is essential to the future of the just war tradition. When we say "peace" after the smoke clears, these criteria are necessary to help us make sure that there really is peace, a just peace that in turn will hopefully prevent future outbreaks of conflict.

THE STRUCTURE OF THE ARGUMENT

The book contains two major sections. The first part, consisting of two chapters, covers just war theory in more detail and the emerging category of *jus post bellum*. Chapter 1 offers an overview of the just war tradition. It gives an account of the historical development of the just war tradition, which includes theological and nontheological dimensions. The traditional categories of *jus ad bellum* and *jus in bello*, along with their respective criteria, are also delineated and discussed. Moreover, attention is given to criticisms of the just war tradition by pacifists and others. Finally, the chapter proposes a theological basis, rooted in Augustine's work, for an understanding of just war as an expression of, or duty flowing from, love for neighbor, which includes the enemy and all those who are caught up in war and its wake. In short, just war aims at establishing a just peace, the *tranquillitas ordinis*, which theologically is restorative and reconciling in nature.

Chapter 2 examines incipient elements of *jus post bellum* considerations and criteria within the Christian just war tradition. Prominent theologians through the years have touched on aspects of post war justice, so we need not start completely from scratch to begin formulating the category and criteria of *jus post bellum*. In addition, recent scholarship in the fields of philosophy, political science, international relations, and military science offers some helpful soundings into the emerging area of post war ethics and *jus post bellum*. However, this body of work is still in an early developmental stage and, as such, includes some overlap, convergences, and consensus, as well as ongoing points of disagreement. This chapter thus provides an account of the current state of the question, setting the stage for a more theological contribution to the discussion.

The second part of the book proposes and details four *jus post bellum* criteria. These are not treated in any particular chronological sequence or order of importance. All should be implemented in tandem and more or less concurrently. The first criterion, just cause, is examined in chapter 3. The result of any just war should be the accomplishment of the objectives that served as the grounds for just cause in the *jus ad bellum* phase. Moreover, satisfying the just cause demands is different from returning to the *status quo ante bellum*, which is precisely what led to war in the first place. The goal of a just war must be to establish social, political, and economic conditions that are more stable, more just, and less prone to chaos than what existed prior to the fighting. The just cause principle has three primary theoretical objectives: (1) hold parties accountable until mission is accomplished, (2) restrain parties from seeking additional gains, and (3) stem overly zealous *post bellum* responses. In practice, this criterion entails both the return of unjust gains and the prohibition of unconditional surrenders.

Chapter 4 focuses on the second criterion: reconciliation. If the primary objective of a just war is a just and lasting peace, then there can be no peace without reconciliation. The goal of reconciliation is to transform a relationship of animosity, fear, and hatred into one of tolerance, if not respect, to turn enemies into friends and to bring emotional healing to the victims of war. Parallels between the sacrament of Reconciliation in Catholicism and recent work on restorative justice are instructive here. This phase is not about cheap grace or taking a forgive-and-forget approach. It involves acknowledgment of wrongdoing, admission of responsibility, punishment, forgiveness, and perhaps amnesty.

Ideally, reconciliation should lead to the return of the offending party to communion. The goal of reconciliation, in short, is justice tempered by mercy. In practice, the reconciliatory aims can be promoted through ceasefire agreements, restrained post war celebrations, public and transparent post war settlement processes, and apologies.

Chapter 5 provides an account of the third *jus post bellum* criterion: punishment. Here the primary objectives are justice, accountability, and restitution. The legitimacy of punishment depends on several factors: publicity and transparency (punishments ought to be meted out through public forums to which many, if not all, have access); proportionality and discrimination (appropriate punitive measures ought not be excessively debilitating and must make distinctions based on level of command and culpability); and legitimate authority (punishments ought to be assigned by an authority that all sides recognize as legitimate). In all likelihood, the legitimacy of the punishment phase depends on an independent authority (meaning a third party) in order to avoid even the appearance of victors acting as judge, jury, and executioner of the vanquished (which is otherwise pejoratively referred to as "victor's justice"). In practice, the punishment phase involves compensation (restitution) and war crimes trials.

The fourth criterion, restoration, is the subject of chapter 6. The goal of a just war is not simply the cessation of violence, but political, economic, social, and ecological conditions that allow citizens to flourish. In other words, a just war should seek to create an environment that permits citizens to pursue a life that is meaningful and dignified. Doing so involves a number of practical concerns, including providing and establishing security, policing, and the rule of law; enabling sufficient political reform whereby a functional government can promote the common good and provide public services such as education, health care, and electricity; fostering economic recovery by helping with the transition from a post war to a peacetime economy; providing social rehabilitation for people who have been victimized by war and soldiers who may suffer from injuries and trauma; and ecological cleanup efforts to address the lingering pernicious effects of weapons such as cluster munitions on people's lives and livelihoods.

Our view is that a just war ought to end justly. It should result in a just peace, in conditions that are better than those that existed prior to—and indeed may have led to—the outbreak of war in the first place. And if a war is evaluated as morally unjust—due to the failure of adhering to either *jus ad bellum* or *jus in bello* considerations—then the obligations for justice *post bellum* are all the greater. In any event, we intend for these criteria of *jus post bellum* to enrich and to buttress the just war tradition—to give it more teeth, as Mennonite pacifist theologian John Howard Yoder called upon Christian just war proponents to do—by emphasizing that moral responsibility for war does not come to a halt when combat ends.[34]

AN EXPLANATION OF TERMS USED

Jus ad Bellum

The *jus ad bellum* category of the just war tradition addresses the necessary conditions for declaring a just war. Typically, *jus ad bellum* comprises seven principles:

1. *Just cause.* War is seen as legitimate if it is waged in self-defense, to protect the innocent, in defense of human rights, or in response to acts of aggression.

2. *Competent authority and public declaration.* The use of force is permissible if a legitimate authority engages in due process and publicly declares its intention to go to war.

3. *Comparative justice.* Meeting the just cause requirement does not grant carte blanche rights to any state; its objectives in war must be limited. No party to war has absolute justice on its side.

4. *Right intention.* The only just motives for waging war are those prescribed by the just cause principle. Ulterior motives (revenge, geopolitical power plays, seizing natural resources, and so on) cannot be rationalized within the just war tradition.

5. *Last resort.* This principle requires that all reasonable peaceful alternatives to war must be fully exhausted before going to war.

6. *Probability of success.* A war cannot be considered just if

it will have no positive influence on the situation. The intent is to prevent futile attempts to change a situation when one side has a substantial advantage or when engaging in conflict is the equivalent of mass suicide.

7. *Proportionality (or macroproportionality)*. The good expected to result from engaging in war must be worth it. The benefits that result from defeating the aggressor must be proportionally better than the inherent evils of war.

In theory, all seven criteria must be met in order for a war to be considered justified. In practice, just cause is often seen as sufficient to justify a war, which has led critics of the just war tradition to claim that it serves as a rationalization or moral cover-up story for the rush to war.

Jus in Bello

The *jus in bello* category of just war theory concerns ethical behavior in combat. These rules of war enjoy international legal status in a host of war conventions such as the Geneva Convention. This category comprises two basic criteria, although contemporary secular versions of just war theory often include more criteria:

1. *Discrimination*. Soldiers must distinguish between combatants and noncombatants, and between military targets and the infrastructure necessary for life (water supplies, sewage treatment facilities, hospitals, crops, and so on). The intentional targeting of civilians is never justified and is rightly condemned as murder. This principle forbids all weapons that fail to discriminate between soldiers and civilians (including nuclear weapons and devices such as land mines).

2. *Proportionality (or microproportionality)*. The use of military force must be proportionate to the objective. This principle forbids all weapons of mass destruction (WMDs).

PART 1

THE JUST WAR THEORY
AND
JUS POST BELLUM

1

THE JUST WAR TRADITION

Its History, Categories, and Flaws

"Reality is deep and wide."[1]

Before delving into justice in the wake of war from a just war perspective, we need to review the development of that tradition to establish our bearings. This chapter begins with some history of just war reasoning. Initially examining ancient Greek and Roman philosophical thoughts on just war, the chapter then narrates the transition from early Christian pacifism to the church's adoption and adaptation of just war. In giving particular attention to Ambrose's and Augustine's theological accounts of just war and its core considerations or criteria, we seek to retrieve a more Christian theological framework for just war theory. This discussion is followed by an overview of how the just war tradition developed across subsequent centuries, focusing especially on key figures and concepts important for understanding the just war categories and criteria.

The second section of the chapter describes the traditional bipartite categories of just war—*jus ad bellum* and *jus in bello*—and their respective criteria. The third section addresses and examines some prominent criticisms of just war theory, setting the stage for the concern that we tackle in the rest of the book: that just war theory has not paid sufficient attention to *jus post bellum*.

Just war is not set in stone. Composed of many theories, just war is a living tradition that has changed and continues to develop in light of new circumstances, technologies, and insights. As John Howard Yoder, a Mennonite pacifist theologian who has written extensively on just war theory, observed, "It is appropriate to speak rather of 'tradition' than of a 'doctrine' or a 'theory,' for there is not one official statement of this approach to which all would subscribe."[2]

Just war thinking, of course, has analogues in other religions, in international law, and the laws of war, including the rules of engagement of today's U.S. military. While overlap exists between contemporary laws of armed conflict and the just war tradition, and it could be argued "that the law of armed conflict is, in essence, a codification" of just war theory, there are differences.[3] In this chapter and the rest of the book we concentrate on the ethics of just war thinking rather than the laws of war, but unlike most philosophers, political scientists, and military experts, we write from an explicitly theological perspective.

Moreover, because just war is more a tradition than a doctrine or theory, its categories and criteria should not be viewed merely as a "checklist"[4] or some sort of "rulebook."[5] In what follows, therefore, as we trace the development and components of the just war tradition, we focus in particular on those threads that are consonant with theological convictions, especially with regard to establishing a just peace for all concerned following an ostensibly just war.[6]

HISTORICAL DEVELOPMENTS

Ancient Greek and Roman Thought

Just war thinking did not begin within the Christian tradition. It has its roots in the ancient Greek and Roman worlds. We turn now to the Greek and Roman philosophers in order to highlight key elements of their thinking about just war. Some of these ingredients were retained, and others modified or even set aside by later Christian theologians in their attempt to baptize just war thinking.

The Greek philosopher Plato (427-347 B.C.E.) wrote extensively about politics and justice, but actually very little explicitly about war. In his view, war was not an end in itself although it was sometimes justified in the pursuit of peace, which he understood to be constituted by a well-ordered society. In his dialogue *Statesman*, he warned about too much peacefulness, on the one hand, and excessive readiness for war, on the other, both of which are at odds with the good of the *polis*.[7] He thus offered a mean between these extremes. Education and formation in the virtues were important, moreover, so that warriors would exercise, for instance, justice, fortitude, prudence, and temperance in their military service to protect the common good.

In all of this we have the beginnings of what would come to be known as the principle of right intent. In addition, because the object of war should be the restoration of peace, the amount of violence (such as the burning of houses and the land, or the despoiling of the dead) ought to be kept to the minimum necessary for obtaining satisfaction from the enemy; accordingly, there was always "an eye to reconciliation,"[8] or what today might be referred to as restorative justice. It has been said that Plato was "one of the originators of the just-war idea," given that the "recurring point in Plato's dialogues is that war should not be considered apart from justice."[9]

Plato's student Aristotle (384-322 B.C.E.), who also served as tutor to Alexander the Great, continued this line of his teacher's thinking and was the first actually to employ the phrase "just war."[10] Critical of the Spartan warrior culture, Aristotle firmly rooted war in the demands of justice, and like Plato, he, too, regarded war not as an end in itself but instead as a means for achieving higher goals like peace and prosperity.[11] A combination of natural law reasoning and the virtues functioned as a foundational backdrop for his thinking about just war.

After the Hellenistic hegemony waned over the Mediterranean world, the Roman Empire sank its talons in the region, with thinkers such as Cicero (106-43 B.C.E.) picking up the Greek ideas about just war. This Roman orator, philosopher, and legal scholar taught that war should be fought and won through virtue, especially fortitude, and that treacherous means, including vices, were to be avoided. He, like Aristotle, believed the universe is governed by a moral law, the natural law. In *De Officiis*, he wrote that it is more in accordance with rational human nature, since we naturally seek peace, to settle disputes by discussion rather than physical force, but that force is justified "in case we may not avail ourselves of discussion."[12] Peace is our goal, and peaceable means of resolving conflicts are to be preferred over the use of force.

Here we see an early reference to what will come to be known as the just war criterion of last resort. Similarly, the criterion of just cause appears in *De Republica*, in which Cicero wrote, "Those wars are unjust which are undertaken without provocation. For only a war waged for revenge or defense can actually be just.... No war is considered just unless it has been proclaimed and declared."[13] For a war to be considered just, it had to have a cause, some incident or transgression, a *casus belli*, such as defense against an invading army. Another just cause for war was righting wrongs that had been perpetrated. Although Cicero used the word "revenge" in the above quote, he probably had in mind bringing the guilty party to justice, so that the punishment would fit the offense.

In addition, in *De Officiis* Cicero noted the importance of a public declaration of war by a legitimate governing authority, which put the enemy on notice and gave it an opportunity to make amends and to right the injustice. Cicero taught that soldiers must rightly intend not the enemy's destruction, but the restoration of peaceful relations and community. Victors were to be merciful toward the vanquished. Although the Romans did not always adhere to Cicero's guidelines, and although they did not apply these rules consistently to everyone, such as pirates and barbarians, the just war reasoning that he set forth would prove influential upon the thinking of early Christian theologians on just war.

From Pacifism to Just War: Just War in the Early Christian Church

Scholars generally accept that the early church understood that its call to be peacemakers required rejecting participation in war. Before examining how the church came to see just war as a faithful form of practicing Christian love for neighbor, we must turn to the pacifism of the first few generations of Christians. In his slim book *Nevertheless: The Varieties and Shortcomings of*

Religious Pacifism, Yoder points out that there is "no such thing as a single position called 'pacifism,' to which one clear definition can be given and which is held by all 'pacifists.' "[14] He proceeds to identify and describe twenty-nine kinds of pacifism.

One must remember not to impose anachronistic assumptions about pacifism onto the early church. As Methodist theological ethicist Stanley Hauerwas has observed, these first generations of Christians did not deduce or begin with some theory about pacifism; rather, through the Christian community's experiences and practices of forgiveness and reconciliation the early Christians believed that in a world of violence and war "we cannot be anything but nonviolent as worshipful followers of Jesus the Christ."[15] Indeed, the early Christians did not refer to themselves as pacifists at all. Their pacifism was part and parcel of their way of life as Christian disciples.

To be sure, there is no straightforward evidence of Christians serving in the Roman military until approximately 170-180 C.E., though there probably were a few soldiers who converted to Christianity prior to that time, as mentioned in the New Testament (Lk 7:9; Acts 10:47).[16] Also, given the Roman custom that soldiers' sons in turn usually became soldiers—a compulsory practice for one son (or his substitute) of an officer—it may be inferred that when further evidence is found of Christians in the military in the late second century, there must have been some Christians in the same legion in the previous generation and perhaps a few in the generation prior to that. Nevertheless, a number of sociological and theological-ethical reasons may have contributed to why most Christians did not serve as soldiers during the first three centuries of the early church's existence.

During this time Christians, a minority sect, periodically suffered persecution at the hands of the Romans, which understandably gave rise to their reluctance to serve in the oppressor's army. Second, because most Christians belonged to social groups, including slaves and freedmen, that were not eligible for such service, not many were able to join the army. Third, the Roman Empire tended to recruit for the military from rural areas, and since most of the early Christians lived in urban areas, few of them volunteered to be in the military.

In addition, Roman officers were required to observe religious rituals, which soldiers had to attend, including sacrifices to and worship of the Roman emperor Caesar. Many military units had their own cult, wherein a particular deity was worshiped in return for that god's favor and assistance. For Christians, because "Jesus is Lord" (Phil 2:11), they refused to join the Roman military and participate in such idolatrous practices. Along similar lines, these early Christians rejected swearing oaths, which were required in the military and which usually involved an idolatrous and binding invocation of some deity. Sexual immorality, such as prostitution, was also associated with being in the military, and Christians were appalled by, and prohibited from participating in, such behavior. It too was viewed as an expression of idolatry, worshiping a creature rather than the Creator (Rom 1:25).

There was also an intense eschatological anticipation among the early Christians of Jesus's return with the coming of the reign of God and the end of the present age. Given this fervent expectation, most Christians did not bother to join the ranks of the Roman military. Finally, aside from some police functions such as the guarding of prisoners, the protection of the roads, and fighting fires, being a Roman soldier might entail killing during war. Because the early Christians abhorred the shedding of blood, they refused to kill as part of the Roman military.

Early Christian pacifism, therefore, was not based solely on some absolute prohibition against killing, although this appears to have been an important reason, especially as most early Christians viewed it as incompatible with Jesus's teachings and example. In his Sermon on the Mount, Jesus commanded his disciples to love their enemies (Mt 5:44) and not to resist evil in the way that others did (Mt 5:39).[17] They saw or remembered how Jesus himself adhered to his own teaching, especially during his arrest, trial, and execution on a cross. For early Christians, Jesus's nonviolent death on the cross abrogated all need for sacrificial practices and exemplified God's love for others, including enemies. It was a clear witness to the way in which God overcomes evil, reconciling people with God and one another. Through the gift of God's spirit and grace, they believed that all Christians, individually and as a new community, were called to follow the way of Jesus. Their pacifism was both integral to and an outgrowth of a way of life faithful to their Lord Jesus Christ.

During the period prior to 325 C.E. most theologians and bishops who addressed the subject opposed Christian involvement in the military, including Justin Martyr (c. 100-165), Clement of Alexandria (c. 160-215), Tertullian (c. 160-225), Origen (c. 185-254), Cyprian of Carthage (c. 200-258), and Lactantius (c. 250-330). The primary theological reasons given for the Christian avoidance of military service—including repugnance toward idolatrous sacrifices, oaths, or killing—varied among these writers. The thread that runs through each of these is idolatry. At the same time, many of these patristic writers critically presupposed or alluded to the gradually growing "acceptance by *other* Christians of participation in war and military service."[18]

How, then, did Christians come to accept and serve in the military? While there may have been some Christians serving in the army in order to help protect against criminals within the borders of the Roman Empire or against invaders on the frontier, this gradual shift continued in 313 C.E. with Emperor Constantine's Edict of Milan, which proclaimed that Christianity would no longer be a persecuted religion within the empire.

According to Daniel M. Bell Jr., "It would be a mistake to attribute to Constantine a sudden and wholesale shift in the church's moral evaluation of warfare," since there were some voices sanctioning military service by Christians prior to his reign and voices opposed to it afterward.[19] Even so, more Christians subsequently came to be found among the ranks of the Roman military. By 416 C.E., only Christians were permitted to serve.

Ambrose, Augustine, and Gratian

Ambrose of Milan (c. 340-397) and Augustine of Hippo (354-430) were two of the earliest Christian theologians (and bishops) to offer a justification for and rules to govern Christian participation in military service and war. In their book *Faith and Force: A Christian Debate about War*, David L. Clough and Brian Stiltner identify four historical stages in the development of just war thinking. In their model, Ambrose and Augustine represent the first stage.[20] The following is a brief summary of these helpful stages.

As governor and then bishop of the city where Constantine's

famous edict was promulgated, Ambrose was deeply familiar with Roman tradition and with the thought of Cicero. The Roman Empire, in his view, was God's instrument for keeping the peace. For Ambrose, like Cicero, the moral life was understood primarily as having to do with the virtues, with justice as the highest social virtue. He thus allowed Christians to fight in just wars when called upon by their governing authorities, but they could do so only by practicing the virtues, and they should be merciful to the enemy. In their conduct during battle, Christian soldiers were to risk their lives to protect the innocent. In other words, Ambrose taught that lethal force was to be used only out of love for the neighbor who was being unjustly attacked. Indeed, the bishop of Milan instructed Christians to forego self-defense if attacked as a private citizen, for this would be an example of excessive self-love. However, when the lives of innocent third parties were threatened, those who were authorized to do so had a duty to defend them. He made an exception for clergy and religious, though, who were to abstain from the use of arms because association with the shedding of blood rendered them ritually impure (and thus unable to preside over sacraments), which hints at lingering discomfort with war, even just war.[21]

According to Clough and Stiltner, Ambrose's aim "was not to provide guidance to rulers about how and when to wage war but to instruct Christians of their civil duties, which include fighting in wars for the protection of social order."[22] Yet he did excommunicate Emperor Theodosius, who was a Christian, because of an incident that occurred in 389. After a group of angry citizens in Thessalonika rebelled against the demands of the Roman Army and killed the commanding officer stationed there, Theodosius ordered a retaliatory strike whereby seven thousand Thessalonians were rounded up and slaughtered. This military action thereby violated right intent, in that it was done out of vengeance rather than justice, and it involved the killing of civilians; killing civilians was later prohibited under the principle of discrimination.

In response, Ambrose wrote a letter to Theodosius informing him that he was to be excluded from the Eucharist until he publicly did penance. When Theodosius submitted to Ambrose's invitation to do penance, during the Christmas celebration in 390, he was reconciled with the Christian community. This example shows how Ambrose understood just war reasoning as not merely a way to justify going to war but more important as a means for keeping it within certain moral parameters, even on the part of rulers—and especially for holding Christians accountable to church teaching concerning war.[23]

As Aristotle was a student of Plato, Augustine was a student of Ambrose. Indeed, he converted to Christianity due to Ambrose's preaching. Augustine is regarded as the father of the just war tradition within Christianity, though he did not provide a full-blown account comparable to what we associate with just war today. Like Ambrose, he followed Cicero, especially with regard to tethering the justice of war to a universal moral order. Unlike Cicero, however, Augustine ultimately anchored the justice of war with God's divine will in creation, wherein God created humankind to live in a just and peaceable community. Just wars were supposed to restore and maintain a semblance of that tranquil order.[24]

As with Plato and Cicero, the aim of a just war—its right intent—should be to restore peace. In his letter to Boniface, a Roman general in Africa who, after his wife's death, desired to retire and become a monk, Augustine wrote,

> Peace should be the object of your desire. War should be waged only as a necessity and waged only that through it God may deliver men from that necessity and preserve them in peace. For peace is not to be sought in order to kindle war, but war is to be waged in order to obtain peace. Therefore even in the course of war you should cherish the spirit of a peacemaker.[25]

Although Augustine recognized that earlier Christians adhered strictly to nonviolence, he offered a number of reasons—some more convincing than others—that he thought participation in military service was congruent with being a Christian.[26]

Indeed, like Ambrose, he anchored just war in loving defense of an innocent neighbor who is under attack. A Christian, however, must not defend himself, for that would be an example of excessive self-love. Augustine wrote,

As to killing others in order to defend one's own life, I do not approve of this, unless one happen to be a soldier or public functionary acting, not for himself, but in defence of others, or of the city in which he resides, if he acts according to the commission lawfully given him, and in the manner becoming his office.[27]

Not only do we have here what would come to be referred to as the just war criterion of legitimate authority, but also just cause. For Augustine, just cause included not only the defense of the innocent but also avenging injuries, punishing wrongs, and getting back what was wrongfully taken.[28] In all of this, Augustine did not have in mind revenge and vengeance, let alone mere retributive justice. Rather—and this tied back to his understanding of right intent—the hope was to have evil persons repent and reform, and thereby restore the peace. He wrote that "we do not ask for vengeance on our enemies on this earth. Our sufferings ought not constrict our spirits so narrowly that we forget the commandments given to us.... We love our enemies and we pray for them. That is why we desire their reform and not their deaths."[29] In other words, the aim of a just war is restorative justice.

Accordingly, Augustine did not think that just war contradicted Jesus's injunction to love one's enemies. Just war is a form of love in going to the aid of an unjustly attacked innocent party; however, it is also an expression of love, or "kind harshness," for one's enemy neighbor.[30] It aims at turning the enemy from their wicked ways, making amends, and helping the enemy to rejoin the community of peace and justice. Augustine wrote, "Therefore, even in waging war, cherish the spirit of a peacemaker, that, by conquering those whom you attack, you may lead them back to the advantages of peace."[31]

But, one may ask, how is this a benefit or how is it loving for those enemies who are killed on the battlefield? Augustine replied, "Let necessity, therefore, and not your will, slay the enemy who fights against you."[32] A mournful mood should accompany this, too. In his view, the "real evils in war are love of violence, revengeful cruelty, fierce and implacable enmity, wild resistance, and the lust of power,"[33] all of which would be at odds with restoring a just peace. Of course, even though he regarded just war as congruent with Christian love, Augustine ultimately held onto the belief that "it is a higher glory still to stay war itself with a word, than to slay men with a sword, and to procure or maintain peace by peace, not by war."[34]

Augustine, continuing the trajectory begun by his teacher Ambrose, significantly influenced how subsequent Christian tradition accepted and understood just war. For the next several hundred years, little was added to what Augustine set forth. Indeed, around 1148 a monk named Gratian collected various official legal pronouncements from church authorities that had been issued over the centuries, and referred to as canon law, which he published with a commentary. Gratian's *Decretum* highlighted Augustine's teachings on just war even as it developed his work in some ways.

As with Augustine, for Gratian just war was supposed to lead to a just peace involving the benevolent and restorative punishment of the evildoer. Just cause also remained essentially the same. Gratian agreed with Augustine on the function of legitimate authority, but revived Cicero's requirement for a public declaration of war. According to Bell, "Gratian's work stimulated an outpouring of commentaries on existing canon law," ensuring "that Augustine's thought [would] serve as one of the cornerstones of the church's thought on just war for the next thousand years."[35]

The Early Medieval Period

Before turning to the second historical stage of just war that Clough and Stiltner identify, it is important to note three other practices of the church related to just war during this early medieval period. One was the church's practice of requiring soldiers who participated in a just war to do penance on their return. Not only was penance expected of those who violated just war principles, such as when Ambrose excommunicated Theodosius, but it was enjoined on those who fought justly—probably as a "medicinal" and healing effort in recognition of the evils experienced during combat.[36] This practice existed from the sixth to the twelfth centuries and may be found in the *Penitentials*, which were guides the clergy used for the sacrament of Confession. We revisit this practice later in this book.

The second practice had to do with protecting noncombatants from harm and was known as the "Peace of God." As warfare came to involve more siege engines and the siege of cities became a military strategy, noncombatants were increasingly in danger. Also, there was the growing threat of roving bandits and unemployed mercenaries on the highways and in the villages of Europe. Along with the chivalric codes for knights to defend the helpless at the time, the church developed the Peace of God to designate persons and places—such as clergy, merchants, peasant farmers, pilgrims, and women, along with churches, monasteries, vineyards, and farms—as off-limits for killing and destruction. A third practice, the "Truce of God," prohibited violence during certain times of the week or year, such as saints' feast days, holy days, and church seasons such as Lent.[37] Collectively these practices indicate an attempt to limit the brutality of war and hint at a lingering discomfort with facile acceptance of war by religion founded on the life and teaching of Jesus Christ, the prince of peace.

Thomas Aquinas

The second stage in the historical development of the just war tradition, according to Clough and Stiltner, centers on Thomas Aquinas (1225-1274), the Dominican friar who taught at the University of Paris and whose most famous work was the *Summa Theologica*. His influence on Christian theology, and on just war, is comparable to that of Augustine. Aquinas treated the subject of just war within a section of his *Summa Theologica* devoted to a discussion of the theological virtue of charity, or love. To the question, "Whether it is always sinful to wage war," Aquinas replied, relying on the thought of Augustine, that for a war not to be sinful, it must be a just war in which the meeting of three criteria is necessary: legitimate authority, just cause, and right intention.[38] On intent, Aquinas continued Augustine's teaching that the goal was to bring, via a harsh kindness or punishment, the benefits of peace to the enemy, but to this Aquinas gave more prominence to the concept of defending the common good. Just war seeks to undo the harm wrongdoers inflict upon themselves by sinning against their neighbor and against justice, and to address the damage the wrongdoer has inflicted upon the common good of the community.

In a few other areas also, Aquinas slightly departed from or advanced earlier teachings on just war. Concerning legitimate authority, he carved out a space for the possibility of the people led by a local magistrate or prince overthrowing a tyrant. However, such a course of action, in his view, should be rare, a last resort, and, as an initial nod to the principle of proportionality, result in a better state of affairs than under the rule of such an oppressive (and, thus, illegitimate) ruler.

Aquinas also departed from Ambrose and Augustine in connection with killing in self-defense. Elsewhere in the *Summa*, when discussing the question of whether it is lawful to kill someone in self-defense, Aquinas argued that self-preservation is natural, and a private individual may not *intend* to kill an attacker even though the death of the assailant may result.[39] Aquinas reasoned as follows: One action may have two effects, one of which is intended and the other is not. A private individual may therefore intend to defend herself from harm, with the intended effect being the saving of her life. The death of the assailant, however, is a possible effect that should not be intended. The individual who employs force in self-defense, according to Aquinas, is not guilty of any crime or sin as long as she did not use more force than necessary for her defense. This mode of reasoning came to be known as the "principle of double effect," and although Aquinas introduced it in reference to private self-defense (rather than war), it has been firmly incorporated into just war thinking, and also other areas of moral theology, including medical ethics. The impact of Aquinas's thought on just war would prove significant in the centuries following his death.

Secularizing Just War Thought: Vitoria, Suarez, and Grotius

The third stage in the history of the development of the just war tradition, according to Clough and Stiltner, included the systematizing and secularizing of just war thought, with a number of major figures and developments from the fifteenth to the nineteenth centuries. Three important thinkers during this time were the Spanish Dominican, Francisco de Vitoria (c. 1486-1546); a later disciple of his, Francisco Suarez (1548-1617); and the Dutch Protestant lawyer, Hugo Grotius (1583-1645). They gave more specificity to the just war criteria, added criteria, and ensconced the tradition in emerging international law, which included significant attention to international laws of war.

In his books *On the Indians* and *On the Law of War*, Vitoria critically addressed Spain's conquests of the indigenous peoples of the Americas. He invoked natural law to argue that these native populations have rights and, as such, should not be treated inhumanely by the conquistadors. As the natural occupants of the so-called New World, the Indians should not be forced by arms to convert to Christianity.

In addition, Vitoria opened the door further for soldiers to question the justice of a war, and he honed further the principle of proportionality by including a consideration of the way one wages battle with regard to the costs and benefits of going to war. Moreover, he explicitly discussed the distinction between *jus ad bellum*, the right to embark upon war, and *jus in bello*, the laws to be adhered to during the conduct of war.

Vitoria also introduced the notion that opponents in a war can sincerely believe that justice is on their side (one side, though, is attributed to invincible ignorance), a recognition that would come to be known as simultaneous ostensive justice, an insight that should remind belligerents to wage war with restraint and moderation. And Vitoria applied Aquinas's double-effect reasoning on self-defense now to warfare itself in order to reinforce the principle of noncombatant immunity. Finally, Vitoria devoted some attention to areas that pertain to justice after war, to which we return in the next chapter on incipient elements of *jus post bellum* in the tradition.[40]

Suarez, a Spanish Jesuit, studied Vitoria's theological work and translated it into more philosophical and legal language, setting the stage for the codification of just war principles into international law. He also expanded the criteria of last resort and noncombatant immunity. Suarez argued that a state's authority derives from the consent of the governed, and that all people have a natural right to liberty and to property. For these reasons, many regard him as the founder of contemporary international law.[41]

Grotius is also considered a father of international law. He who wrote in response to the vicious and devastating Thirty Years' War (1618-1648), a time also of the "collapse and fragmentation of the Christian vision ... in a world where Christian convictions do not seem to hold or where they are not shared."[42] Now that there no longer existed a unified Christendom in Europe, Grotius sought to establish just war in legal rather than in theological terms.

In his magnum opus, *On the Law of War and Peace*, he developed a "law of nations" or "peoples" (*jus gentium*) in addition to natural law. As Bell points out, Grotius operated with a two-tiered ethic, whereby the precepts of natural law and the law of nations offered a minimum standard of justice by which anyone—Christian or not—could be expected to abide. The precepts of the new law of the gospel, which are more demanding and robust, were applicable primarily to Christians. As Bell puts it, "His intent was not to separate just war from Christianity but to reconnect the two in a situation where he deemed that the link between Christian morality and war had been weakened."[43] What was for Grotius a distinction later became a separation.

Grotius is remembered for the work he did in connection with a universal moral minimum for just war. Coinciding with this development, Grotius devoted very little attention to right intent in his treatment of just war. Instead, his treatment of just cause overshadowed his treatment of the rest of the criteria. He narrowed just cause for war to self-defense, while at the same time allowing for the possibility of preemptive strikes or anticipatory attacks in the face of a grave and imminent threat (but not what later would come to be referred to as preventive war, which involves attacking a possible threat that is more distant in the future).[44] Moreover, he offered the first systematic account of rules governing the protection of civilians and prisoners of war.[45] To be sure, the legacy of Grotius has been significant for the international laws of war to this very day. However, as we are writing from an intentionally Christian theological perspective, we maintain that a retrieval of the importance of right intent, which is expressed in and informs the other criteria, must be given greater weight.

The Period after the World Wars

The fourth stage in the history of the development of the just war tradition, according to Clough and Stiltner, corresponds with the recovery and rethinking of just war during the second half of the twentieth century, not only in international law but also in theology and the churches. As political scientist Serena K. Sharma puts it, here we have "a veritable rebirth in just war thinking, in large part owing to the two World Wars."[46]

During the nineteenth century, Napoleonic warfare, revolutionary wars, and the U.S. Civil War marked a shift to total war, which involved whole populations, and the purpose of war transitioned from convincing an enemy to surrender to bringing about its destruction. The death and devastation of World Wars I and II thus provoked Christian theologians such as John Courtney Murray, S.J., and Methodist ethicist Paul Ramsey to invoke the just war tradition as a way of morally evaluating the Cold War nuclear standoff between the United States and the Soviet Union, as well as the Vietnam War.

At the same time, there was a revival of pacifism—although it too was always a living tradition over the centuries—among Christian individuals and groups, such as Dorothy Day, Peter Maurin, the Catholic Worker Movement, Martin Luther King Jr., and the Fellowship of Reconciliation. In 1965 the Second Vatican Council officially affirmed pacifism in *Gaudium et Spes* for "those who renounce the use of violence in the vindication of their rights ... provided that this can be done without injury to the rights and duties of others or the common good."[47]

In 1983 the U.S. Catholic bishops issued their pastoral letter, *The Challenge of Peace*, in order "to help Catholics form their consciences and to contribute to the public policy debate about the morality of war" during a time when the threat of nuclear war was an important concern of the church and indeed the rest of the world.[48] John Howard Yoder believed that *The Challenge of Peace* familiarized people in the church and in wider society with the existence of the just war tradition, as evident in the use of just war language by politicians, military commanders, the media, citizens, and church members in connection with Grenada, Panama, and the Gulf War of 1990-1991.[49] In the view of Drew

Christiansen, S.J., this document had "two important byprod-ucts": increased public awareness of just war principles and also a growing acceptance of nonviolence as a legitimate alternative to just war within the Christian tradition, both of which share what the bishops refer to as a common presumption against war.[50]

To be sure, as Clough and Stiltner note, this fourth stage of development is still under way, with new developments possible, including further conversations between Christian just war think-ers and Christian pacifists, resistance to a punctual approach to warfare by giving more attention to addressing the root causes of conflict, a more critical stance toward governments and their (ab)use of just war language, a stricter application of just war criteria, and a recovery of the theological foundations of the just war tradition.[51] We add here the consideration of *jus post bellum*.

Obviously, this historical survey of the just war tradition is not intended to be exhaustive. Many other important contributors were omitted because of space limitations. Similarly, we have not devoted attention to developments in the pacifist tradition, and we refrained from treating the Crusades of the Middle Ages, a development that certainly related to or affected the just war tradition (although, in our view, being at odds with it).[52] We have sought to highlight some of the key persons and relevant ideas of the just war tradition, especially within Christianity, demonstrat-ing how the tradition has changed and developed over time.

OVERVIEW OF THE TRADITIONAL CATEGORIES

Although just war thinkers such as Augustine and Aquinas did not explicitly divide the criteria for a just war into specific categories, the kind of moral reasoning that goes with the different temporal dimensions of war was indeed present in their contri-butions to the tradition. Sharma is technically correct when she writes that the "medieval architects of the tradition recognized no such distinction between *ad bellum* and *in bello*," and that con-cerns about the conduct of war were built into the *jus ad bellum* considerations.[53] Yet we find identifying these categories—while emphasizing their "tight conceptual" interconnections—is important in order to prevent conflating, downplaying, or neglecting the criteria, principles, and practices for justice at each phase of war.[54] In this section we delineate how the two traditional major categories of just war, and the criteria associated with each, are understood today, particularly in the Catholic Church. We take our cue from the U.S. Catholic bishops' *The Challenge of Peace* for the following explication of categories and criteria.[55]

Jus ad Bellum—Before War

The first main set of criteria in just war theory is known as *jus ad bellum*. This category includes criteria that ought to be satisfied prior to embarking upon war. That is, these principles have to do with why and when going to war is justified. Seven criteria or principles fall under the umbrella of *jus ad bellum*. While these criteria are not necessarily listed in any order of importance, all of these criteria are supposed to be met before engaging in warfare can be justified.

Just Cause

This criterion deals specifically with the *why* aspect of going to war. A just war is undertaken in response to something. Wars of aggression are patently unjust. In the past, as we saw above, just cause included defense against aggression to defend the vulnerable, punishing other grave wrongs and injustices (such as human rights abuses), and regaining what was wrongfully taken or withheld (including restitution and redress). At the time *The Challenge of Peace* was written, the scope of just cause had been narrowed and focused on a nation's defense against an unjustified attack or act of aggression by another nation. During the 1990s, in view of horrific genocides in the Balkans and in Rwanda, discussion arose about extending defense to include others beyond one's country. This came to be referred to as humanitarian intervention, and more recently this norm is being called the responsibility to protect (R2P) by the United Nations and the World Council of Churches.

Pope John Paul II claimed that when people suffer at the hands of their government or because their government lacks the ability to protect them, other nations "no longer have a 'right to indifference' [and it] seems clear that their duty is to disarm this aggressor if all other means have proven ineffective."[56] Note that John Paul used the language of obligation, duty, or responsibility when it comes to protecting others. More recently, both the *Catechism of the Catholic Church* and the *Compendium of the Social Doctrine of the Church* underscore the right and the duty of nations to use force of arms to protect (under the rubric of "legitimate defense") their own citizens and innocent victims in other countries that are unable to defend themselves.[57] Although the *Catechism* does not deny governments "the right of lawful self-defense,"[58] as William L. Portier has pointed out, it is worth noting that the *Catechism* delineates the "strict conditions for legitimate defense by military force [that] require rigorous consideration."[59] In Portier's view, the Catholic Church has reoriented its moral discourse about war and peace, so that "what we have called 'war' or 'just war' is pushed to the edges of the moral conversation where it can survive only in the form of what the *Catechism* calls 'legitimate defense by military force' (n. 2309)."[60]

To be sure, this line of thinking seems evident in recent statements by Pope Benedict XVI. For example, in accordance with a tradition of observing a World Day of Peace, Benedict XVI devoted his second World Day of Peace message to "certain recent situations of war."[61] While the pope affirms that "in Christ we can find the ultimate reason for becoming staunch champions of human dignity and courageous builders of peace," he has not entirely jettisoned the church's traditional position that sometimes force is justified to defend the innocent. Indeed, Benedict calls on

> the international community [to] reaffirm international humanitarian law, and apply it to all present-day situations of armed conflict, including those not currently provided for by international law. Moreover, the scourge of terrorism demands a profound reflection on the ethical limits restricting the use of modern methods of guaranteeing internal security.[62]

He urges nations to establish "clearer rules" and "norms of conduct" for defending the innocent and limiting "the damage as far as possible," while concurrently he repeats the refrain that "war always represents a failure for the international community and a grave loss for humanity."

What might these "clearer rules" or "norms of conduct" look like? Here Benedict footnotes the section of the *Catechism* (pars. 2307-2317) that lists "the traditional elements enumerated in what is called the 'just war' doctrine" (par. 2309), and which the pope regards as offering "strict and precise criteria."[63]

Accordingly, defense of the innocent is just cause for armed force and intervention at this time. It should be noted, moreover, that just cause allows for preemptive strikes (but not preventive war) in order to defend against an imminent and grave threat (clear and present danger). As the *Catechism* puts it, however, "the damage inflicted by the aggressor on the nation or the community of nations must be lasting, grave, and certain."[64] The threat cannot be speculative or simply possible; it must be probable and sure. At the same time, if the threat were to be carried out, the consequences on the attacked nation would have to undermine its capacity to defend itself or indeed threaten its very existence.

Legitimate or Competent Authority

Only duly appointed authorities who bear responsibility for protecting the common good may declare and wage war. Private individuals and groups cannot do so. We as two authors, the College Theology Society, General Electric, al Qaeda, the Ku Klux Klan—none of these private individuals or groups are considered a legitimate authority permitted to declare and engage in war. As public authority varies from nation to nation, it might rest with a president, monarch, parliament, or congress. In Article 1, Section 8 of the U.S. Constitution, Congress possesses the prerogative to declare war and provide for the common defense of the United States. According to James Madison, "In no part of the Constitution is more wisdom to be found than in the clause which confides the question of war and peace to the legislature and not to the executive department."[65] Moreover, since the inception of the United Nations, except for cases of self-defense under Article 51 of the U.N. Charter, authorization from the Security Council is expected before the United Nations undertakes any armed interventions.

The adjectives "legitimate" and "competent" are important.

Some authorities may be tyrannical and actually at fault for the suffering of the innocent in their nation, and in Catholic teaching—as well as increasingly in international circles with R2P—such authorities are illegitimate. This is why in recent centuries just war theory has cautiously permitted just revolution.[66] With regard to humanitarian intervention, national sovereignty, while respected, is not absolute. In such cases where intervention is necessary to safeguard innocent human lives due to the malicious acts of an illegitimate government or because of the authorities' failure or inability to protect these lives, the international community has a duty to intervene.

Still, as the *Catechism* notes, "The evaluation of these conditions for moral legitimacy belongs to the prudential judgment of those who have responsibility for the common good."[67] However, prudence, it should be noted, is a political and moral virtue that requires formation, practice, and a community. It is not a virtue that only governmental authorities possess. Especially in democratic nations, citizens ought to exercise this virtue and convey their views about any given war to their governmental representatives. John Howard Yoder pointed out that while the just war tradition originated in a different time when it was "assumed that decisions about war belong to sovereigns," today the citizens of democratic nations need "the availability of usable nonsectarian language like that of the just war tradition ... because there must be debate" in order to cut through the fog of governmental disinformation, propaganda, and spin.[68]

Right Intent

This criterion is related to just cause in that the purpose for going to war is to address the wrongs that an aggressor has committed or is on the verge of committing. As the bishops point out, "During the conflict, right intention means pursuit of peace and reconciliation, including avoiding unnecessarily destructive acts or imposing unreasonable conditions (such as unconditional surrender)."[69] Ultimately, the goal is to restore order, which means setting in motion necessary conditions for establishing a just peace. This is the *telos* of just war. Rear Admiral Louis V. Iasiello, the twenty-third chief of navy chaplains, agrees when he writes that this is "the ultimate goal of all just conflicts—the establishment of a just and lasting peace."[70] Joseph Capizzi and H. David Baer similarly point out, "Just intention expresses love for the enemy by stipulating that the end of war be peace."[71]

A just war is not fought out of vengeance, revenge, or hatred; nor should it be about conquest, expansionism, and imperialism. Rather, "this respect for the well-being of the enemy is expressed through the criterion of just intention," as well as through the rest of the criteria. This "peaceful order must be a just order—one that includes and recognizes the claims of the enemy. This just order requires more than conceiving peace as a return to the status quo ante."[72] This is why right intent is not reduced to just cause. The aim of the criterion of right intent "can never be to restore a problematic order that gave rise to conflict in the first place."[73] For this reason Baer and Capizzi follow in the footsteps of their teacher Theodore Weber, arguing that just war and its criteria ought to be configured around right intent, which also "requires placing just war theory within the larger framework of peacemaking."[74] We return to this point later when we begin to construct what should be part of *jus post bellum*.

Probability of Success

There must be a reasonable hope of winning the war and achieving the aim of restoring a just peace. As the *Catechism* puts it, "There must be serious prospects of success."[75] The purpose of this criterion, according to the U.S. Catholic bishops, is to prevent "irrational resort to force or hopeless resistance."[76] Embarking upon war should not be an exercise in futility nor the equivalent of mass suicide.

This criterion should also help guard against protracted wars. While this is a difficult criterion to assess, and discerning this in advance does not involve quantitative certainty, the key words here are "probability" and "likelihood." By "success," though, we mean more than merely achieving military victory. Implementing a just peace must also be factored into the equation.

Last Resort

The use of lethal military force should, if possible, not be the first option. If at all feasible, nonviolent means must be seriously tried and exhausted. As the *Catechism* stipulates, "All other

means of putting an end to it must have been shown to be impractical or ineffective."[77] These means may include smart sanctions,
diplomatic efforts, third-party negotiations, or an ultimatum to
surrender, to sue for peace, or to give up the perpetrator(s).[78] In
addition, appeal should be made to the United Nations to help
provide a resolution to the problem. Also, a declaration of war
should be made so that the nation defending itself is accountable
to the world community and so the offending party can sue for
peace on the stated grounds.[79] Of course, if bombs are already
falling and people are dying, this does not preclude the immediate
use of force for defensive purposes.

Proportionality

In connection with *jus ad bellum*, the principle of proportionality takes into account the evils associated with going to war:
they must not outweigh the evils already present that political
authorities are seeking to prevent. In other words, proportionality asks for an accounting of whether going to war will result
in more harm, damage, and costs than any good that might be
achieved. As the *Catechism* states, "The use of arms must not
produce evils and disorders graver than the evil to be eliminated."[80] Allman refers to this criterion, in connection with *jus ad
bellum*, as macroproportionality, in order to distinguish it from
the proportionality criterion in *jus in bello*.[81]

Proportionality is not limited in scope to the nation embarking upon war, but it encompasses anything and all who will be
affected by the war, including those who live in the aggressor
nation. Indeed, those who claim that modern war is total and
thus too destructive—especially were nuclear weapons to be
used—are actually employing this criterion to make their point.
The U.S. bishops, moreover, note that proportionality must be
taken into account not only before embarking upon war but also
"throughout the conduct of the war," since unforeseen developments occur along the way. The example they give in this connection is the Vietnam War, which the bishops did not explicitly
say was unjustified until 1971 when they "ultimately concluded
that the conflict had reached such a level of devastation to the
adversary and damage to our own society that continuing it could
not be justified."[82]

Comparative Justice

Because war involves so much destruction, displacement, suffering, and death, the U.S. Catholic bishops identified the new criterion of comparative justice in *The Challenge of Peace*. This criterion is meant to put a brake on the rush to war, and it asks whether one side is sufficiently right in the dispute. (As we noted earlier in the section on the historical development of the just war tradition, some thinkers such as Vitoria had already considered the concerns it raises.) As the bishops put it,

> In a world of sovereign states recognizing neither a common moral authority nor a central political authority, comparative justice stresses that no state should act on the basis that it has "absolute justice" on its side. Every party to a conflict should acknowledge the limits of its "just cause" and the consequent requirement to use *only* limited means in pursuit of its objectives.[83]

As such, comparative justice is intended to rein in the strong impulse toward self-righteous crusades. It encourages a sense of humility and restraint, and it underscores the importance of right intent and the goal of restoring a just peace for all involved.

Jus in Bello—Justice during War

The second major set of criteria for just war is known as *jus in bello*. This category has to do with how the war is conducted once hostilities have begun. These criteria are concerned with the means that are employed, including weapons, tactics, and targeting. From the top-ranking officers making decisions about targets to strike with a missile to the soldier armed with a rifle and looking for insurgents in a city neighborhood, the *jus in bello* criteria are supposed to hold. That is, these criteria are meant to restrain violence and prevent slippage into total war. It is worth noting that the Catholic just war tradition usually identifies only two *in bello* criteria (discrimination and proportionality), but other sources, including secular just war theories, often include a longer set of criteria.[84]

Discrimination

Also known as noncombatant immunity, the criterion of discrimination holds that civilians should not be directly or intentionally targeted or harmed.[85] To intentionally target or kill civilians during war is equivalent to murder. Militaries are supposed to discriminate, or distinguish, between combatants and noncombatants. Their intent should be to strike a legitimate military target or accomplish a military objective. Noncombatant injuries and deaths should not be intended. Paul Ramsey posited that in the Christian just war tradition this principle expresses love and respect for the aggressor enemy and its citizens. The criterion typically includes a prohibition on intentionally targeting infrastructure necessary to sustain civilian population (e.g., electricity grids, sewage treatment facilities, hospitals, water supplies), as long as the infrastructure does not support military efforts. If the infrastructure is used in support of the war effort it may be a legitimate target.

In connection with this criterion, the Second Vatican Council declared in *Gaudium et Spes*, "Every act of war directed to the indiscriminate destruction of whole cities or vast areas with their inhabitants is a crime against God and man, which merits firm and unequivocal condemnation."[86] As an extension of this criterion, wounded soldiers and prisoners of war should also be respected. Moreover, certain places, such as hospitals and sacred buildings (e.g., mosques, synagogues, and churches), should not be targeted or destroyed. This criterion has its historical roots in the medieval practice known as the Peace of God, which attempted to protect from warfare particular categories of people and places.

The other side of the coin, however, is that some unintentional injuries and deaths of civilians (and damage to nonmilitary property) may be permitted and excused. The unfortunate euphemism for this is "collateral damage." According to the *Catechism*, "Unintentional killing is not morally imputable."[87] At play in this distinction is the so-called principle of double effect, which recent scholarship has shown to be more of a framework of moral reasoning that consists of a number of principles.[88] For example, American Catholic moral theologian John C. Ford, S.J., in a well-known article that appeared in 1944 in the Jesuit journal *Theological Studies,* employed this double-effect mode of reasoning to criticize the strategy of obliteration or carpet bombing during the Second World War. Ford outlined double effect as follows:

> The foreseen evil effect of a man's action is not morally imputable to him, provided that (1) the action in itself is directed immediately to some other result, (2) the evil effect is not willed either in itself or as a means to the other result, (3) the permitting of the evil effect is justified by reasons of proportionate weight.[89]

Ford culled many quotes from British and American sources at the time, indicating that the United Kingdom and the United States employed a "strategic plan of wiping out German cities."[90] The air forces of these nations aimed "on purpose" to destroy industrial centers, railroads and communications, and residential districts where workers lived, "so that absenteeism will interfere with industrial production."[91] The justification that was given was essentially consequentialist, namely, that this strategy would demoralize the population, deflate their support for the German war effort, and destroy industry upon which their military depended—all of which would lead to the defeat of the enemy. The action of carpet bombing was thereby, as the first point of double effect requires, directed to some other result.

Ford's use of the word "immediately" in explaining the double effect is crucial, as the war's termination was a more distant objective. Moreover, where workers lived, their spouses and children did also. When employees were injured and killed, so too were their families. And the quotes Ford cited made it clear that these deaths and injuries were indeed intended as a means to an end. For this reason, he wrote, "The principal moral problem raised by obliteration bombing, then, is that of the rights of non-combatants to their lives in war time."[92]

Oliver O'Donovan offers the following hypothetical question as a test of intention concerning means: "If it were to chance that by some unexpected intervention of Providence the predicted harm to non-combatants did not ensue, would the point of the attack have been frustrated?"[93] If the answer is yes, then the noncombatant deaths were not accidental, but instead were intended as either part of the means or even the goal of the attack. In O'Donovan's view, the dropping of the atom bombs on Hiroshima and Nagasaki failed this test.

This does not, however, mean that all unintended and accidental civilian deaths are morally acceptable. As the *Catechism* goes on to say, "But one is not exonerated from grave offense if, without proportionate reasons, he has acted in a way that brings about someone's death, even without the intention to do so."[94] After all, under several circumstances one can be blamed for unintended side effects.[95] For instance, if someone drives under the influence of alcohol and kills someone with his car, such an effect from driving while intoxicated should have been foreseen as a possibility. The driver is thus morally blameworthy. He or she has not committed murder, but manslaughter. The death was neither intended nor totally accidental. The agent did not foresee the bad side effect of his action, though he should have foreseen it as a distinct possibility, which then could have been prevented or avoided.

Another example of when an agent is morally responsible for unacceptable side effects that are unintended but foreseen is sometimes referred to as "depraved heart murder."[96] If a person who owns an airplane blows it up for the insurance money, foreseeing but not intending the passengers' deaths that result from the explosion, this is a type of murder—usually second-degree murder—though it is not an intentional killing. The agent in this action has exhibited a "callous disregard for human life" that results in death.

Such scenarios in which agents are responsible for foreseen side effects were addressed centuries ago by Aquinas, whose discussion of whether an innocent person may kill an unjust attacker in self-defense, as we saw earlier, is often regarded as exhibiting double-effect reasoning. Recall that his account of justified self-defense requires two conditions: first, one may only intend to defend oneself, but not intend to kill the attacker; and second, the act of defense must be proportionate to the end.[97]

Perhaps more often overlooked, though, is what Aquinas had to say about harms that are both foreseen and certain. For example, in his several references to the parable of the Wheat and the Tares (Mt 13:24-40), Aquinas interpreted Jesus's story as a warning against harming innocent persons, even unintentionally, when one is dealing with evil.[98] Furthermore, in his treatise "On Evil," Aquinas referred to a scenario in which a branch falls as a result of a woodcutter's chopping a tree in a forest. If the forest is not regularly traveled by persons, no moral blame is attributed to the lumberjack if the branch kills someone. The victim's death is unintended, even if it is foreseen as a somewhat remote possibility. However, if the forest is indeed regularly traveled by people, the woodcutter is morally culpable if the falling branch kills someone.

According to Aquinas, "But if evil is always or in most cases associated with the good intrinsically intended, the will is not excused from sin, although the will does not intrinsically intend the evil."[99] In a way resembling the case of depraved heart murder, Aquinas believed agents are morally responsible for unintentional effects if they are foreseen as probable or certain. Why is all of this important? It shows that the principle of discrimination—and its concern for noncombatant population of an enemy nation—should be very important in the Christian just war tradition.

Proportionality

Allman terms the *jus in bello* version of proportionality "microproportionality" to distinguish it from *ad bellum* proportionality ("macroproportionality).[100] Militaries must use only the amount of force necessary, and not excessive force, to achieve their objective. A parallel concept that proves illuminative exists in policing. Police officers are expected to use discriminate force, intending only to subdue or stop a dangerous suspect, and they are supposed to employ proportionate force. That is, microproportionality requires not only weighing the consequences—good and bad—but also weighing possible alternative options and using the appropriate, fitting means.

Often referred to as a use-of-force continuum, police officers possess a range of use-of-force options that may be utilized depending on a subject's level of resistance or noncompliance.[101] For example, if a suspect resists arrest with punches, an officer is not justified in resorting to his firearm. He has at his disposal several intermediary options, such as a baton or pepper spray.

As moral philosopher G. E. M. Anscombe has noted, Aquinas may also have had in mind proportionate means rather than ends or effects in his use of double-effect reasoning when dealing with the question of self-defense.[102] One ought not to use a sledgehammer to swat a mosquito on her neighbor's forehead; it would be disproportionate and morally wrong, notwithstanding any good intention. This same sort of understanding of proportionate force applies to the conduct of war.

By now it should be clear that the categories and criteria of the just war tradition over the centuries have been, as Iasiello puts it, "in a state of perpetual transition."[103] Those principles present in the thought of Cicero or Augustine have remained part of the tradition, even if they have been revised or understood in new ways over time. Similarly, new criteria have been developed and added, while some others have been set aside. The current framework of just war theory delineated by the U.S. Catholic bishops in *The Challenge of Peace*, with its two categories of *jus ad bellum* and *jus in bello* criteria, is a recent expression of this living and dynamic tradition. Perhaps this clarifies why we see a need for similar considerations and criteria for the *jus post bellum* period.

WEAKNESSES AND STRENGTHS OF THE JUST WAR TRADITION

Criticisms have been and continue to be leveled against the just war tradition.[104] One common charge made against the just war tradition is that it has been and continues to be used as a cover for the nation-state; stated another way, there never has been a truly just war. Governmental authorities invoke the language of just war to justify all sorts of wars that are actually undertaken for other reasons. Doesn't every nation or group declare its war to be just? When fighting a putatively just war, nations tend not to abide by the rules. Still, while just war language and principles, admittedly, have more often than not been "honored in word more than deed" and misused "to rationalize war," we hold, as the ancients put it, that *abusus non tollit usum* (because something can be abused does not mean it cannot be used rightly).[105]

More than half a century ago, John Courtney Murray, S.J., responded to this criticism. While acknowledging that "the traditional doctrine was irrelevant during World War II," and that it had "not been made the basis for a sound critique of public policies, and as a means for the formation of right public opinion," Murray added that all this "is not an argument against the traditional doctrine." If anything, this shows the need for a serious retrieval of the just war tradition. Indeed, he countered, "The Ten Commandments do not lose their imperative relevance by reason of the fact that they are violated. But there is place for an indictment of all of us who failed to make the tradition relevant."[106]

Likewise, Yoder cautioned that the question "Has there ever been a just war?" may be unfairly asked of just war proponents. He wrote, "The basis of moral obligation is not the record of past successes in doing right. Has there ever been a perfectly monogamous spouse? A faithful Christian church? The fitting question is whether *in the current case* those who claim that heritage are *in fact* letting it set the limits of their action."[107] To be sure, Yoder respected and challenged his fellow Christians who purport to adhere to the just war tradition to be honest in their use of it and to adhere to it in a way that has teeth. He advised his fellow Christian pacifists, "The doctrine of the 'just war' must be dealt with far more respectfully than most pacifists have been willing to do. It takes seriously, as the other available thought patterns do not, that there can be an ethical judgment upon the use of violence in the name of the state."[108] Yoder, as much as anyone else, was highly critical of Christian just war, but he engaged it and tried to hold his fellow Christians and others accountable to it. "Wherever any new opening for the moral criticism of violence arises," he believed, "it is in some way a use of the just war logic, and should be welcomed as at least an opening for possible moral judgment."[109]

After all, although during World War II many of the principles of just war were largely set aside or flat out violated, the article by Ford on obliteration bombing stands as a testament to how the just war tradition can indeed be invoked to critique a war or its conduct. Appearing in print with the war still under way, Ford's essay is now widely regarded as a milestone in twentieth-century just war thought. Indeed, in a recent book about Ford,

Eric Marcelo O. Genilo notes that this article is considered "the most influential article in the journal's history."[110] It inspired similar treatments of weapons and their use over the subsequent decades and in other conflicts. For example, in an article appearing in 1964, James W. Douglass extended Ford's incisive analysis to address the morality of nuclear bombing and deterrence.[111] Similarly, in 1995 when the United States, the United Kingdom, and France were threatening air strikes against Serbs in Bosnia, J. Bryan Hehir drew on Ford's work to emphasize the importance and nonnegotiability of the principle of noncombatant immunity.[112]

Ford began his article by affirming the abiding relevance of the principles of the just war tradition. Although a number of moralists held that modern war was necessarily total and indiscriminate, and although Ford acknowledged that much of the warfare of the early twentieth century involved devastation heretofore unimaginable, he nevertheless adamantly maintained that limited, and thus just, war is possible.[113] Not only did he condemn Germany's policy of blitzkrieg, but Ford turned critical attention to the Allies' carpet bombing of cities in Germany and Japan.

We wish to locate ourselves within this serious strand of the Christian just war tradition. Yoder suggested that it "can (theoretically) have teeth at several points: refusal to obey an unjust order, 'selective conscientious objection' when called to serve an unjust cause, suing for peace when one cannot win without using unjust means, [and] prosecuting a war crime."[114] In Yoder's view, the church unfortunately has not done enough to form and inform its members to embody and practice a disciplined version of just war theory. While there are undoubtedly a number of things that the church ought to begin doing in this connection (especially with regard to practices, virtue formation, and discernment) we submit that teasing out another phase of just war, the *jus post bellum* category of criteria, will also help just war Christians to be more accountable to their convictions and criteria, particularly for establishing a just peace. Moreover, we invite pacifist Christians to invoke and use these criteria to hold their fellow just war Christians and others accountable.

Clough and Stiltner raise the greatest possible objection to the just war tradition from a Christian theological perspective.

That is, in view of what Jesus taught and did, there would appear to be "an insuperable obstacle to a Christian ethic of justified warfare."[115] In their view, Christians who accept and support the possibility of just war need to provide an account for their stance that does not distort Jesus or dismiss his teachings about love for enemy. We agree. That is why we wish to offer an account of just war that takes seriously Jesus Christ, who came that all might have life. As Christians, we believe that just war, if it has any place in Christianity, must somehow be an expression of, and witness to, our faith in the loving and peaceable kingdom of God as revealed in Jesus Christ. This makes a difference in how just war is understood and practiced.

We think it is important that Christians recall and retrieve the theological seedbed that Ambrose and Augustine planted, from which the just war tradition in Christianity grew. As Adrian Pabst has noted, "For the Church Fathers and medieval theologians, 'just war' was a matter of practical judgement … [and] reflections on 'just war' were part of a larger framework grounded in the specific praxis of Christian beliefs, namely the belief that peace is the highest truth and constitutes the ontological shape of the world."[116] This account of just war does not view it as a compromise or as something less than a faithful following of Jesus. It is still rooted in love and does not deviate from the moral vision of Jesus and the early church, but is instead an extension of that vision into different circumstances. We seek to understand just war as an organic development in a living tradition that is consonant with fundamental convictions of our faith in the God revealed to us by Jesus Christ.

While we certainly disagree with Methodist ethicist Paul Ramsey on a number of counts, we find very helpful his basic point about love serving as the fundamental basis for the Christian just war tradition. Augustine, according to Ramsey, showed how, "in a world of conflicting neighbor relations," it is "possible to move from the presumption of universal love for all to preference for some neighbors, and to the idea of a justifiable use of lethal force."[117] In other words, in a trilateral relationship where one neighbor is (or imminently will be) guilty of aggression against another innocent neighbor who is (or imminently will be) a victim, the Christian must intervene, forcibly if necessary, in defense of the latter neighbor *and* out of love/concern for the former, for as the psalms proclaim, "Let the just strike me; [for] that is kindness" (Ps 141:5).

As an example of "the *logic*, the heart and soul, of such protective love,"[118] Ramsey mentions the Good Samaritan who assisted the man victimized by thieves on the Jericho road. While in this parable the Samaritan showed love for the man who was attacked by bandits earlier in the day, Ramsey asked what Jesus would have suggested the Samaritan do "if he had come upon the scene while the robbers were still at their fell work?"[119] Too bad we have no record of anyone asking Jesus this important question! In his disturbing and challenging book *Killing Civilians: Method, Madness, and Morality in War*, Hugo Slim shares the story of the Liberian village of Bakedo, a mostly Muslim community of Mandingo people of traders and farmers in West Africa. In June 1990 a massacre happened in the mosque nestled in the town's center:

> After launching their successful insurgency from Côte d'Ivoire further to the east, Charles Taylor's NPFL (National Patriotic Front of Liberia) forces burst into Lofa County. On that June day, people were farming and going about their business as usual when news came that armed fighters were on their way to the village. The town's elders met quickly and agreed to meet the soldiers in a spirit of peace with an offering of two cows and some money as a token of their hospitality. Sure enough, a little later that day, two pick-up trucks full of armed NPFL men drove fast into town, led by a woman commander. Most of the soldiers quickly fanned out to surround the town and block routes out of it. Others pushed the villagers' reception committee into the "palava hut" near the mosque and forced them to lie on the floor. The minds of the soldiers were made up and their orders were clear. After taking some drugs and dancing around, they got serious. The commander shouted at the cowering people in the "palava hut" and said: "You, together with your belongings, belong to us. We will kill you because you are Mandingo people, strangers and not citizens. So we will kill all of you on this land." The soldiers then opened fire on everyone in the hut, immediately killing 36 people—men, women and children—at point blank range.

Panic then ensued as people all over the village ran for the forest or scrambled to hide in their houses. As people fled, the sentries posted at the exits of the village shot them one by one, killing men, women and children outright or wounding others who then ran on into the bush where many of them later bled to death. Soldiers inside the village stormed every hut, killing anyone they found and firing up into the thatched roofs where people were hiding, their blood then dripping to the floor below. The shooting lasted for thirty minutes ... , the surviving villagers think they counted 350 people killed in that half hour.[120]

What should a good Samaritan do when a crime such as this is happening? While we believe that much can be done, including the practices of just peacemaking, to prevent such scenarios from happening in the first place, unfortunately, force is sometimes necessary to put a stop to horrific crimes that are already under way against the innocent.

For Ramsey, whenever a choice must be made between the unjust perpetrator and the innocent victim, circumstances dictate that the latter is to be preferred. As Augustine put it earlier, necessity requires such action. By necessity, however, we use it in the strict sense of employing lawful and indispensable means, and not in the sense that was critiqued by Yoder: "that one may legitimately break the rules whenever one 'really has to,' which tends to boil down to being useful (saving lives, shortening the war) rather than to the real lack of any other means."[121] The latter was the reasoning that supposedly justified the U.S. decision to drop atomic bombs on Hiroshima and Nagasaki. But let us be clear, this is not what we mean by necessity.

What, it may be asked, has happened to the Christian call to love the enemy neighbor? In Ramsey's view, such love is not altogether extinguished or absent. What he referred to as the "twin-born" justification for war involves a preferential love for the wronged innocent neighbor, but it must also extend to the wrongdoing guilty neighbor, through the principle of non-combatant immunity.[122] To illustrate, Ramsey thought that the two elements—"(1) a specific justification for sometimes killing another human being; and (2) severe and specific restrictions upon anyone who is under the hard necessity of doing so"—are both again "exhibited in the use of force proper to the domestic police power."[123] The first element correlates with just cause, which is one of the criteria of the *jus ad bellum* category, and the second element correlates with noncombatant immunity, which is one of the criteria of the *jus in bello* category of the just war tradition. In our view, following recent work by Baer and Capizzi, this love for the enemy also finds expression in the other criteria, including those of *jus ad bellum*. Indeed, it is especially evident in right intention, which, as Baer and Capizzi claim, "expresses love for the enemy by stipulating that the end of war be peace."[124]

This point brings us to another important criticism of the just war tradition, namely, that it lacks "historical thickness."[125] It tends, in other words, to ignore the larger historical context (meaning the decades preceding the war) and instead looks only to the period immediately prior to conflict. Along the same lines, Yoder cautioned against the tendency to "punctualism" in moral decision making and casuistry, including in the just war paradigm: "What is either right or wrong is that punctual decision, based upon the facts of the case at just that instant, and the just war tradition delivers the criteria for adjudicating that decision. This procedure undervalues the longitudinal dimensions of the conflict."[126] In real life, the moral questions we face and the decisions that are made are deeper and wider than can be served by punctualism.

For this reason, Christian pacifists and just war theorists in recent years, as noted in the Introduction, have devoted more attention to just peacemaking practices that should help to create conditions for a just peace that effectively diminish the likelihood of war. Just peacemaking focuses on addressing the root causes of conflict. It seeks to give more teeth to the just war tradition's criteria of right intention and last resort.[127] Thus, the charge of punctualism is not necessarily a damning criticism. It has already inspired Christian ethicists to be more creative and constructive in addressing *jus ante bellum*. As political theorist Michael Walzer has suggested, just war theory has "no fixed temporal limits; it can be used to analyze a long chain of events as readily as a short one."[128]

However, we believe that expanding the just war tradition to encompass *jus post bellum* will actually "close the loop" or make for a more honest just war theory by bringing us back to the practices of just peacemaking. A Christian just war theorist must be a vigilant peacemaker *ante bellum* and a strict adherent to the norms of *jus ad bellum*, *jus in bello*, and *jus post bellum*.[129] Christians should never be comfortable with war or tolerate facile interpretations of just war theory, otherwise what once was interpreted as an unfortunate/sinful but necessary form of neighbor love becomes nothing more than a Christian gloss on crass political realism. We take seriously Yoder's charge that Christian just war theorists should take just war theory seriously. In grafting the practices of just peacemaking to the front end of traditional just war theory and *jus post bellum* to the back end, we are proposing a more comprehensive and honest just war theory—one that is fully committed to justice and peace *ante*, *ad*, *in*, and *post bellum*.

As philosopher Brian Orend points out, "Conceptually, war has three phases: beginning, middle and end. So if we want a complete just war theory—or comprehensive international law—we simply must discuss justice during the termination phase of war."[130] While we agree with Orend's concern about *jus post bellum*, what we have in mind actually amends his three-phase paradigm by reconnecting full circle with a fourth phase that ought to be considered: the period *ante bellum*, best exemplified by the just peacemaking approach. As we have seen in this brief survey of the history of the Christian just war tradition and of the criteria of the *jus ad bellum* and *jus in bello* categories as outlined in the bishops' *The Challenge of Peace*, very little attention has been given to post war justice. In recent years, although some philosophers, political theorists, military experts, and others have begun to address this area, to date it continues to be a relative lacuna or at best a footnote in Christian just war thought. The category of *jus post bellum* cannot be "simply appended as a separate just war category, completely autonomous from the *jus ad bellum* and *jus in bello*."[131] We agree that planning for a just peace ought to be undertaken prior to the initiation of hostilities, and we believe that the categories and criteria of each phase of just war are interlocking. In short, the goal of establishing a just peace for all involved and affected by war should be furthered and reinforced by making more explicit *jus post bellum* criteria and practices.

2

JUS POST BELLUM

An Emerging Category

"Peace is not sought in order to provoke war, but war is waged in order to attain peace. Be a peacemaker, then, even by fighting, so that through your victory you might bring those whom you defeat to the advantages of peace."[1]

In the previous chapter we traced the history of just war thinking, including major philosophers and theologians, from the ancient world to today. We also identified and briefly examined the two primary categories of just war theory, along with their respective criteria, that we have inherited up to this point in time, *jus ad bellum* and *jus in bello*. After considering and addressing some criticisms of the just war tradition, we put forth our own criticisms, principally, that insufficient attention has been given to post war justice and that insufficient attention has been paid to how just peacemaking as a type of *jus ante bellum* relates to just war theory. What we did not highlight, however, were some of the nascent elements of *jus post bellum* present among the contributors to this living and developing tradition. In addition, in recent years *jus post bellum* has become an emerging category in disciplines other than Christian theological ethics, including political science, philosophy, and military science.

This chapter begins by turning to the just war tradition for insights that point toward and can be used to construct criteria for *jus post bellum*. Then we turn to a quick survey of recent contributions from philosophers, political scientists, and military researchers to the development of criteria that can bring about justice once the smoke of war has cleared. This chapter concludes by pointing out the need for a perspective that is both theological and ethical.

NASCENT ELEMENTS OF *JUS POST BELLUM* IN THE TRADITION

Concern for post war justice is not new. Military strategists have for centuries talked about exit strategies. Some evidence of concern about post war justice may be found among classic just war thinkers, though much of it was in connection with thinking about *jus ad bellum* and *jus in bello*. We now turn to some of the philosophers and theologians discussed in the first chapter, while others previously mentioned are notably absent. In addition, some whose work received little or no attention now come to the fore to demonstrate how their thought is being mined today to develop the just war category of *jus post bellum*.

The Ancient World

Classic authors, in the ancient Greek and Roman worlds, differentiated between war with barbarians and conflict among fellow Greeks or Romans. Still, Aristotle did not regard war as an end in itself, but instead a means to achieving higher goals, such as peace and justice. "No one chooses to be at war or provokes war for the sake of war," he wrote, "[We] make war that we may live at peace."[2] The Romans tended to view war more through the legal lens of contractual obligations. According to Frederick H. Russell, "The etymology of *pax* stems from *pangere*, to make a pact or contract wherein the rights and duties of both parties were specified."[3] While war against barbarians involved conquest and enslavement and not just the mere military defeat of the enemy, conflict between city-states was considered more of a breach of contract that required compensation and redress from the guilty offender who had provoked the conflict. Within this context, some attention to post war concerns may be found among classic Greek and Roman writers.

For example, Plato exhorted Greeks to fight "as those who intend someday to be reconciled." Concrete examples of what not to do if a just and lasting peace is the goal included the following:

> They will not devastate Hellas, nor will they burn houses, [nor] suppose that the whole population of a city—men, women, and children—are equally their enemies, for they know that the guilt of war is always confined to a few persons and that the many are their friends. And for all these reasons they will be unwilling to waste their lands and raze their houses; their enmity to them will only last until the many innocent sufferers have compelled the guilty few to give satisfaction.[4]

Plato thus distinguishes between the guilty and the innocent, and punishment should not be exacted upon all inhabitants indiscriminately. The leaders who were responsible for the unjust act that provoked the war in the first place are the guilty ones who owe some form of satisfaction.

In addition, Plato urged his fellow Greeks not to construct monuments to honor the victors of war and not to erect trophies in the temples. As Louis Iasiello notes,

> In doing so he displayed extraordinary insight into the *post bellum* psyche. He apparently understood the dynamics of a constructive *post bellum* environment, fearing that such public observances might fuel hard feelings and thus impede the healing process. Perhaps celebrations meant to convey the profound thanks of a grateful nation to its troops might translate into the unintended consequence of prolonging hostilities or fueling insurgencies.[5]

Although Plato did not explicitly deal with the *jus post bellum* category—just as he did not explicitly refer to *jus ad bellum* and *jus in bello*—its seeds are certainly evident in some of his texts.

Plato's student, Aristotle, in turn taught Alexander the Great. During the battle of Halicarnassus in 334 B.C.E. against the Persians, Alexander's siege engines broke into the city, but he forbade any reprisals against its civilian population. Also, after a victory at the Hydaspes River, he ordered his troops to bury not only their own dead but also "the bravest of the enemy."[6] Traces of the spirit of Plato's teachings therefore continued to characterize Alexander's practices of war.

According to Roland Bainton, the Greeks and the Romans occasionally exhibited magnanimity as an expedient way to make peace and avoid another war. As an example, he refers to Nikolaos, who addressed a Sicilian assembly to dissuade them from being brutal toward the defeated Athenians:

> Let no one accuse me of softness toward Athens. Have I not lost two sons in the war? ... Nevertheless mercy should be extended to Athens, partly on the grounds of the law since the common usage of the Greeks forbids the slaughter of the vanquished, and partly on the grounds of humanity.... Why did the ancients set up their trophies in wood rather than in stone? That the memory of their victories might be short.... In the fluctuations of Fortune the victor of today may be the vanquished of tomorrow and how can he expect to find mercy if he refuse it? Magnanimity will be the best way to establish peace and make the Athenians ashamed of their unjust war. Recall their contributions to Greek culture and the common loss which will be sustained in the destruction of their citizens.[7]

While he invokes the way in which fellow Greeks ought to treat each other in armed conflict, Nikolaos also appeals here to a more universal morality rooted in our common human nature, which Romans and Greeks share. He also warns that their roles might someday be reversed, so it would be wise to be merciful now so as to someday in turn receive mercy. Adhering to principles of justice and mercy will also serve as a testimony to one's enemies. Finally, Nikolaos notes the way in which the destruction of others actually affects us all.

As we saw in the previous chapter, the Roman philosopher

Cicero held that wars ought to be won through adherence to the virtues, not by vicious or treacherous means. The latter were not honorable, and they could moreover pave the way for conflict to erupt again in the future. Similarly, Cicero encouraged victors in war to be merciful to the vanquished and when dealing with besieged cities; they were to punish only those guilty of resisting while sparing the majority of the innocent population.[8] Soldiers must not intend the enemy's utter destruction, but rather the restoration of peaceful relations and community. In *De Officiis*, he advised,

> When the victory is won we should spare those who have not been bloodthirsty and barbarous in the warfare.... Not only must we show consideration for those whom we have conquered by force of arms but we must also ensure protection to those who lay down their arms and throw themselves upon the mercy of our generals.[9]

This is not to say, of course, that the Romans abided by such considerations consistently. Bainton relays some negative judgments from some of the vanquished of the time. For example, the Britons said, "The Romans are robbers of the world. After denuding the land, they rifle the sea. They are rapacious toward the rich and domineering toward the poor, satiated neither by the East nor by the West. Pillage, massacre and plunder they grace with the name of empire and where they make a desert, call it peace."[10] Noting such violations of their just war principles, however, does not entail that such rules had no effect whatsoever.

Another instance when the Romans failed to act magnanimously occurred when Carthage rearmed itself after its defeat in the first Punic War. Rome, which regarded this as a threat, leveled Carthage and enslaved its people. According to Bainton, "When subsequently Rome was rent by civil wars, later Romans reproached the ruthlessness of their sires."[11] Calling to mind the ancient adage about how "you reap whatever you sow" (Gal 6:7), which more recently has been dubbed "blowback,"[12] the Romans here were reminded of the wisdom of Cicero and, before him, Plato, with regard to the importance of ending a war in a way that laid the groundwork for a just and lasting peace for all. These early theorists of *jus post bellum* tend to frame their concern primarily in pragmatic terms, as opposed to pursuing *jus post bellum* out of principle or duty.

The Christian Tradition

The Christian adoption of just war thinking began, as we saw for Ambrose and Augustine, with an emphasis on proper intent, namely, a love that seeks a just and lasting peace for all parties involved in a conflict. Augustine believed that peace "is the purpose of waging war ... What, then, men want in war is that it should end in peace."[13] He exhorted the just warrior to "be a peacemaker, even in war so that by conquering them you bring the benefit of peace even to those you defeat."[14] This peace, in Augustine's view, was not merely the absence of hostilities but rather the restoration of a tranquil and just order. According to Bainton, Augustine echoed the rules of conduct from classical antiquity, including no wanton violence, profanation of temples, looting, massacres, or conflagration.[15] While these are concerns for *jus in bello*, they certainly have implications for the wake of war. To be sure, Christians did not always abide by these standards, especially during the Crusades or in the conquest of the Americas.

A thousand years after Augustine, the Dominican theologian Francisco de Vitoria took the Spanish king to task for the conquistadors' treatment of Amerindians. Reminding the monarch that just war ought to be embarked upon "only under compulsion and reluctantly," Vitoria added that "it must not be waged so as to ruin the people against whom it is directed, but only so as to obtain one's rights and the defense of one's country and in order that from that war peace and security may in time result."[16]

Moreover, he held that moderation and humility ought to shape how victory is implemented. Reports of massacres, plundering, and looting, he said, cast doubt on the justice of the enterprise. He attributed significant weight to the criterion of proportionality on both the macro *jus ad bellum* and micro *jus in bello* levels. War should not be embarked upon if it leads to greater evils outweighing the possible good that is sought. Nor should the conduct of war involve wanton and excessive violence and destruction. Any killing and damage should not pose an obstacle to, but rather should be in line with the justice and peace that are the purpose of a just war.[17]

Vitoria argued that any plundering and looting during war should be circumscribed by proportionality. Goods may be seized, from both the guilty and the innocent, but only in accordance with what justice requires as fitting reparations and punishment bestowed upon the enemy.[18] If looting occurs without authorization from a superior officer, offending soldiers ought to make restitution to the victims. Rape was especially regarded as a horrible crime and denounced by Vitoria.

He also turned his attention to the question of deposing princes, taking over governments, and dissolving kingdoms (what today might be called regime change or nation-building) by acknowledging that there are occasions when such drastic measures may be justified, as when the continuing rule of a prince or government would pose an ongoing threat. However, in this and everything else he said in connection with post war justice, Vitoria encouraged victors to refrain from doing everything they lawfully might and instead to be merciful and moderate where possible.[19]

Vitoria's student Francisco Suarez identified three "periods" that must be distinguished with respect to war: "its inception; its prosecution, before victory is gained; and the period after victory."[20] This clearly shows concern about just conduct in the wake of war. In his attention to punishment, satisfaction, and reimbursement for incurred losses, Suarez basically echoed what Vitoria had to say concerning what ought to be done after victory.[21]

As for Grotius, post war justice was not altogether absent from his thought. Book 3 of his 1625 work *De Jure Belli ac Pacis* (Laws of War and Peace) contained rules governing the conduct of war, as well as practical principles for the termination of a just war, including rules on surrender, good faith, and interpretation of peace treaties.[22]

Summing up the contributions of these just war theorists of the sixteenth century, Oliver O'Donovan notes that they assumed that *post bellum* practices would include "an attempt on the part of the victors to punish the vanquished, by confiscations, executions, and possibly the deposition of the ruler," but, even so, they discouraged and attempted to limit such actions out of concern for vices that are inconsistent with the attitude requisite to a just war, concern about the difficulties in distinguishing levels of guilt, and worry that "judicial zeal might provide further fuel for conflict."[23] Indeed, these latter just war thinkers echo the incipient attention to *jus post bellum* that was evident among the ancient Greeks and Romans. However, perhaps less emphasized in their work is the earlier Christian concern, especially pronounced in Augustine's thought, for right intent as entailing the restoration of a just peace for all, including one's enemies. As noted in the previous chapter, Grotius devoted hardly any attention to right intention. According to Sharma, Grotius's contribution to the just war tradition "marks a sharp contrast with Augustine, for whom the preliminary issue was justifying Christian participation in warfare," so that the focus will come to be more on *bellum legale*, or a legalist approach that seeks merely to regulate war, rather than *bellum justum*.[24]

The Work of Immanuel Kant

During the Enlightenment, treatments of war came to be found even more within the domain of political philosophy and international law than in theology. The English philosopher John Locke (1632-1704), in his *Second Treatise on Civil Government*, devoted attention to politics and war, including the topics of conquest and the dissolution of a defeated nation's government.[25] Locke's work obviously proved influential, particularly in connection with the American War of Independence, for subsequent political thought. Jean-Jacques Rousseau (1712-1778) and other Enlightenment thinkers could also, of course, be tapped here. However, because the work of the German Lutheran Immanuel Kant (1724-1804) is receiving a revival of interest in connection with post war ethics among some philosophers today, we now highlight some relevant aspects of his thinking before turning our attention to the current state of the question about *jus post bellum* among disciplines other than theology.

With works such as his *Critique of Pure Reason* and *The Metaphysics of Morals*, Kant has no doubt left his mark on Western philosophy and was a seminal figure in cosmopolitanism. For him, human reason is the foundation upon which morality rests, and through reason international laws could be formulated to establish a social contract involving a league of nations to guarantee peace. Famous for his deontological ethics, including the categorical imperative, Kant devoted considerable thought to peace treaties, regime change, post war reconstruction, and the requisites for longer-term peace between nations. Interestingly, until recently scholars have considered Kant to be more of a pacifist. As Brian Orend observes, "Kant tended to be regarded either as a dogmatic pacifist—for how could the categorical imperative permit war?—or else as a hopeless utopian, what with all this stuff about 'perpetual peace.'"[26] Nevertheless, Orend has persuasively demonstrated that Kant should more accurately be viewed as a just war theorist. That is not to say that Kant snugly fits into the traditional just war mold. As Orend acknowledges, Kant deviated from traditional just war thinking in that he gave less attention to *jus in bello*, he rejected consequentialist appeals to proportionality and probability of success, and he focused more attention to *jus ad bellum* and *jus post bellum*, going beyond what the tradition had previously set forth.[27]

Of particular significance for our project, in part 1 of *The Metaphysics of Morals*, Kant treats the topic of international rights, which is being "concerned partly with the right to make war, partly with the right of war itself, and partly with the questions of right after war, i.e., with the right of states to compel each other to abandon their warlike condition and to create a constitution which will establish an enduring peace."[28] Here Kant references not only the two traditional categories of just war criteria—*jus ad bellum* (*Recht zum Krieg*, "the right to make war") and *jus in bello* (*Recht im Krieg*, "the war itself")—but also *jus post bellum* (*Recht nach dem Krieg*, "right after war").[29] Kant opposed the view that might makes right. Although he made room for the possibility of regime change in serious cases of blatant aggression, he believed that the victor in war must respect the rights of the people of the defeated nation to become sovereign and self-determining. A constitution and government that is more rights-respecting and democratic—what Orend views as a precursor to what is now called "the democratic peace thesis"—would help prevent future conflict from arising.[30]

Kant also thought that the end of a war provided an opportunity to bolster the prospects for a just peace among the international community of nations.[31] Similarly he began his *Critique of Perpetual Peace* by outlining ways to eradicate incentives to war and instead build an atmosphere of mutual trust between states (as advocated by just peacemaking); he viewed such trust as an essential springboard to constructing a lasting peace. He maintained that during the conduct of a war, nothing should be done to extinguish such trust, for that would undermine prospects for building post war peace. Assassinations and treacherous espionage, for example, might "make mutual confidence impossible during a future time of peace."[32]

Although Kant clearly devoted significant attention to the importance of *jus post bellum*, this phase of the ethics of warfare was curiously neglected over the next couple of centuries. According to international law scholar Carsten Stahn,

> Surprisingly, this "third leg" in the theory of warfare disappeared in the conceptualization of the laws of war in the 19th and 20th century. The *jus in bello* was codified, later the *jus ad bellum*. The *jus post bellum*, by contrast, did not receive much attention. It was only treated in a cursory fashion in some treatises at the beginning of the 20th century.[33]

As a result, *jus post bellum* currently is, according to Michael Walzer, "the least developed part of just war theory."[34] This state of affairs, however, is beginning to change. Indeed, during these initial decades of the twenty-first century, international law scholars such as Stahn, along with philosophers, political scientists, and military experts, are giving *jus post bellum* "renewed attention."[35]

PHILOSOPHY, POLITICAL SCIENCE, INTERNATIONAL LAW, AND MILITARY SCIENCE

As philosophical thinkers such as Aristotle and Cicero had already laid some of the foundations in just war theory for Christian theologians to build upon, so too today philosophers and thinkers from other secular disciplines such as the political and military sciences have already begun to develop and debate *jus post bellum*. As we noted in the Introduction, Catholic moral theology engages signs of the times as it seeks to formulate an ethical perspective on issues we face in the world. That philosophers, political scientists, and military experts in recent years are devoting so much discussion and debate to *jus post bellum* is surely such a sign that we should read before bringing a Christian theological account to bear on the question.[36] In particular, we highlight the contributions of four scholars from the fields of philosophy and international relations.

Brian Orend

One of the key and more prolific writers in the philosophical literature on *jus post bellum* is Brian Orend. Currently a professor of philosophy and director of international studies at the University of Waterloo, Orend has written several articles, book chapters, and books on the subject. He approaches the topic not through international law, but from the perspective of philosophical just war theory. As we noted in the previous section, Orend draws deeply from the well of Kantian thought in connection with *jus post bellum*. Indeed, he believes that Kant is "historically the first figure to offer us truly deep, systematic and forward-looking reflections on justice after war."[37]

In Orend's view, "Violations of *jus post bellum* are just as serious as those of *jus ad bellum* and *jus in bello*."[38] Orend begins his delineation of *jus post bellum* by asking, "What are the ends or goals of a just war?" Although this sort of question is addressed by the *jus ad bellum* criterion of right intent, Orend links it more with just cause when he writes "that the proper aim of a just war is the vindication of those rights whose violation grounded the resort to war in the first place."[39] Moreover he calls upon political authorities to declare at the outset of a war their intention to abide by the *jus in bello* and *jus post bellum* criteria, an expectation that will function as an extra incentive for limiting the conduct of war, ruling out policies of unconditional surrender, and requiring that post war settlements are committed to and fully implemented.

Orend offers six principles for *jus post bellum*: (1) rights vindication (not vindictive revenge but resecuring the violated rights that triggered the conflict, such as rights to life, liberty, and territorial sovereignty); (2) proportionality and publicity (measured and reasonable settlement, publicly proclaimed); (3) discrimination (distinguishing between leaders, soldiers, and civilians); (4) punishment (war crimes trials to deter, to foster rehabilitation/"atonement," and to hold soldiers accountable on all sides of the conflict); (5) compensation (financial restitution); and (6) rehabilitation (demilitarization of aggressor state, political rehabilitation).[40] Orend thinks all of these requirements should be met for there to be an ethical exit strategy from a war. Any violation or neglect of these principles should be punished.

Orend then offers some principles for forcible post war regime change, which involves "the timely construction of a minimally just community" to rehabilitate a defeated aggressor.[41] The regime being put in place should not have the nature of a crusade or be imperialistic, but should have the goal of respecting human rights. Orend demonstrates that this is empirically possible by citing the examples of governments established in Germany and Japan (1945-1955). He offers an "ideal 10-point recipe for transforming a defeated aggressor into a minimally just regime,"[42] noting that success takes seven to ten years.

Orend holds that "when or if an aggressor wins a war, the peace terms will necessarily be unjust. The injustice of cause infects the conclusion of the war."[43] In Orend's view, the three categories are so deeply interconnected that injustice in any one of them negatively affects hopes for justice in the others. He adds, "This is not to say that meeting *jus ad bellum* will automatically result in your meeting *jus in bello* and *jus post bellum*. But it *is* to say, conversely, that failure to meet *jus ad bellum* results in automatic failure to meet *jus in bello* and *jus post bellum*."[44] The relationship between the three categories and Orend's notion of infection is explored in the next chapter.

Gary J. Bass

Another philosopher who has written about *jus post bellum* is Gary J. Bass, an associate professor of politics and international affairs at Princeton University. He observes, "Political leaders often invoke postwar developments like bringing democracy or stability as part of justifying or condemning a war: but political theorists have not yet fully come to terms with which of these arguments are morally compelling."[45] He quotes from George W. Bush and Jimmy Carter, who both referred to the responsibility to make a defeated nation more stable and secure. In Bass's view, *jus post bellum* rights and obligations stem from extant just war and, in particular, just cause and the *jus in bello* criteria.

With regard to just cause, he writes that "the declared ends that justify a war—whether stopping genocide or preventing aggression—impose obligations on belligerent powers to try, even after the conclusion of the war, to bring about the desired outcome."[46] As for the *jus in bello* criteria, he says that proportionality requires restraint during combat in order to avoid total war and total conquest. "If political transformation of the enemy is the objective of a war, then that war will likely be a total war."[47]

Bass offers an account of *jus post bellum* that is based on what he calls "the liberal approach to just war theory" espoused by theorist Michael Walzer, or what Walzer refers to as the "legalist paradigm" of just war theory. Bass also draws from the work of political philosopher John Rawls.[48] The focus is on justice; "if a war has a just cause, and is fought justly, the war still must lead to a just post war settlement."[49] Bass writes,

> Just postwar actions cannot redeem a war that was unjust to begin with, but we think somewhat worse of an aggressor state that annexes conquered territory than of an aggressor state that evacuates it, just as we think worse of an aggressor state that targets civilians in the war it started than of an aggressor state that does not.[50]

In connection with avoiding conquest, Bass mentions three areas to consider. First, the victorious nation has no right to reconstruct the defeated nation out of self-interest. This prohibits either setting up puppet regimes or undertaking reconstruction with the goal of the victor's economic, military, or political gain.[51] Second, the *in bello* criterion of proportionality requires restraint in transforming a society. Third, the winning country has no right to impose cultural reconstruction.

Bass has a rather minimalist account of post war reconstruction obligations and is very concerned about self-interested nation-building. "The duty to respect to the greatest extent possible the sovereignty of the defeated nation and to seek the consent of the defeated in any project for reconstruction is thus both an obligation of justice and a counsel of political prudence."[52] Bass argues that if just cause has to do with self-defense, "then there is little justification for reshaping a defeated society."[53] Our account of just war, however, allows for more than self-defense, for we include legitimate defense of the innocent, which encompasses humanitarian intervention or R2P. Thus, our account of post war reconstruction obligations might involve elements akin to nation-building, though nation-building does not constitute a just cause for embarking upon war. To illustrate his view, Bass says the George H. W. Bush administration was correct not to invade deeper into Iraq to take over Baghdad in the first Gulf War. For Bass, "The end of war must entail the restoration of national sovereignty," and that is pretty much it.[54] Accordingly, Bass calls for a "presumption against any right of the victors to reconstruct a defeated country."[55] Of course, part of this depends on what is meant by "reconstruct."

Bass does maintain, as we do, that the goal should not simply be a return to the *status quo ante*. Another flare-up of unjust war by the aggressor nation must be prevented. The most compelling case for a *jus post bellum* duty to reconstruct a defeated country arises when dealing with genocidal states: "Without some reconstruction, there would be another war, and that is an injustice itself."[56] The example he cites is Nazi Germany, which was not merely about dictatorship. "My argument, then, is that there is a *jus post bellum* duty to reconstruct genocidal states."[57] Orend makes a similar case for regime change, which he says can be a just cause from the onset—a concept explored in greater detail in chapter 6. A country on the verge of anarchy after the defeat of its dictatorial regime may be a case for "a more limited kind of foreign reconstruction," in Bass's view.[58]

He further notes that spelling out *jus post bellum* duties in advance is difficult to do in the abstract, because it involves duties of positive assistance—whereas *jus in bello* criteria are phrased as negative duties of justice.[59] At first glance, this seems true. However, the *jus in bello* criteria could be stated more positively—for example, targeting only combatants and saving as many noncombatant lives as possible. *Jus post bellum* criteria do seem to be open to more positive possibilities. Bass cites three provisos on reconstruction: first, the victor nation ought not be neutral; it should have any "eye to chastening the perpetrators and comforting the victims."[60] Second, it should include the participation of other governments from the international community. Third, it should set realistic goals—"the point is to dispose of cruelty, not to build a utopia." In the end, though, Bass argues "that in most cases the primary *jus post bellum* responsibility of a victorious state is to get out as soon as possible."[61]

Doug McCready

Doug McCready, a retired Army Reserve chaplain with a Ph.D. in religious studies from Temple University, has one foot firmly planted in the world of theology and the other in international relations. He was a Senior Service College Fellow at the Fletcher School of Law and Diplomacy. In his article "Ending the War Right: *Jus Post Bellum* and the Just War Tradition," McCready aptly criticizes most *jus post bellum* with its means. The end is establishing a just and lasting peace that is substantially more just and more stable than what preceded the war. This includes war crimes trials, truth and reconciliation commissions, security, reconstruction efforts, and so on, none of which are proper ends in and of themselves, but ways of establishing a just and lasting peace.

We take this criticism seriously. However, a theory of *jus post bellum* that fails to offer concrete examples is irrelevant. As McCready himself notes, "The purpose of a *jus post bellum* category is to increase the likelihood of a just and lasting peace, not provide an additional topic for academic papers and conferences."[62] Thus we illustrate the criterion of our *jus post bellum* theory with concrete examples of how these principles have been upheld and violated. To suggest there is a one-size-fits-all blueprint for post war justice is untenable. Too many variables (history, culture, ethnic identities, religious convictions, conditions on the ground, etc.) require *jus post bellum* principles to remain thin, leaving the thicker task of application to those responsible for post war reconstruction and reconciliation.

McCready identifies three unresolved issues concerning the construction of a *jus post bellum* category:

1. Identifying when the *post bellum* phase begins. *Jus post bellum* considerations often overlap with the *jus in bello* phase because the end of formal and significant combat doesn't always coincide with the end of the war, as the most recent wars in Iraq and Afghanistan illustrate.
2. What should be done when a state fails to fulfill its *post bellum* responsibilities? Should political leaders be held responsible legally? What mechanisms ought to be set up to hold people accountable for *jus post bellum*?
3. Identifying when a victor can leave the defeated nation. In other words, when has *jus post bellum* been achieved, and how much does the victor owe the defeated?

Again, our model addresses these concerns.

Mark Evans

Mark Evans, a senior lecturer in politics at Swansea University and an expert on just war theory, makes several keen observations about the emerging category of *jus post bellum*. First, he distinguishes between "restricted" and "extended" conceptions of *jus post bellum*, which can conflict with one another. Restricted interpretations "focus on the norms to govern the ending and immediate aftermath of a just war," while extended interpretations focus on the more lofty, elusive, and long-range goal of establishing a just and lasting peace.[63] Second, he offers five *jus post bellum* criteria or guidelines that just combatants must be prepared to pursue:

1. Set peace terms that are proportionately determined to ensure a just and stable peace as well as to redress the injustices that prompted the conflict.
2. Take full responsibility for their fair share of the material bur-

dens of the conflict's aftermath in constructing a just and stable peace.

3. Pursue those national and international political initiatives for conflict prevention (which is similar to the objectives of just peacemaking).

4. Take full and proactive part in the ethical and sociocultural processes of forgiveness and reconciliation, which are central to the construction of a just and stable peace.[64]

5. Where just combatants occupy the defeated unjust aggressor, or are present in another territory in the aftermath of a humanitarian intervention, they have a duty to restore sovereignty/self-determination to the territory as soon as reasonably possible.[65]

Evans notes that this final criterion may not always be relevant, as in cases when "there are good reasons (such as ethnic tensions) why a state should not in fact be reconstituted in its antebellum form" (such as Yugoslavia following the ethnic cleansings in the 1990s).[66] He posits this final criterion to prevent "mission creep," when the responsibilities of the occupying force continually expand, thereby lengthening the period of post conflict occupation.

In addition, Evans proffers the possibility of "justified early termination" for situations in which prolonged occupation prevents just occupiers from securing a just and stable peace. In other words, there could be instances when a just occupier can simply take too long and in which extending their mission in the name of securing a just and lasting peace actually prevents the very end they pursue. In such instances Evans advocates settling for a "suboptimal 'acceptable peace' recognizing that sometimes one has no reasonable alternative but to sacrifice elements of what one ideally ought to do (or what one set out to do)."[67]

Evans's recognition that demanding explicit *jus post bellum* commitments in the *ad bellum* phase foolishly ignores that war is a Pandora's box; no one can accurately predict what the situation on the ground *post bellum* might entail is a welcomed dose of realism, but it is also a slippery slope. It essentially allows an easy out for occupiers who can cut and run, claiming, "If we stay any longer we will prevent the defeated from achieving self-sufficiency." This paternalistic argument was popular once the

U.S. occupation of Iraq proved more arduous than anticipated, with pundits and some elected officials essentially arguing, "We must stand down, so the Iraqis will stand up."

Evans seems aware that he has stepped on the slippery slope. He sets a hedge around this argument by articulating six considerations necessary to excuse occupiers from their responsibilities.[68] While the nod to realism is appreciated, we contend that just war theory's rationale for the use of deadly force is the *tranquilatitis ordinis*, a just and lasting peace. The moral force of *jus post bellum* is precisely that it holds those claiming to fight a just war responsible for the just cause(s) identified in the *ad bellum* phase. Any stepping back from this rigorous interpretation of the criteria makes for a less honest just war theory.

Finally, several other scholars have made contributions to the *jus post bellum* debate that are worthy of note (albeit brief). Michael Walzer, one of the most prominent contemporary just war theorists, identifies self-determination, popular legitimacy, civil rights and a commitment to the common good as criteria of *jus post bellum*, while E. Patterson proposes three *jus post bellum* goals: order, justice, and reconciliation.[69] James Turner Johnson and Alex Bellamy separately question the necessity and wisdom of a *jus post bellum* category, arguing in large part that its concerns fall properly under *jus ad bellum*.[70] Finally, Darrel Mollendorf, a philosopher at San Diego State University, argues for the need to develop *jus ex bello*, a "set of considerations that govern whether a war, once begun, should be brought to an end and if so how," which he regards as "a middle phase doctrine, and therefore distinguishable from *jus post bellum*."[71]

A THEOLOGICAL PERSPECTIVE

Adrian Pabst, who lectures on politics, international relations, and religion at the University of Kent, in "Can There Be a Just War without a Just Peace?" helps transition this current discussion of *jus post bellum* toward a more theological perspective. For him, the current philosophical efforts to construct a framework for *jus post bellum* rest upon an "account of justice [that] is predicated on abstract ideas and disembodied practices of justice which derive from minimalist principles."[72] This is perhaps why debate continues among philosophers, political scientists, and others about whether *jus post bellum* entails simply a return to the *status quo ante*. According to Pabst, justice in these more philosophical accounts "constitutes neither the overcoming nor the resolution, let alone the reconciliation of violence; it is mere regulation."[73] Peace, in that view, is reduced to the cessation of hostilities and the imposition of abstract principles in a defeated society. It is a kind of negative peace, rather than the positive, restorative form we saw earlier in the thinking of Augustine. In short, the outcome for these philosophical (Pabst refers to them as "liberal" just war theories) approaches to just war is "un-reconciled conflict."[74] Interestingly, in this connection Pabst also accuses neoconservatives, such as Catholic thinkers Michael Novak and George Weigel, who espouse a "unilateral" just war theory, of being similarly lacking when it comes to restoring a truly just peace in the wake of war.

As Catholic theological ethicists who seek to take seriously the theology undergirding Christian just war theory, we believe Pabst rightly calls for "an alternative vision" for justice before, during, and after war:

> Genuine justice is transcendent, substantive and inclusive. Transcendent because true justice requires discernment beyond ethnic, economic and social division. It negates self-interest as ultimately destructive. It envisages an equitable peace and reconciliation between all parties. Just interventions must really deliver systematic transformation, not merely regime change. Most importantly, a just settlement must not be a pale imitation of western variants but instead an inclusive process that blends universal values with particular traditions. Only if the indigenous cultures believe that the intervention was conducted justly and nobly by a legitimate force will there be any hope for genuine reconciliation and a lasting permanent peace.[75]

While subsequent chapters develop the four *jus post bellum* criteria we are proposing (including a chapter devoted to post war reconciliation), for now we wish to highlight the way that

Pabst emphasizes reconciliation. This is a positive vision, one that we believe is congruent with the just and lasting peace that the Christian just war tradition initially envisioned but has become either lost altogether or subordinated to other criteria such as, in the work of Weigel and Novak, just cause. Of course, if we are going to hope for this sort of restorative justice and lasting peace, we must intend it.

Pabst seeks to recover the *telos* of just war for the early Christian theologians, "namely the belief that peace is the highest truth and constitutes the ontological shape of the world."[76] For the earlier theological tradition, just war was less a theory than a matter of practical judgment grounded in specific practices aimed at restoring a just peace for all. Pabst argues that during the transition from a more theological to a more universal natural law approach (represented by Vitoria, Suarez, Grotius, and others), the focus shifted from a more substantive account of just war to more "abstract legal considerations on the justice of war," including the rise of the language of rights (the "right" to resort to war, the "right" to use force during war, and the "right" to conclude a post conflict settlement), with the result that "violence came gradually to be granted the same ontological station as peace and thus could only be regulated, rather than resolved."[77]

In Pabst's view, therefore, Kant's approach to just war theory, even with its attention to *jus post bellum*, yielded too much ground to the ontological priority of violence, which can only be regulated, and would thus prove ultimately to be self-defeating. And modern versions of political liberalism, represented by Rawls and Walzer (and, by extension, Orend and others today), with its "minimalist principles," continue this trajectory that "merely regulates antagonistic interests and values rather than attempts to overcome and reconcile them."[78] Pabst believes we can and should do better by aiming higher. It appears to us that what he is calling for formerly was encompassed under the *jus ad bellum* criterion of right intent.

Iasiello appears to agree:

From war's inception (*jus ad bellum*) and throughout its prosecution (*jus in bello*), the goal of all should be the establishment of a just and lasting peace. Therefore, the long-term consequences of even a justified use of force require that just intention extend into the *post bellum* stage, thus demanding our consideration of a third category of just war theory (*jus post bellum*).[79]

As a navy chaplain, Iasiello recalls how Christian just war thinking has as its goal this restorative vision of a just and lasting peace, otherwise known as the *jus ad bellum* criterion of right intent. Indeed, his claim is that right intent should guide and direct each phase and all of the criteria of just war.

As we saw earlier, right intent was especially pronounced in the work of Augustine and other Christian theologians until the sixteenth century, when it received significantly less attention by, for example, Grotius. For this reason, we suspect it is not a mere coincidence that *jus post bellum* received only cursory attention during the centuries following, even with the attention given to it in the work of Kant.[80] With Pabst and Iasiello, we believe that right intention is fundamental for Christian just war thinking. Interestingly, other theological ethicists today are also rediscovering the importance of right intent for just war theory.

For example, Lutheran ethicist Helmut David Baer and Catholic moral theologian Joseph E. Capizzi have recently argued, drawing on the efforts of their teacher, Methodist ethicist Theodore Weber, "that just intention be assigned a governing role in just war theory."[81] In their view, reconceiving just war in this way would reestablish it as an actual politics rather than "as an assortment of criteria."[82] Like Pabst, they are critical of current approaches to just war theory that tend to "regulate the conduct of states."[83] As an alternative, they propose an account of just war that revolves around right intent, which is the teleology of political power. They write,

> Thus, just intention expresses love for the enemy by stipulating that the end of war be peace. Peace is a principle of order. A lasting order, however, must encompass the point of view and interests of the enemy; that is, a peaceful order must be a just order—one that includes and recognizes the claims of the enemy. This just order requires more than conceiving peace as a return to the status quo ante. War

brings about a new set of relationships. The newly encoun-
tered neighbor must be brought into an equitable and stable
relationship with us.

The similarities here with what Pabst called for are striking. Baer
and Capizzi are calling for reconciliation and thereby "placing
just war theory within the larger framework of peacemaking."[84]
Like Pabst, they are according ontological primacy to peace.
Unlike Pabst, however, Baer and Capizzi stop short of explicitly
discussing *jus post bellum*.

The most recent voice to enter into this discussion is that of
Methodist theological ethicist Daniel M. Bell, whose work seeks
to get the church to reclaim just war as a discipline that requires
certain theological practices and formation in the virtues in order
to shape persons who truly embody and adhere to the criteria.
Instead of merely ticking principles off a checklist, Christians must
demonstrate, as an expression of right intent, love that seeks to
restore a just and lasting peace. In Bell's view, "If one's intent in
waging war is indeed just, if one really loves one's enemies and
intends to bring the benefits of peace and justice to them, then
one will not abandon them when the shooting stops but will be
involved in the restoration of a just peace."[85]

In making this point, however, Bell nevertheless posits that
the addition of the category *jus post bellum* "is unnecessary."[86]
Yet he goes on to consider briefly how right intent might require
"exit strategies," regime change, maintaining security, providing
health care for returning soldiers, reparations, criminal prosecu-
tions of the guilty, and a number of other things—all of which are
typically covered under the rubric of *jus post bellum*. While we
obviously are sympathetic with Bell's project and agree that just
war ought not be seen simply as a checklist of criteria, we believe
that the categories and criteria are necessary and helpful tools for
Christians who seek to put their right intent into practice—and
to hold them accountable. After all, if adding a category of *jus
post bellum* is unnecessary for the reason that Bell gives, then
so too is having the other two categories of criteria. In our view,
right intent is necessary but not sufficient. The three categories
and their associated criteria are also necessary to help guide how
to put into practice and implement this just intention.

CONCLUSION

While the contributions from philosophers such as Orend and Bass are engaged and drawn upon in the remaining chapters, we want it to be clear that we seek to offer concrete ideas and practices of justice that derive from this deeper theological soil. Our proposal, to use Walzer's language, is both thin and thick (in other words, it includes theoretical universal principles that are grounded in and tested by the mud and blood of human experience). We also see this project as a service to our own Christian community. For, although the U.S. Catholic bishops recently have emphasized the need for a "responsible transition" in Iraq, they have done so in a way that is only on the surface connected with this theological account of the just war tradition.

In "Toward a Responsible Transition in Iraq," a statement released in January 2006, Bishop Thomas G. Wenski, then chairman of the United States Conference of Catholic Bishops Committee on International Policy, wrote, "It is important for all to recognize that addressing questions regarding the decisions that led us to war, and about the conduct of war and its aftermath, is both necessary and patriotic."[87] Thus, he alluded to each of the three categories of just war. As evident in this brief eight-page public statement, the bishops, who had earlier expressed grave concerns about the morality of embarking on war in Iraq, were beginning to give attention to what justice requires in the wake of war, that is, *jus post bellum*. Indeed, Wenski conveyed the sadness the bishops felt about the deaths of U.S. military personnel and of Iraqis during the years since the initiation of the war. Even though a brutal dictator, Saddam Hussein, had been deposed, and although democratic elections had been held, "the human and social costs" connected with these two achievements weighed heavily on the bishops' hearts. The ongoing lack of stability, the uneven rebuilding efforts, and the continuing absence of adequate security spurred the bishops to "seek to offer some moral reflections to help guide our nation along the difficult road ahead." They called for a genuine, nonpartisan dialogue, and toward this end the bishops suggested that "an honest assessment of our moral responsibilities toward Iraq should commit our nation to a policy of *responsible transition*."

The rest of the statement consisted of some reflections about the timing of U.S. military withdrawal from Iraq and the nature and extent of a combination of American and international participation to promote stability for the people of Iraq. The bishops noted that U.S. military forces ought to remain in Iraq "only as long as it takes for a responsible transition, leaving sooner rather than later." They then provided a series of "basic benchmarks" that would eventually allow American troops to leave: achieving an adequate level of security, establishing the rule of law, promoting economic reconstruction, and supporting the development of political structures to advance stability, civic participation, and respect for fundamental human rights, including religious freedom. Particular attention was also given to human rights violations, not only by terrorists who target civilians, but by some members of the U.S. military. Such actions, especially torture, "simultaneously undermine both the struggle against terrorism and the prospects of a responsible transition in Iraq." These instances also undermine the United States' moral credibility and any efforts to win the hearts of the population of Iraq; they also jeopardize the possibility of humane treatment of captured American military personnel.

Another key area of concern that the bishops identified is the plight of refugees and asylum seekers, including but not limited to Christian minorities in Iraq. At the same time, the statement devoted a couple of paragraphs to pastoral concern for U.S. military personnel and their families. In the end, Bishop Wenski noted that statements like this are insufficient, and that the "time has come for public reflection that leads to action."

The statement noted that these activities and practices are important because in Catholic social teaching peace is more than the absence of war. Peace is built on justice, including economic, political, criminal, and other forms of justice. Here the bishops touched upon the underlying theological basis that we are seeking to recover for just war and post war justice. Yet, in our view, this document, along with subsequent statements from the bishops reiterating its points (including a December 18, 2009, letter to retired Marine General James L. Jones from Bishop Howard J. Hubbard of Albany, New York, regarding President Barack Obama's goal of a "responsible transition" in Afghanistan), focuses more on exit strategies and thus come close to seeming like a checklist of considerations that err on the side of minimalism.[88] We believe that a more theological account of just war and *jus post bellum* would not only offer a contribution to the wider public discussion among other disciplines but it would also provide a richer foundation for this "responsible transition" that the bishops have in mind.

As we have seen in this chapter, while the just war tradition has largely developed within Christian circles, theologians and church leaders have for the most part, but not altogether, ignored *post bellum* ethics. Still, even with the nascent ingredients that we identified and discussed in this chapter, this dimension of just war theory has not received nearly the degree of attention that the *jus ad bellum* and *jus in bello* categories have enjoyed.

Moreover, while *jus post bellum* ethics have been developing today in secular disciplines such as political and military science, concerns have been raised that these treatments might be minimalistic. Until now, there has also been a failure to address post war justice substantively from within the Catholic and Christian tradition, which is why we are proposing four main criteria, each consisting of a number of considerations and practices, to promote justice in the post war period. This approach does not provide, of course, a one-size-fits-all blueprint. Rather, the criteria we propose for *jus post bellum* "can be amended, as details demand, in particular as well as unconventional cases."[89] Even so, we believe that the right intent of restoring a just and lasting peace requires serious and systematic attention to *jus post bellum* by Christian theologians and the church.

PART 2

FOUR *JUS POST BELLUM* CRITERIA

3

THE JUST CAUSE PRINCIPLE

"Just Cause: force may be used only to correct a grave, public evil, i.e., aggression or massive violation of the basic rights of whole populations."[1]

Having laid a foundation for just war theory (its history, interpretations, and critiques) and having explored the emergence of *jus post bellum* as a new category in the just war tradition, we turn to the heart of the matter: the development of a systematically coherent and theologically grounded set of *jus post bellum* criteria. Our *jus post bellum* framework draws on the work of Brian Orend—the principal architect of *post bellum* ethics, who approaches just war thinking from a philosophical perspective— but, as we noted in the previous chapter, we at times disagree with or go beyond what he has proposed. The remainder of this book provides a four-part framework or skeleton for a theory of *jus post bellum* that is consistent with Christian just war thinking. It is organized around four principal categories: just cause, reconciliation, punishment, and restoration.

JUS POST BELLUM AND THE TRADITION

Centuries ago Augustine noted that the goal or *telos* of a just war is not simply victory on the battlefield, but the *tranquillitas ordinis*, the tranquility that comes from order, or what today we might call a just and lasting peace. This right intention gives rise to and directs the other just war criteria. Although recent just war thinkers seem to conflate the *jus ad bellum* criteria of right intent and just cause, we do not. Establishing a just and lasting peace cannot constitute a just cause for war, since such a goal could be used to justify a crusade to spread a religion or even democracy and human rights or a war to end all wars. Just cause has to do with the actions that provoked the war in the first place. Once a just cause has indeed been identified, then right intent immediately kicks in, so that the other *jus ad bellum* criteria are carefully considered and satisfied before embarking upon war, the *jus in bello* criteria are strictly adhered to, and the war ends in a way that fosters a just and lasting peace. As Annalisa Koeman, in attempting to understand Orend's approach to this, notes, "Right intention is ... a normative thread through all three phases of war and impose[s] firm moral limits and constraints on aims and conduct in order to achieve an appropriate (just) war termination and ensure the original intent is effectively secured."[2] Right intent thus includes, but is not limited to, addressing and rectifying the injustice(s) that served as the grounds for "just cause" in the *jus ad bellum* phase.[3]

According to Augustine, "A great deal depends on the causes for which men undertake wars."[4] Classical just war theory identifies self-defense, defense of human rights (for example, humanitarian intervention), restitution (regaining what was wrongfully taken), redress (taking possession of what is wrongfully withheld), and legitimate punishment as the only "just causes" for going to war.[5] Just cause *post bellum* is related but not identical to just cause *ad bellum*. This chapter focuses on just cause *post bellum*. Furthermore, satisfying the just cause demands of the post war period is different from returning to the *status quo* before the war. As Michael Walzer notes, the *status quo ante bellum* is precisely what led to war in the first place.[6] Minimally, the goal of a just war must be to establish social, political, and economic conditions that are substantially more stable, more just, and less prone to chaos than what existed prior to the fighting.[7] Maximally, it means a social, political, and economic environment that allows citizens to pursue lives of meaning and enables humans to flourish.

Accountability

The *post bellum* just cause principle has three primary objectives. First, it seeks to hold accountable the party claiming to fight a just war. It requires the party to achieve the objectives that were identified as the legitimate reasons for going to war in the first place. As Gary Bass observes,

> *Jus post bellum* is connected with *jus ad bellum* ... in that the declared ends that justify a war—whether stopping genocide or preventing aggression—impose obligations on belligerent powers to try, even after the conclusion of the war, to bring about the desired outcome. If a state wages war to remove a genocidal regime, but then leaves the conquered country awash with weapons and grievances, and without a security apparatus, then it may relinquish by its postwar actions the justice it might otherwise have claimed in waging the war.[8]

In other words, the "good" of a just war (*ad bellum* and *in bello*) can be undone *post bellum*. Parties claiming to fight for a just cause must stay the course until the mission is accomplished.

In the 2003 U.S. invasion of Iraq, for example, some of the reasons cited under this principle were: to eliminate weapons of mass destruction that could be transferred to terrorists, to liberate the people of Iraq from a violent dictator, to enforce U.N. sanctions because weapons inspectors were prevented from doing their jobs, to eradicate a safe haven for global terrorists, and to bring democracy and stability to the Middle East. However, as the cost of the war in terms of dollars and lives mounted, popular support for the war evaporated and Americans began calling for a pullout. To do so, though, would have been a direct violation of this principle. The supposed "just cause" had/has not been accomplished.

Long after President George W. Bush stood on the deck of the USS *Abraham Lincoln* on May 1, 2003, under a banner proclaiming "Mission Accomplished," Iraq remained in a state of anarchy and the region was unstable. As we write, the future of Iraq is still in serious doubt as factional violence claims scores of civilians. The United States has a *post bellum* responsibility to provide security until it has accomplished the mission(s) it claimed as its objective(s). Furthermore, considering that bringing democracy and regime change are dubious just causes from an *ad bellum* perspective in the first place, such causes only make the *post bellum* responsibilities that much greater. In short, the United States' *post bellum* responsibilities under the just cause principle demand sustained U.S. involvement in Iraq—until it can finance and support a responsible transition to Iraqis or an international third party—regardless of the cost to the United States in terms of dollars or U.S. soldiers' lives.

A Means of Restraint

The just cause *post bellum* principle also restrains parties from seeking additional gains. To go beyond what was identified as the just cause would be an act of aggression. The just cause principle prohibits shifting rationales for going to war after the conflict has begun. Once a nation has achieved its declared mission, the conflict must end. For example, assuming (for the sake of illustration) the 1991 Gulf War met the *jus ad bellum* criteria, President George H. Bush was criticized for not marching to Baghdad once the Iraqi forces were driven beyond the Kuwaiti border. The allied forces had the advantage, and it is reasonably assumed that they could have toppled the Hussein regime. However, to do so would have been rightly condemned as an act of aggression because the rights of the Kuwaiti people (the just cause of the war) had been vindicated. Any additional gains would be unjust.

As we noted in the previous chapter, Orend draws on, and seems to conflate, both the just cause and right intention criteria of *jus ad bellum* to create the rights vindication criteria of his *jus post bellum* category. Nevertheless, for him the just cause criterion functions to put the brakes on war making.

> The just goal of a just war, once won, must be a more se-
> cure and more just state of affairs than existed prior to the
> war.... The proper aim of a just war is the vindication of

those rights whose violation grounded the resort to war in the first place.... The principle of rights vindication forbids the continuation of the war after the relevant rights have, in fact, been vindicated. To go beyond that limit would itself become aggression.[9]

Thus, just cause *post bellum* can serve a restraining purpose against wars of conquest.

Proportionality

This principle also seeks to ensure proportional (in other words, measured and restrained) *post bellum* behavior by the victors. As Orend observes, it prevents "war from spilling over into something like a crusade, which demands the utter destruction of the demonized enemy. The very essence of justice in, and after war is about there being firm limits, and constraints, upon its aims and conduct."[10] A proportionate *post bellum* response accomplishes the just cause it seeks. It achieves its declared objectives, and it constrains zealotry.

Practical Implications

The practical implications of the just cause principle are clear. Any unjust gains made during war (for example, acquisition of land, capital, war booty, or seizure of financial assets or natural resources) must be returned to their original owners. Furthermore, an unconditional surrender cannot be made a provision of ending the conflict. It is well established in just war theory that demanding unconditional surrender is patently unjust. Walzer and Orend argue that requiring unconditional surrender is unjust and impractical because it is a disproportionate response that will most likely prolong the war.[11]

Having a publicly declared *post bellum* plan in place before the shooting starts is essential to create an environment in which the nearly vanquished will see surrender as a viable option. When states publicly declare their cause(s) and intentions and their commitment to seek no additional gains once the initial cause(s) of war has been achieved, the prospect of a negotiated settlement is stronger than when the vanquished are asked to simply trust that its enemy will show mercy.

In short, the just cause principle acts as a tenet of restraint and accountability. The remaining *jus post bellum* criteria explored in the following chapters are congruent with and complementary to the just cause principle. Of course, it should be again noted that the criteria we are delineating are best characterized as *phases* or *stages* in that they are not only moral principles (or norms and rules) but also include concrete steps necessary for achieving *jus post bellum*.[12]

JUS POST BELLUM: CAN YOU GET GOOD FRUIT FROM A BAD TREE?

There is a tendency to treat the three categories of just war theory in isolation from one another as if each category were a series of checklists—that is, once the *ad bellum* criteria have been satisfied, one can progress to the *in bello* list, and finally move on to the *post bellum* list. We reject this segmented approach, as the three categories are intimately related. There is disagreement, however, over the nature of the relationship between them. If a war is unjust *ad bellum*, is whatever follows automatically unjust? Can an unjust aggressor fight a just war? Can a victorious unjust aggressor establish a just peace in the aftermath? In other words, can one get good fruit from a bad tree?

Before more developed criteria emerged for the post war period, the question of the relationship between *jus ad bellum* and *jus in bello* focused on the moral responsibility of soldiers fighting in a war that failed to meet the *ad bellum* criteria. For example, were soldiers who fought for Germany in World War II guilty of murder because their aggressive war was unjust? Walzer takes up this question in his classic work *Just and Unjust Wars* and concludes that soldiers "are not responsible for the overall justice of the wars they fight; their responsibility is limited by the range of their own activity and authority."[13] In other words, soldiers are responsible for their own violation of *in bello* restraints, but not for whether the war itself is justified.

Walzer struggles to make this case by offering several reasons that soldiers are not responsible for the overall justice of the wars in which they kill, including (1) their knowledge of such matters is limited, (2) they have been habituated to follow orders and instilled with a strong sense of patriotism, (3) allowing soldiers to select the wars/battles in which they are willing to participate (selective conscientious objection) would imperil military effectiveness, and (4) custom: it is a longstanding social convention not to hold soldiers responsible for the overall justice of a war (as, for example, the Nuremburg trials).[14]

This notion that soldiers are responsible only for *in bello* concerns and not for *ad bellum* concerns poses problems. If a war is unjustified and the architects of the aggression can be held responsible for the crime of aggression, then why not also those who carried out the actual acts of aggression? Certainly there are mitigating circumstances: soldiers may be ignorant of the facts that led to the war or they may be victims of propaganda; they may have been conscripted with severe penalties for refusing to fight; or they may be young, uneducated, or easily manipulated into fighting for what they think is a just cause.

Orend's Position on Just Cause and *Jus Post Bellum*

Orend offers a nuanced approach to this quandary:

> There should be *a presumption against* holding soldiers responsible for the crime of violating *jus ad bellum*. But this presumption does *not* preclude us from concluding, in particular cases based on public evidence: that some soldiers of a particular aggressor state either *did* know, or *really should have* known, about the injustice of the war they were fighting; that they could have refused to participate in it; and thus that they may be held responsible, albeit with much lesser penalties than the elites.... Soldiers who fight for an aggressor do not have strict moral equality with those who fight for a victim or defender. The former are not mainly to blame for the aggression but they *are* to blame, in a smaller but material sense.[15]

Orend's careful effort to be fair in ascribing moral blame reminds us of the Catholic moral theological distinction made between vincible and invincible ignorance. If someone does an act that is objectively immoral, even though she in her conscience thought it was morally right, she is not morally guilty, *if there is no way that she could have known better*. This is known as a case of invincible ignorance. However, if someone should have known better but did not take the time to inform himself about an issue or decision, then he is indeed morally blameworthy, which is an example of vincible ignorance—though not necessarily as blameworthy as someone who does know better, but nevertheless commits an evil act.[16] While the debate that Orend is seeking to address does have *jus post bellum* implications vis-à-vis war crimes trials and punishments (see chapter 6), our concern here is simply to illustrate that the three categories of just war theory cannot be treated in isolation of one another; they are interrelated.

For Orend, if a war fails to meet the *ad bellum* criteria (especially just cause), then it can never be just in the way it is prosecuted or just in the post war period. He uses a number of analogies to make this point. He describes the just cause principle as "a bright red thread [that runs] through each of the three just war categories, *tying them into a coherent whole*";[17] as similar to calling one's shot in billiards; and as like a virus whereby the lack of just cause *ad bellum* infects all that follows.[18] For Orend everything, and especially just cause, hinges on *jus ad bellum*:

> *Jus ad bellum* sets the tone and context for the other two categories, and to that extent is probably the most important. That is *not* to say that meeting *jus ad bellum* will automatically result in meeting *jus in bello* and *jus post bellum*. But it *is* to say, conversely, that failure to meet *jus ad bellum* results in automatic failure to meet *jus in bello* and *jus post bellum*. *Once you're an aggressor in war, everything is lost to you, morally*.[19]

Orend maintains that "it is axiomatic that if there was no justice at the start of the war, there will be no justice at the end. In other words, the less just your start of war, the fewer your rights in the postwar phase. Coherence entails that injustice in the beginning *infects* both the middle and the end of war.... It seems more accurate to quip that it is 'garbage in, garbage out.' "[20] Clearly, according to Orend, you can't get good fruit from a bad tree.

Three additional reasons are identified by Orend to link *jus ad bellum, jus in bello,* and *jus post bellum.* First, echoing Kant, he argues, "A state should commit itself to certain rules of conduct, and appropriate war termination, *as part of its original decision to begin war.* ... Because if it cannot so commit, it ought never to start the process."[21] In other words, war is serious business, and nations must declare how they intend to prosecute a war from start to finish before the first shot is fired.

Orend's insistence (and, for that matter, Kant's) that *jus post bellum* be fully considered in the *ad bellum* phase makes for a more honest just war theory and guards against using just war thinking as moral camouflage for political realism. In an ideal world, nations would fully and adequately consider all three categories and would call their shots. Practically speaking, war is a Pandora's box. Rarely can one accurately forecast what one will find once the smoke of the battlefield has lifted. It seems unrealistic at best and could be detrimental to insist that nations be held accountable for their *post bellum* predictions, when such forecasting is marginal. If nations have committed themselves (in the *ad bellum* period) to certain *post bellum* courses of action, then what are their responsibilities if the post war period turns out far worse than predicted? Can aggressor nations then claim not to be responsible beyond what they originally pledged to do? This is different than the "suboptimal acceptable peace" argument put forward by Mark Evans (outlined in the previous chapter). Evans argues in favor of allowing victors to exit before they have achieved a just and lasting peace, when the period of occupation drags on too long and works against establishing peace and order. But the intent to establish a just and lasting peace (the *tranquillitas ordinis*) validates just cause. Predicting what one will find after the smoke clears is extremely difficult, but that does not therefore grant permission to "cut and run," it merely indicates that post war planning must take into account that realities on the ground will be shifting and require alternative plans. These very real practical concerns notwithstanding, a robust *jus post bellum* category must become normative to just war theory and international law.

Second, Orend recognizes that while it is possible for a state to have multiple reasons for going to war, the publicly declared causes and intentions should be limited to the primary objective(s) in order to dissuade the " 'scatter shot' approach to justifying war, where you throw out every possible argument in favor of war, hoping some will stick in terms of persuading the public or attracting evidence which will stand the test of time and scrutiny,"[22] as was the case with the 2003 U.S. invasion of Iraq. The overall justice of war is measured by whether the cause(s) that justified the use of force has been met and by the other just war theory criteria.

Finally, the responsibility for fulfilling *jus post bellum* requirements rests primarily on the shoulders of political leaders and not the military leaders or soldiers in the field. This is certainly true regarding the overall prosecution of the *post bellum* phase, especially in terms of resources devoted to post war security and reconstruction. However, in the days and months immediately following the formal combat phase, the military leaders are often responsible for justice *post bellum*, especially in terms of practical matters like where and how security forces are deployed, how weapons are rounded up, and the capture of war criminals.

To cast *jus post bellum* as primarily the responsibility of political leaders runs the risk of excusing other sectors from taking their post war obligations seriously. While military leaders tend to focus on the period immediately after formal combat has ended (usually addressed as part of the exit strategy) and bear some responsibility for this period, *post bellum* responsibilities also fall on the larger civil society, of both the vanquished and vanquishing nations. War efforts typically involve the entire nation (political, military, and the whole of civil society, including business and religious sectors), and as such the *post bellum* responsibilities ought to be proportionally distributed.

A Critique of Orend's Position

Orend's position is appealing in its logic and its purity, but we disagree with him in three areas: (1) his interpretation of just cause (including how he conflates it with right intention), (2) his insistence that the failure to satisfy the *jus ad bellum* criteria renders *jus in bello* and *jus post bellum* impossible, and (3) for practical reasons. For Orend, *jus ad bellum,* and especially just cause, are the crux of just war theory. He goes so far as to call *jus ad bellum* "probably the most important" consideration.[23] For him, all other criteria (*ad bellum, in bello,* and *post bellum*) are contingent on just cause. Without denying the importance of just cause, philosophically and chronologically, placing such heavy emphasis on just cause reduces the other criteria to subservient roles, which only supports the all-too-common abuse of just war thinking (most often by politicians and political pundits) wherein the totality of just war theory is reduced to just cause. In our thinking, when judging whether a war is just, the criteria are equally important and relevant.

Concerning Orend's assertion that "if a war fails to meet the *ad bellum* criteria (especially just cause), then it cannot be *jus in bello* or *post bellum*" (in other words, you can't get good fruit from a bad tree), we respond that while this position may make sense in a purely academic setting or in a theoretical discussion, it is nonetheless too rigid a position to hold in practice and it has the potential for disastrous results.

John Langan, S.J., uses the phrase "imperfectly just"[24] to capture the notion that just war theory presents ideals, but that when these ethical principles are applied to real-life scenarios, ethical purism is often unattainable. More recently John DiIulio used the phrase "tolerably just" to describe President Obama's decision to increase U.S. troops in Afghanistan in 2009, which sounds similar to Evans's "suboptimal acceptable peace," and which also hints at the idea that there are degrees of justice.[25] Justice is not an either/or category. Orend himself suggests this distinction when he says, "The less just your start of war, the fewer your rights in the post-war phase." However he prefaces it with a more absolutist position: "it is axiomatic that if there was no justice at the start of the war, there will be no justice at the end."[26]

Admitting a dose of realism takes just war theory out of the ivory tower and brings it down into the mud and blood of human existence; yet, this recognition that the just war criteria might be imperfectly just in their application should not be seen as opening the door to crass political realism or to Walzer's "supreme emergency" exception, which permits overriding or ignoring the traditional restraints of just war thinking in situations in which the threat is both imminent and horrifically devasting.[27] Walzer creates the supreme emergency to cover unique cases such as the threat posed by the Nazi regime. Recognizing he has stepped onto a slippery slope, though, he argues that the case for supreme emergency exceptions must present rigorous proof. As contemporary just war theologians who take all of the categories and criteria seriously, we do not accept Walzer's allowance for supreme emergency cases. We expect each and every criterion to be adhered to as best as possible. They ought never be ignored or suspended. All we are acknowledging here is that the application of these criteria may not always, if ever, be perfectly just, and that sometimes (rarely) we might have to settle for a "tolerably just" or "suboptimal acceptable" *post bellum* peace.

A Theological Perspective

It is helpful at this point to introduce a theological perspective. Perfect justice, as Reinhold Niebuhr—the great American Protestant theologian and champion of Christian realism—reminds us, is unattainable by humans due to human sinfulness. In this world we strive for relative justice, the attainable approximation of perfect justice in an imperfect world. Perfectly just wars do not exist. When we speak of a "just war," we are really talking about a "mostly just war." The intent behind just war theory is to limit what nearly all agree is an evil. War is sometimes tolerated because we live in an imperfect world rife with sin and greed, and under certain circumstances war represents the lesser of two evils. Even so, war always remains an evil.

Of course, not all of these evils are moral ones, for Catholic moral theology distinguishes between nonmoral (also referred to as ontic or pre-moral) evils and moral evils.[28] But even nonmoral evils can have an intransitive effect on human and societal character. We think the medieval practice of requiring penance for soldiers who participated even in a just war was a recognition of this effect. Kant himself recognized that the justified use of deadly force taints all involved when he recommended, "At the end of war, when peace is concluded, it would not be inappropriate for a people to appoint a day of atonement after the festival of thanksgiving. Heaven would be invoked in the name of the state to forgive the human race for the great sin of which it continues to be guilty."[29] Atonement and forgiveness for the sins/crimes of war is addressed more fully in the next chapter.

This distinction is useful in the debate about good fruit from a bad tree. While a failure to satisfy the *ad bellum* criteria taints the *in bello* and *post bellum* phases, it does not render approximate justice impossible. If Orend's position always held, then no war could ever be considered just, and just war theory would become no more than an ethical ideal, a thought experiment with little real-life application.

For example, many argue that Allied resistance against Germany, Italy, and Japan in World War II satisfied the *ad bellum* criteria, but the use of nuclear weapons and carpet bombing and other atrocities were an injustice and a violation of *jus in bello*. But the reconstruction plans in post war Germany and Japan are upheld by many (including Orend) as models of post war justice. By the logic of "garbage in, garbage out," one would have to conclude that all sides in World War II fought an unjust war and that the post war reconstruction efforts were also in fact unjust. It would place the Allied forces in the same moral category as the so-called Axis of Evil because no one fought a perfectly just war. Such a purist stance renders talk of just war meaningless, whereas in admitting degrees of justice one can distinguish imperfectly just wars from perfectly unjust wars and praise what is good or condemn what is bad *ad bellum*, *in bello*, and *post bellum*. We are not suggesting that the *ad bellum*, *in bello*, and *post bellum* phases be treated in isolation, but rather that a lack of perfect justice in the *ad bellum* phase ignores the morally praiseworthy acts of ordinary soldiers (certainly some German soldiers exercised restraint and discrimination in World War II) and demands moral perfection, which the Christian tradition deems as unattainable by human efforts alone.

A war that fails to meet all of the *ad bellum* criteria is unjust. But a war that fails to meet all of the *ad bellum* criteria *and* ignores the restraints of *jus in bello and* the obligations of *jus post bellum* would obviously be more unjust than one that was fought and ended in accordance with the *jus in bello* and the *jus post bellum* criteria. A war that fails to meet the *jus ad bellum* requirements, but observes the *in bello* restraints and fulfills the *post bellum* responsibilities does not turn an unjust war into a just war, but it does make it less unjust than it would have been if the *in bello* and *post bellum* obligations had been ignored. We envision the justice of war on a sliding scale of sorts, although a strict algorithm is impossible (see Figure 1, below).

Figure 1: Just to Unjust Wars, Sliding Scale

Perfectly Just War
Satisfies all jus ad bellum, jus in bello,
  and jus post bellum criteria

Imperfectly Just War
Satisfies jus ad bellum with only minor isolated
  violations of jus in bello and jus post bellum

Unjust War
Any war that fails to meet all jus ad bellum
  criteria
Any war that satisfies jus ad bellum, but systematically violates jus in bello and/or ignores jus
  post bellum

Perfectly Unjust War
Fails jus ad bellum, jus in bello, jus post bellum

We anticipate a chorus of objections to this schema and the notion that any war that fails to fully meet the strictures of *jus ad bellum*, *jus in bello*, and *jus post bellum* could be called just (even imperfectly just). To those who insist that the term "just" be reserved for wars that are perfectly just, we cede the logic of the argument, "How can justice be imperfect? If it is imperfect, then it's not justice!" However, "imperfect justice" is not synonymous with "unjust."

The Christian tradition has long affirmed that perfect justice, true justice, or what many may simply call justice is eschatological. This side of the *Parousia*, all we can hope to attain is an approximation of justice (and an approximation of love). Nonetheless, this must not become a reason to interpret the criteria of just war theory loosely or to cry, "Perfect justice is impossible! Let slip the dogs of war!" Let us be clear. We are contemporary just war theorists who insist on the strictest interpretation of the *ad bellum* principles and seriously espouse the tenets of just peacemaking. If Christians wish to be just war theorists, then they must be equally committed, if not more, to proactively eliminating the conditions that lead to war. They must be vigorous peacemakers.

While there are some differences between us (Allman and Winright) in terms of application of these various criteria, we are in substantial agreement in terms of the larger framework and especially in terms of the *jus post bellum* criteria outlined here. Regardless of one's position in the debate about whether a war can be just during its course or afterward, if the reasons for going to war are unjust, then the obligations *post bellum* are all the greater. In other words, while you may not get good fruit from a bad tree, some fruit is more rotten than others.

Practically speaking, if this rigid moral purism were ensconced in international law and practice, then aggressor nations without a just cause for going to war would have no incentive to observe *in bello* restraints or pursue post war reconstruction and reconciliation. If nothing praiseworthy is to be found in practicing justice during and after a war, then the unjust aggressor would see fighting to the bitter end as a viable alternative.

In many ways, this argument is similar to the reasons that demanding unconditional surrender is patently unjust. Such an action is disproportionate and could prolong and intensify a war. The purpose of just war theory is not to rationalize the rush to war but to limit its brutality and duration. Anything that prolongs war or increases bloodshed runs contrary to just war thinking. Furthermore, following the logic of Orend and other ethical purists, nothing could ever be called just in a nation founded on injustice. For example, is everything done by the United States inherently unjust because the founding of our nation came via injustices done to Native Americans? Is it impossible to call the emancipation of slaves of African descent "just" because the original action was so patently unjust? Is not the righting of a wrong still right? So, too, an unjust war (*ad bellum*) can be fought according to *in bello* norms, and an unjust war (*ad bellum* or *in bello*) can be ended justly. This does not excuse or wipe out the previous injustices, but it is certainly better than a war that is undertaken for an unjust cause, is carried out in an unjust manner, and ends with a lack of justice for the vanquished people.

CONCLUSION

Just war theory has had many nursemaids: philosophers, theologians, political scientists, military leaders, and politicians. The introduction of a theological perspective into the debate of *jus post bellum* is long overdue. While *jus post bellum* ethics is still in the early stages of development, the absence of a theological perspective leaves *jus post bellum* wanting in at least two ways.

First, *jus post bellum* offers a clearer connection between just cause and right intent. Just cause figures prominently in nearly every theory of *jus post bellum*. The just cause(s) of war originally articulated in the *ad bellum* phase must be accomplished for a war to be considered just. The "vindication of rights," as Orend first called it, perfects or completes just cause *ad bellum* and *post bellum*. The logic is simple and clear: the end of a just war must be accomplishing the objectives that served as the grounds for going to war in the first place. Where we part company with Orend is on his conflation of just cause and right intent. Here the Christian theological just war tradition has maintained a stricter (more traditional) interpretation. This is not surprising considering Christian morality's emphasis on sin, conscience, and intent. While many political science just war theories dismiss the category of right intent as indiscernible and immeasurable, philosophical and theological just war theories maintain it is crucial. Intent matters in moral judgments.

Second, Christian realism grounds just war theory. Academic ethicists have no problem articulating theories of perfect justice. But as Augustine reminded us centuries ago and Reinhold Niebuhr did so more recently, we do not live in the City of God.

Ours is a world mired in sin and greed, selfishness and violence. While it is also home to the growing reign of God, a world of perfect justice and love has not yet been firmly established. It is what we hope for. In the meantime, our ethics must balance the ideal with the real.

The remaining three criteria of our *jus post bellum* ethic are the natural consequences of the just cause principle and are best characterized as phases in that they are not only moral principles but also include concrete steps necessary for achieving *jus post bellum*.

4

THE RECONCILIATION PHASE

"We must deal effectively, penitently with our past or it will return to haunt our present and we won't have a future to speak of."[1]

If the primary objective of a just war is a just and lasting peace, then there can be no peace without reconciliation, or as Pope John Paul II noted in his 2002 World Day of Peace message, there is "no peace without justice, no justice without forgiveness."[2] The goal of reconciliation is to transform a relationship of animosity, fear, and hatred into one of tolerance, if not respect. Perhaps a more realistic way to characterize this transformation is to say that reconciliation aspires to move people from hatred to benign indifference, from indifference to tolerance, from tolerance to respect, and ultimately from respect to friendship. In short, the reconciliation phase seeks to turn enemies into friends and to bring emotional healing to the victims of war. A parallel is present between *post bellum* reconciliation and the sacrament of Reconciliation.[3] The reconciliation phase contains the basic elements of the sacrament of Reconciliation: admission of guilt, absolution, penance, and the return of the offending party to full communion. The goal of both sacramental and *post bellum* reconciliation is justice tempered by mercy.

RECONCILIATION: WHAT IT IS, WHAT IT ISN'T

In their work on "transitional" or "post conflict" justice, Rachel Kerr and Eirin Mobekk observe that while reconciliation is "almost always touted as a key objective of transitional justice processes ... often it is unclear what is meant by it."[4] Many, such as Davida Kellogg, object to making reconciliation an aim of the *post bellum* phase. Seeking or forcing reconciliation, they argue, trivializes the brutality of war. It reduces the crimes of war to an area of disputation and fails to recognize war as a violent crime. Forcing or even pressuring the victims of war to reconcile with their perpetrators is akin to expecting the rape victim to forgive her rapist. "It is the height of presumption" to imagine that victims of the crime of aggression and of war crimes should ever forgive their attackers.[5] Instead, they argue, prevention should be the primary aim of *post bellum* ethics.

We believe that such worries possibly evince an impoverished understanding of reconciliation, seeing it primarily as a forgive-and-forget approach, whereas a richer understanding of reconciliation demands acknowledgment of guilt, contrition, reparations (penance), and—only then—absolution. If, as Kellogg admits, the purpose of a just war (and in particular, of the *post bellum* phase) is "the establishment of a lasting peace," then the need for reconciliation is paramount, lest the punishment phase be nothing more than retribution.

Critics such as Kellogg also tend to fall into a dualist trap. They often see the choice as reconciliation *or* prevention, or sometimes reconciliation (including forgiveness and amnesty) *or* justice. These are false dichotomies. A more holistic approach aims at reconciliation, justice, and prevention. While reconciliation might seem a lofty ideal, the relationships between the Allied forces of World War II and Germany, Italy, and Japan reveal that adversarial relationships can be reconciled in a relatively short period of time. More recently, the success of truth and reconciliations commissions, such as those used in South Africa, Guatemala, East Timor, Peru, Sierra Leone, Morocco, Liberia, and elsewhere, provide further evidence of the power of truth telling, admission of guilt, apology, and forgiveness.[6]

Forgiveness

Already we have used a number of terms that need to be clarified. Forgiveness is not the same as reconciliation, and justice need not be opposed to forgiveness, reconciliation, and amnesty. According to Walter Wink, forgiveness is unilateral. Stemming from the Greek *aphiemi*, it means "to let go, loose, set free, acquit, dismiss, remit."[7] Forgiveness in the political arena differs from interpersonal forgiveness. As William Bole notes,

> To look at forgiveness as a political prospect is to look away from some conventional wisdom. For one thing, forgiveness in politics is never about forgetting, but about remembering.... Forgiveness is not simply about personal piety, but about social change.... Forgiveness is not a denial of human responsibility; rather it rests on the moral judgment that an act was wrong. Forgiveness is compatible with justice, never with vengeance. As Hannah Arendt also said, "Men cannot forgive what they cannot punish."[8]

Bole concludes,

> Forgiveness as a political strategy has seldom appeared on the diplomatic radar screen.... Nevertheless, the notion has slipped into an array of initiatives aimed at building trust and relationships, especially in post-conflict societies.... A durable peace requires more than political accords and ceasefires. It requires social healing, which may only come through the introduction of a radical new factor, such as forgiveness.[9]

Forgiveness seeks reconciliation, which is mutual. It is an action directed toward the other. It does not imply condoning or accepting the behavior of the other, only that one wishes to set oneself and the other free, to move on. Reconciliation is relational, mutual. It is the result and goal of forgiveness.[10]

Reconciliation and Justice

Advocates of post war reconciliation are serious about just war theory's claim that the aim of a just war is a lasting or sustainable peace. In many ways, honestly seeking *post bellum* reconciliation perfects and heals the sins and evils of war; it is the litmus test of whether a particular war can truly be deemed justifiable. Unfortunately, the *post bellum* phase is often entered into under the banner of justice alone, as if justice without reconciliation and peace were possible.

Trudy Govier, who has written extensively on reconciliation and revenge, observes that *post bellum* approaches that focus primarily on justice, as opposed to sustainable peace, tend to ignore or dismiss attempts at reconciliation. While "justice and peace are in some contexts contending values ... social justice presupposes peace."[11] Often the clamor for post war justice is not much more than a call for payback or even revenge. "Scholarly and popular commentators on war's aftermath often comment that peace cannot be achieved without justice. One does not have to probe deeply to find out just what sort of justice they have in mind: it is justice under the law and most fundamentally, penal justice" that involves indictments, arrests, trials, prison terms, and executions, all under the logic that "those most guilty should be made to pay for what they have done."[12]

Reducing post war justice to merely penal or retributive justice misses the point that justice and peace are not competing values. They are complementary. Likewise, talk of reconciliation does not preclude the demands of penal and retributive justice (such as trials, punishments, or reparations). Robust post war justice includes elements of restorative justice alongside retributive, social, procedural, and criminal justice. Restorative justice is the dominant model for post war reconciliation. Restorative justice approaches conflict by engaging "those who are harmed, wrongdoers and their affected communities in search of solutions that promote repair, reconciliation and the rebuilding of relationships. Restorative justice seeks to build partnerships to reestablish mutual responsibility for constructive responses to wrongdoing within our communities" rather than "privileging the law, professionals and the state."[13]

This approach is remarkably similar to the biblical notion of justice. John Donahue, in his seminal work "Biblical Perspectives on Justice," distills down to a single definition the many notions of justice in the Bible: "fidelity to the demands of relationship."[14] Justice is relational. It, like reconciliation, is interpersonal. One cannot decouple justice from peace, just as one cannot seek peace without justice. They are symbiotic.

Pope John Paul II, writing in the aftermath of the September 11, 2001, terrorist attacks, operated out of a biblical and restorative justice paradigm. In his 2002 World Peace Day message he declared, "My reasoned conviction, confirmed in turn by biblical revelation, is that the shattered order cannot be fully restored except by a response that combines justice with forgiveness. *The pillars of true peace are justice and that form of love which is forgiveness.*"[15] He goes on to dismiss notions that "justice and forgiveness are irreconcilable," because such notions see justice exclusively in terms of vengeance.

> But forgiveness is the opposite of resentment and revenge, not of justice. In fact, true peace is "the work of justice" (Is 32:17).... True peace, therefore, is the fruit of justice.... But because human justice is always fragile and imperfect, subject as it is to the limitations and egoism of individuals and groups, it must include and, as it were, be completed by the *forgiveness which heals and rebuilds troubled human relations from their foundations*.... Forgiveness is in no way opposed to justice, as if to forgive meant to overlook the need to right the wrong done.[16]

Here we find an understanding of forgiveness that is richer than the cheap grace of the forgive-and-forget model. Post war reconciliation contends that forgiveness and ultimately reconciliation (understood as restoration of shattered relations) flow out of justice. This notion that justice, peace, and forgiveness are interrelated is biblical—"Love and truth will meet; justice and peace will kiss" (Ps 85:11 NAB; see also Ps 89:15; Mt 9:13)—and includes the demand that the truth be told. This is the rationale of the various truth and reconciliation commissions that have proved successful in post war restoration efforts. Having laid a theoretical/theological foundation for *post bellum* reconciliation, we turn now to questions of practice.

SIX ELEMENTS OF *POST BELLUM* RECONCILIATION

Practically speaking, *post bellum* reconciliation attends to six key areas: the period immediately after the conflict ends, acknowledgment of wrongdoing, apologies, punishments, forgiveness, and amnesty.

Immediate Post Conflict Period

Typically the *post bellum* phase begins with a cease-fire agreement, an armistice, or surrender. Cease-fire agreements are a necessary precondition to reconciliation. Warring parties cannot begin to work on the thornier issues—such as assuaging mutual fears, addressing hatreds and prejudices, reparations, war crimes, and so on—until they stop shooting at each other. Because reconciliation requires a willingness to engage in relationship building, it must be based in trust, which cannot be established by fiat.[17] Trust is built up over time, typically beginning with small but symbolically significant gestures of respect.

The period of surrender provides a crucial opportunity for laying a foundation of trust and respect. Rear Admiral Louis Iasiello stresses the importance of an honorable surrender in creating "a healing mind-set" in the immediate post conflict period. He presents the surrender of the Confederate Army at the end of the U.S. Civil War as a paradigm of honorable surrender. Union soldiers, at the command of General Grant, extended military courtesies including a marching salute to their defeated former enemy. Grant acknowledged the reconciliatory aim of the *post bellum* phase when he said to his troops, "Gentlemen, the war is over; the rebels are our countrymen again."[18] Symbolic gestures such as honorable surrender, honoring civilian and military dead on all sides, and treating the defeated with basic human dignity signal the end of the formal combat phase and begin the transformation from hostile animosity toward something else.

Restraint in post war celebrations can also contribute to the reconciliatory aims of this phase. Plato warned that constructing monuments to victors can harden the hearts of the vanquished.[19]

Michael Schuck makes a similar observation.[20] Celebrating the end of the war and the return of soldiers is normal; however, when victors celebrate not only the end of the war but the defeat of their enemy as well, they fail to recognize the moral and non-moral evils that accompany all war, including just wars. Post war victory celebrations that laud the killing of others gloss over how the death of an enemy—even though the killing may have been justified—involves a (nonmoral) evil, in that a creature of God now lacks being and no longer exists. Celebrating the return of soldiers is certainly understandable, but to rejoice in the defeat of enemies turns killing itself into a good. Instead of celebrating the defeat of the enemy, the honorable behavior, valorous acts, and sacrifices made by all sides need to be respected and honored. The little good that can be found in war needs to be publicly acknowledged so that all sides might come to see that their former enemy includes decent, kind, brave, and virtuous people.[21]

Acknowledgment

Acknowledgment involves the requirement that those who have committed wrongs or done harm to others admit they are perpetrators. This is not the same as apologizing. A person can admit that he or she has committed such an act without feeling remorse. Nevertheless many victims of war crimes derive some healing from having what was done to them become part of the public record or, minimally, hearing the perpetrators admit they did indeed carry out the atrocities. The desire to hear the truth is often far more important to victims than seeing their abusers brought to justice.[22]

Acknowledgment is about bringing the truth to light, which can take many forms, such as truth and reconciliation commissions; public burials; investigative journalism; memorials, monuments, and museums; art exhibits; and the rewriting of textbooks. Kerr and Mobekk write, "Creating an historical record not only helps identify the patterns of abuse and its actors, thus reinforcing a sense of accountability; it also helps ensure against the setting in of a collective amnesia and reduces the possibility for revisionism."[23] Acknowledgment concerns the truth part of the truth and reconciliation process. It involves a confession of wrong behavior from individuals, collective groups (military, police, paramilitary), and ethnic groups. It includes not only sins of commission, but also sins of omission, the complicity of the silent, those who were aware of the atrocities being committed but chose to remain silent.

The narrative of the old/oppressive regime needs to be replaced with a new narrative, one based in truth and inclusive of the experience of the victims. As Robert J. Schreiter notes, "Victims of violence and suffering must tell their story over and over again in order to escape the narrative of the lie.... Little by little they construct a new narrative of truth," but this must be done within boundaries so that the victims are not overwhelmed or forced to relive the violence through the act of truth telling.[24] As Wink describes it, truth telling is "mysteriously powerful" and "almost magical" in its ability to signal the end of the abusive regime's power.[25] So long as the account of what was done to victims remains buried, it signals to the community that the oppressive regimes should still be feared. Making explicit what was done and by whom (even if everyone already knows) is cathartic, which is why some victims are more interested in the truth being told than in punitive justice. Again, the wisdom behind this is biblical: "The truth will make you free" (Jn 8:32).

Govier places truth telling and acknowledgment of wrongdoing in the larger framework of social trust. Social trust is "a confident expectation that other people in the society (even strangers) will act in a decent and unthreatening way most of the time ... [which] cannot be taken for granted in the aftermath of war."[26] Establishing social trust requires constructing a new consensus on the historical narrative.

> Truth and reconciliation commissions have many goals including investigation, fact finding, acknowledgement, testimony, understanding of causes, and healing. Theirs is a quest to understand what went on and why, to reach some sort of consensus about the historical narrative and value for the future of society, and to establish, on the basis of that consensus, values and commitments for a fresh start.[27]

Practically, the construction of a new historical consensus involves public forums, journalism, and the rewriting of textbooks. The old history of the lie must be laid to rest, and a new historical narrative of truth must be brought forth.

Gleaning from a U.S. Institute of Peace study of thirty-five countries that have emerged from repression, Wink offers seven practical rules of thumb for truth telling/acknowledgment:

1. The truth needs to be told.
2. It needs to be told completely.
3. If the threat posed by the old regime and its forces prevent[s] full disclosure, then as much should be revealed as possible.
4. The truth needs to be sanctioned by an official body. If the new government is too weak to do it, then it should be done by the churches [or other nongovernmental organizations].
5. At least the leading architects and executors of the policy of disappearances, murder, and torture should be prosecuted.
6. If they cannot be prosecuted, they should at least be publicly exposed.
7. Amnesty should not be offered until the truth has been told and, if possible, at least some of those most guilty prosecuted.[28]

Reconciliation requires the deconstruction of the narrative of the lie and the reconstruction of a new historical narrative in which the truth is recorded for history and spoken aloud for all to hear so that victims and the entire community can move forward.

Apologies

Apologies are distinct from acknowledgment, but acknowledgment remains a necessary precondition of authentic apology. According to Govier, apology requires that "those responsible for wrongdoing acknowledge to victims and the broader public that they have indeed committed these acts; they accept responsibility for committing them, express their sorrow or moral regret, and commit to reform and the offering of practical amends to the victims."[29] This secular understanding of apology includes some of the basic elements of the Christian notion of confession (admission of guilt, contrition, and penance). Apologies involve a great reversal as they require perpetrators to surrender the position of power, to become vulnerable (humble) before the ones they have wronged, leaving it to the victims to decide whether the apology will be accepted or rejected.

Wink's understanding of the dynamics of apology is more nuanced. He maintains that apologies by perpetrators make the wrongdoing an indisputable part of the public record: "The principal function of an apology is precisely its putting in the public record a statement of awareness and intent that seeks reconciliation, whether it has the power to accomplish that or not, and whether it is accepted or not."[30] Apologies empower victims because the power to accept or reject the apology is in the hands of the victim, as is the power to forgive. Just because not all apologies are accepted does not mean they are ineffectual.

Acceptance of an apology is not the same as forgiveness. As Wink explains,

> It is possible for those who have been harmed to forgive persons who harmed them.... No one can forgive those who have harmed others [e.g., the dead cannot forgive, nor can anyone but the murdered forgive the murderer].... An apology is a statement of regret [and responsibility] that attempts to elicit an act of forgiveness. Nonetheless, because it is often made long after the crime by those who did not commit the crime, to those who were not themselves the direct victims, it may not be possible for survivors or their descendants to accept it.[31]

Thus, between acceptance and rejection lies the alternative of "acknowledgment without acceptance," when those who receive the apology do not believe they can accept it because they were not the direct victims or instances in which the victim(s) recognizes that the apology has been made but is neither ready to forgive nor condemn.

Finally, Wink includes the notion of collective apologies. Nations, tribes, and other large groups can apologize for wrongs done in the past by members of their own group. For example, Pope John Paul II apologized and repented for centuries of Christian violence against Jews. On an interpersonal level such an apology was not his to give because he was not the perpetrator of the violence. But as the formal head of the largest Christian denomination, a church with a long and ugly history of anti-Semitism, the gesture was extremely powerful. In a similar fashion, heads of state can offer symbolic apologies for wrongs their nations committed in the past. For example, Chile's president Patricio Aylwin apologized for the Pinochet regime's reign of terror. While these collective apologies are not the same as interpersonal apologies, they do contribute to international reconciliation.[32]

If the primary goal of a just war is a just and lasting peace, and if the primary goal of the reconciliation phase is to transform adversarial relationships into relationships of respect, trust, and ultimately friendship, then a formal apology is a necessary condition of the settlement process. Just as there can be no forgiveness without an admission of guilt, so, too, formerly warring parties cannot reconcile without expressions of regret. Obviously, the unjust aggressor needs to apologize for the crime of aggression and for any offenses committed *in bello*; likewise the victors ought to apologize for any crimes, offenses, and insensitivity shown in the course of the conflict. Admissions of guilt are not the same as admissions of criminal activity, which must be punished. Admissions of guilt at this phase can be broadly construed, saving the prosecution of specific war crimes for the punishment phase. Mutual admissions of guilt (apologies) are a necessary first step and augment the long-term healing process of reconciliation.

Punishment

Punishment for the crime of aggression, as well as for *in bello* war crimes, is also necessary for reconciliation. As already noted, a distorted understanding of reconciliation takes a forgive-and-forget approach. Pursuing reconciliation does not preclude penal punishments, reparations, war crimes trials, or other forms of punishment. While punishment is addressed in the following chapter, it is important to note here that punishment must be proportionate and prudential—severe enough so that the evils of war are properly acknowledged and dealt with (for justice's sake) and to serve a deterrent to others. Punishments must not be so severe that they unduly burden those not directly or materially responsible for the crimes of war. Overly punitive punishments fuel resentment and can mitigate post war reconciliation. Excessively burdening the defeated by a victor's justice can simply lay the foundation for future/retaliatory conflict. Thus, in order to quell seething resentments, blunt the pernicious effects of rumor, and ensure that peace agreements enjoy popular support, the post war settlement process must be as public and transparent as possible, and the negotiating parties should be widely recognized as having the authority to be part of this process. Victors in battle ought not to assume that they, by virtue of military victory, are the most competent authority to negotiate post war settlements. In fact, in order to prevent settlements as appearing excessively punitive or vindictive it is better for independent authorities (for example, international bodies such as the United Nations, NATO, the European Union, the African Union, or a third-party state) to negotiate the post war settlement process.

Forgiveness

Forgiveness is the heart of the reconciliation process. It does not excuse or make light of the wrongs done; in fact, it brings them to light. Only that which has been fully disclosed can be forgiven.

Daniel Philpott, a political scientist with the Kroc Institute for International Peace Studies at the University of Notre Dame, calls forgiveness "the crowning practice" of post war reconciliation. "It is also the most dramatic, for it is initiated by the victim, who not only relinquishes his or her claim against the perpetrator but exercises a constructive will toward restored relationship. Theologically, forgiveness is a participation in God's own redemption of the world.... Politically, it can be restorative." [33] Here we see a radically different notion of justice that is primarily restorative, not retributive. Whereas justice in the realm of political science and international affairs tends to focus on the rule of law, due process, punishment, and retribution, justice in the biblical tradition is constructive; it is about restoring relationships between estranged people and with God, or as the *Compendium of the Social Doctrine of the Church* declares,

> *Mutual forgiveness must not eliminate the need for justice and still less does it block the path that leads to truth. On the contrary, justice and truth represent the concrete requisites for reconciliation.* . . . However, in order to re-establish relationships of mutual acceptance between divided peoples in the name of reconciliation, it is necessary to go beyond the determination of criminal behaviour, both of commission and omission, and the procedures for seeking reparation. It is necessary, moreover, to promote respect for *the right to peace.* This right "encourages the building of a society in which structures of power give way to structures of cooperation, with a view to the common good."[34]

Forgiveness not only empowers victims, it can also liberate them from the past. Having the horrid things done to them acknowledged and having the perpetrators ask their forgiveness allows victims to close that chapter of their lives and move on (without forgetting). This is why forgiveness cannot be rushed. It must proceed at the pace the victim sets. Wink warns against "false forgiveness," or cheap grace, because either it trivializes forgiveness as sentimentalism or it rewards insincere signs of contrition that are merely playacting. True forgiveness requires full knowledge of what was done and sincerity on the part of the confessor—in other words, genuine contrition.

As Kerr and Mobekk point out, "It is in the context of TCs [truth commissions] that the concepts of forgiving, healing and reconciliation are most often heard."[35] To be sure, religions (and not just Christianity) appear able to make a unique and effective contribution in the area of forgiveness. As noted previously, some secular approaches to post war reconciliation appear to see justice at odds with reconciliation and thereby tend toward penal or retributive justice. Religious understandings of justice (particularly in the Jewish, Christian, and Muslim traditions) pursue restorative justice and see reconciliation as a constitutive part of a just peace. The principal goal of restorative justice is not punishment (although restorative justice certainly includes punishment); instead restorative justice seeks to heal relationships that violence has torn asunder. This does not exclude other religious traditions that also have an ethos of reconciliation. Buddhism and Hinduism both uphold forgiveness as virtuous, and many of the truth and reconciliation commissions in Africa drew explicitly on indigenous religious teachings, beliefs, and rituals.

Religion is probably the richest resource for reconciliation because it grounds the process not only in the common good (which secular approaches also attempt) but in something much larger: the healing of the cosmic order, *tikkun olam* (healing of the world), and redemption. Judaism, Christianity, and Islam, for example, pursue forgiveness and reconciliation in their understandings of the very nature of God. As Yoder put it, "God is by nature a reconciler, a maker of shalom,"[36] or in the words of Alexander Pope, "To err is human, to forgive divine." We are called to forgive because God has forgiven us. We are called to show mercy because God is all-merciful. "For us to participate in the peacemaking purposes of that kind of God is not just morality," writes Yoder. "It is worship, doxology, praise."[37] Hence, Christianity and other religions are saturated with scriptures, symbols, and rituals devoted to forgiveness and reconciliation: Yom Kippur, Lent, Ramadan, the parable of the Prodigal Son, the sacrament of Reconciliation, the Western Wall in Jerusalem, and so on. These scriptures, symbols, and rituals are part of the deep culture of people. To attempt post war reconciliation without these sacred texts, rituals, and symbols (especially in conflicts that involve people of similar cultural background, such as a civil war) is like trying to build a house without hammer and nails. It is to attempt an arduous task without the most effective tools.

Amnesty

Amnesty, stemming from the Greek *amnēstia*, meaning forgetfulness, is really the wrong word to describe the final step in the reconciliation process. This is not about forgetting, but about pardoning. Etymologies aside, "amnesty" typically refers to an act by an authority (such as a government) of exempting from punishment those who are guilty of a crime. Amnesties run the gamut from blanket amnesties with no requirements or attempts at truth telling to amnesties conditioned on full exposure, which may include prosecution and punishment for the principal architects of the aggression. For Wink, "Amnesty should ideally be the last step in the process of reconciliation."[38] It is an "ideal" because political circumstances always condition the post war period. Sometimes military and police personnel (as well as bureaucrats) sympathetic to the overthrown regime remain in place and prevent full exposure, or the victims may really only care that the truth be told (as fully as possible), but may not want trials.

Moreover, as Kerr and Mobekk note, conditional amnesties can obstruct the aim of achieving reconciliation in the context of a truth commission, as was the case in South Africa where a perpetrator would not risk prosecution if he or she told the truth about past abuses. As they state it, "The result of a structure that incorporates conditional amnesty is that the perpetrator immediately walks free after testifying, whereas the victims are left waiting for reparations which may never come."[39] Hence, impunity is reinforced, which in turn exacerbates lingering fear, instability, and insecurity. For Kerr and Mobekk, conditional amnesties may serve the national reconciliation process, but these must be carefully applied, especially when it comes to individuals involved or affected. Other subsequent truth commissions have learned lessons from this example. "For reconciliation to begin," they write, "the victims need to find the claims of remorse, if they are uttered, to be credible."[40] Just as there can be false forgiveness, so, too, there is false reconciliation, wherein amnesties are granted with no requirements of truth telling or even expressions of remorse by perpetrators.[41] False reconciliation is the appearance of reconciliation without any of the demands of justice.

CONCLUSION

Reconciliation is indeed a principal area of *post bellum* ethics. It is also the phase in which religion can play its most constructive role. Religious understandings of reconciliation (especially Jewish, Christian, and Muslim theologies of reconciliation) provide a much richer understanding of reconciliation than secular models.

Whereas both models speak of reconciliation and justice, the secular models' understandings of justice tend to be backward looking, focusing mostly on what has been done, which leads them to be primarily punitive or retributive. Religious models are forward looking, focusing on what *needs to be done*, which leads them to tend toward restorative justice. The former aims at punishment, the latter at reconstruction.

Religions are also uniquely suited to address post war reconciliation in a practical manner. Religions ground the reconciliation process in something much larger than mere political interest. Drawing on centuries of religious texts, symbols, and rituals, religion grounds post war reconciliation in the nature of God or the cosmic order. Nearly every religious tradition has a theology of forgiveness and reconciliation, as well as powerful symbolic mechanisms that prod people to seek and grant forgiveness. Religions provide rituals that are based on centuries of practice and tailored to the cultural milieu. They provide a blueprint for how to forgive and a theological rationale for why people ought to seek reconciliation. To attempt post war reconciliation without these powerful resources of forgiveness is foolhardy.

While some tend to dismiss the religious models as naively unrealistic, the experience of truth and reconciliation commissions shows that restorative justice works. Restorative justice models can bring perpetrators to justice and augment the healing of nations. Peace is a precondition for any judicial system. Attempting to render punitive justice without the infrastructure of due process and transparency typically relies on ad hoc judicial systems or military tribunals, which appear as nothing other than vengeance. There can be no justice without law and order, and there is no law and order with social stability ... in other words, peace; and there is no peace without reconciliation.

5

THE PUNISHMENT PHASE

"Beloved, never avenge yourselves, but leave room for the wrath of God; for it is written, 'Vengeance is mine, I will repay says the Lord.'" (Rom 12:19)

While reconciliation aims at rebuilding relationships, the punishment phase's primary objectives are justice, accountability, and restoration—none of which are at odds with reconciliation. The legitimacy of punishment depends on

1. *Publicity* and *transparency*. Punishment ought to be meted out via public forums to which many, if not all, have access.
2. *Proportionality* and *discrimination*. Punitive measures ought not be excessively debilitating and must make distinctions based on level of command and culpability.
3. *Competent authority*. Punishments must be assigned by an authority that is recognized as legitimate by all sides.

In all likelihood, the legitimacy of the punishment phase depends on an independent authority in order to avoid even the appearance of victors acting as judge, jury, and executioner of the vanquished. This phase comprises two principal parts: compensation and war crimes trials.

COMPENSATION

Restitution is a basic demand of justice. If John is responsible for the destruction of Maria's property, then John ought to repair or pay for the damage. When it comes to interpersonal relationships, restitution/compensation is fairly clear, straightforward, and safeguarded in law. It is more complicated when it comes to post war compensation programs that can involve international relations and international law and may involve centuries of oppression of minority groups by their own government (such as that of indigenous populations and other minority groups).

Five perennial questions frame the debate about post war compensation: What is post war compensation? Why is it necessary? Who ought to pay, and to whom is it owed? When should it be paid? How much is owed, and how should it be distributed? We address these questions in three clusters.

What Is Post War Compensation, and Why Is It Necessary?

We begin by making distinctions between compensation, reparation, restitution, and penalty. Philosopher Bernard Boxill differentiates between compensation and reparation. He maintains that compensation is "forward looking."[1] Its primary aim is to help victims recover. It does not necessarily involve only victims of injustice but can include victims of natural disasters who seek compensation in order to rebuild their lives.[2] Reparations, in contrast, are "backward looking." Reparations are due only when one has been wronged by another. Reparations are paid because an injustice has been done, and as such require not merely the transfer of resources, but must include "an acknowledgement on the part of the transgressor that what he is doing is required of him because of his prior error," in other words, admission of guilt and responsibility.[3] Haig Khatchadourian, an emeritus professor of philosophy at the University of Wisconsin–Milwaukee, builds on Boxill's point by noting, "Acknowledgment is required not only because it may lead to the repair of wrongful losses but also because it constitutes recognition of the equal rights of the injured party. Denial of a wrong is a continuing affront to the dignity of the victim."[4] The demand of acknowledgment serves as a common touchstone between the reconciliation and punishment phases.

Khatchadourian modifies Boxill's characterization of compensation as "forward looking" and reparation as "backward looking."

It might be better expressed in terms of the *moral conditions or grounds* for reparation and compensation than in terms of their aims. The grounds for reparation are indeed in the past, while those of compensation may be in the past as well as the present. As for their *aims*, however, both are forward looking (as the very term "aims" could suggest). Both aim at the just rectification, correction, or amelioration of the condition of those who have suffered certain kinds of injury or loss.[5]

For Boxill and Khatchadourian, compensation and reparation are forms of compensatory (or corrective) justice and not forms of distributive or penal justice. While Khatchadourian admits that "corrective justice may require punishment [and] penal justice can also include restitution,"[6] he does not explore the difference.

Restitution and the punitive dimension of post war compensation need not be minimized in order to highlight the role of reparations. They can coexist. Restitution refers to restoring a group (or person) to their condition prior to an injury or offense, in other words, returning whatever was unjustly seized and paying for what one has unjustly destroyed. Thus, while reparation includes acknowledgment of responsibility, restitution is akin to the transfer of resources in order to return victims to their prior condition.

At the most basic level, post war restitution refers to returning property unjustly or justly seized during conflict (returning annexed land, seized financial assets, war booty, and so on) or paying for what has been unjustly destroyed. But if reparations are cast only in terms of restitution ("fixing what has been broken or stolen"), then the situation returns to the *status quo ante bellum*, which is rarely a valid objective in a post war scenario since the *status quo ante bellum* is the condition that led to war in the first place. (This point is explored in detail later.)

Post war compensation programs also serve a punitive function, namely to punish wrongdoers and to ensure that crime (the crime of aggression and *in bello* war crimes) ought not to pay. Even the most basic definition of justice, "getting what one deserves," makes this point clear. Those who are the victims of war ought to be compensated for their pain and suffering, *and* the perpetrators, not the victims, should be the ones who bear the burdens and costs of the bad behavior.

Ernesto Verdeja, a political scientist at the Kroc Institute for International Peace Studies at the University of Notre Dame, proffers an alternative "theory of reparations" consisting of four ideal types of reparations that can be plotted along two axes: collective-individual and symbolic-material (see Figure 2, below). "These dimensions trace the scope and type of reparation that should be accorded, and though different mechanisms are appropriate within each created space, each dimension is crucial for a normative theory of reparations."[7]

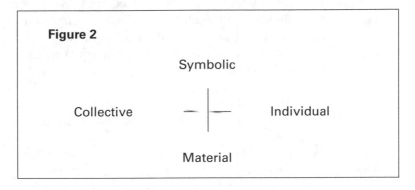

Figure 2

Symbolic

Collective ——|—— Individual

Material

Collective-symbolic reparations include monuments, parks, historical memory sites, national days of remembrance, and formal apologies. Individual-symbolic reparations (such as recording and archiving victim testimonies) address "the need to recognize victims as individuals and not simply to place them in a residual category, reducing them to an amorphous group of passive, voiceless survivors."[8] This can prove difficult because of the sheer number of victims and the need to be sensitive to each individual.

Collective-material reparation is a matter of distributive justice targeted toward groups that have been victimized. These efforts often include housing, education, employment, and other development programs focused on alleviating systemic injustices that have oppressed classes of people, including indigenous populations, ethnic and racial minorities, and religious groups.

While money cannot compensate for death, torture, rape, and

the like, individual-material reparations recognize that the victims of war have real and immediate needs—medical, psychological, legal, and financial, among others. Individual-material reparations address assessable damages due to destroyed or stolen property, as well as the physical and emotional problems that inhibit recovery. They also "maximize individual autonomy" and avoid "the paternalism inherent in collective material reparations."[9]

Reparations are always imperfect. No sum of money or symbolic gesture can compensate victims of war's atrocities. That reparations fall short of perfect justice is not an excuse for doing nothing. Reparations that are strictly symbolic are criticized as a form of cheap grace in which perpetrators shed a few crocodile tears, erect a monument, and walk away. Material reparations can be dismissed as blood money that buys the compliance and silence of the victims too easily because they are often in such dire straits. But as Verdeja notes,

> Such criticisms are fatal only if we think of reparations as free standing, separated from other reconciliatory mechanisms. If presented as the sole method of dealing with the past, then certainly there is good reason to be skeptical. Adequate engagement with the past must include more than symbolic and material reparations, important though these are. For reparatory justice by itself does nothing to end a culture of impunity or to foster accountability, or to promote the rule of law and reformation of corruption and violent state institutions.[10]

Here Verdeja hints at what we would consider to be a crucial absence in his dual axis theory: the lack of an explicit demand for political reparations.

Reparations are not just about the victim and the perpetrator. War is a political act that affects the entire community. Reducing reparations to an interpersonal level only or even using criminal justice analogies (a criminal vs. a victim) ignores the larger sociopolitical context of war. Political reparations involve formal efforts to confront the intentional or accidental alienation of certain groups from political processes. For example, in November 2008 the Iraqi Parliament, as part of its effort to reconstruct the political machinery after the U.S. invasion and the fall of Saddam Hussein, made changes to provincial election laws to guarantee representation of specified ethnic and religious groups.[11]

Finally, reparations are often criticized for being impractical. While in theory the idea that justice demands compensation for victims makes sense, in reality sorting through the ganglion of post war reconstruction makes reparations nearly impossible. However, this criticism falls short in the face of history. In 1995 Brazil compensated 130 families of the disappeared. In Chile nearly 5,000 family members of people killed by the Pinochet regime receive a lifetime monthly stipend of almost $480 from the Chile National Corporation of Reparation and Reconciliation, as well as medical assistance and counseling. In Argentina family members of the disappeared and killed received a one-time payment of $220,000 and waivers from the mandatory military service normally required of citizens. New Zealand's Treaty of Waitangi implemented a reparations/reconciliation program that included apologies, land reform, and compensation for abuses of the indigenous Maori people. The Greenland Home Rule Act (1978) provides measures for self-rule for Inuit populations that were forcibly relocated in the 1950s. To promote Sami languages and culture, Norway has a fund that was established in 2000, with formal apologies by the king and prime minister, for indigenous assimilation programs in the past.[12] While such programs are often criticized for being "too little, too late," they illustrate that reparation programs can work.

While Boxill and Khatchadourian justify reparations as a demand of corrective justice, Verdeja's dual-axis paradigm justifies reparations based on reparatory justice and distributive justice. Verdeja also posits a more utilitarian or pragmatic argument. Reparations contribute to post war reconciliation and reconstruction by (1) returning to victims "some sense of *moral worth and dignity* [because] ... they symbolize society's recognition of victims as equals deserving respect";[13] (2) signaling to society the need to reconceptualize its identity, to "rethink of itself more inclusively, the moral constellation of obligation toward fellow citizens is expanded";[14] (3) "strengthening *public trust* in state institutions," especially police and military forces that may have been complicit;[15] (4) undermining the ideologies of the past and deconstructing the *"justificatory narratives of the perpetrators"*[16] (see the previous chapter for more on the importance of construct- ing a new narrative); and similarly (5) promoting *"an alternate, critical interpretation of the past."*[17]

Verdeja's pragmatic rationale for reparations is framed in a way that presumes the perpetrator is a government and the victims are a minority group within the state, but this can be easily adapted to an international conflict. His theory bears strong similarities to the reconciliation phase discussed in the previous chapter.

Reconciliation and punishment are not at odds with one another. Reconciliation demands accountability. If reparations and compensation programs are nothing more than punishment for its own sake, then they are a form of vengeance. If they are exacted in service of reconciliation and reconstruction, then they are in service of justice and the common good. Indeed Verdeja admits that his theory aims at reconstruction and reconciliation. It "seeks to transform victims into citizens—to give them the status that will allow them to live meaningful lives in a new society."[18] But his pragmatism will not allow him to devolve into idealism. Reparations are not a cure-all for post war reconstruction:

> Such a model provides conceptual clarity to the possibilities and limits of reparations.... Nevertheless, it must be under- stood as part of a broader process of engaging legacies of abuse, including facing the past openly and honestly.... In the absence of some form of accountability, impunity will continue to poison social relations and breed contempt.... Shorn of the rule of law ... reconciliation becomes little more than a euphemism for the power of entrenched elites.[19]

Reparations must thus be cast as one part of many efforts to achieve post war justice.

Who Ought to Pay? To Whom Is It Owed? When Should It Be Paid?

The second cluster of questions surrounding post war com- pensation concerns who should pay, who should get paid, and whether payment has a statute of limitations; in other words, does the right to compensation extend indefinitely, and does it include descendants of the victims?

Concerning who ought to pay, due care needs to be exercised to ensure that the civilian population of an unjust aggressor nation does not bear the burden of decisions made by political and military leaders over which civilians had no control. Michael Walzer and Brian Orend agree that the political and military elite of unjust aggressor nations bears the primary responsibilities of compensation and that the personal wealth of the architects of the aggression should be seized in order to compensate the victims of their crime. Gary Bass rightly expands the list of who ought to pay to include the profiteers of an unjust war.[20]

Walzer, however, argues that if the private wealth of these architects is not sufficient, then it is legitimate to tax the population of the aggressor nation. He considers post war taxes on the populace of the aggressor the price for maintaining national sovereignty. Walzer clarifies his position of collective responsibility by noting that while citizens are not legitimate targets *in bello*,

> They are, however, [valid] political and economic targets once the war is over. Reparations are surely due the victims of aggressive war, and they can hardly be collected only from those members of the defeated state who were active supporters of the aggression. Instead the costs are distributed through the tax system, and through the economic system. . . . In this sense citizenship is a common destiny.[21]

To this he adds the caveat, "The distribution of the costs [of reparations] is not the distribution of guilt."[22] One can oppose the actions of one's government and still be responsible for the consequences of the government's behavior.

For Orend, however, holding individual citizens responsible for the bad behavior of their government violates the principle of discrimination.

> Respect for discrimination entails taking a *reasonable* amount of compensation *only* from those sources: (1) which can afford it; *and* (2) which were materially linked to the aggression in a morally culpable way. If such reparations "can hardly

pay" for the destruction [the] Aggressor meted out on [the] Victim, then the fiscal deficiency does not somehow translate into [the] Victim's moral entitlement to tax everyone left over in the Aggressor [nation]. *The resources for reconstruction simply have to be found elsewhere.*[23]

For Orend, taxing anyone not materially linked to the aggression in a morally culpable way is a case of guilt by association. But Orend fails to explain how one determines culpability or what to do in cases of "fiscal deficiency" other than to look "elsewhere."

Walzer also questions whether the personal wealth of the architects of aggression could ever be sufficient to serve as legitimate reparation. Orend responds by noting that frequently these architects of aggression are tyrants who have amassed small fortunes. Orend, however, fails to take into account that the personal wealth of tyrants is often unjustly acquired (perhaps through the misappropriation of development funds, bribes, or illegal activities) and thus is properly owed not to the victims of the aggression but to the victims of the tyrant's theft and other illegal activities. Paying the victims of a tyrant's aggression with wealth stolen from other victims of the tyrant's bad behavior is tantamount to making one victim pay another victim.

Trade is an additional and often ignored source of revenue that could compensate the victims of aggression. Trade agreements deliberately favorable to the victims of aggression could include no tariffs on goods flowing from the victim nation to the aggressor, and higher, but noncrippling, tariffs on goods flowing from the aggressor nation to the victim nation. Such agreements can be sources of tremendous revenue that hasten post war reconstruction efforts.

As a hypothetical example, imagine if the United States agreed to purchase a set number of barrels of oil from Iraq for a determined period, such as ten years, and promised to pay 1 percent above the market price with a guarantee that the revenue generated from that 1 percent would be used for reconstruction and rehabilitation projects. Such an arrangement, which would not be crippling to the U.S. economy, would generate significant revenue for reconstruction efforts. It could also facilitate economic planning because Iraq could predict future revenue with great accuracy. In a similar vein, in the aftermath of the 2002 Iraq War, the Network of Spiritual Progressives called for a "Global Marshall Plan" similar to the original Marshall Plan in which 1.5 to 2 percent of the U.S. gross domestic product was allocated toward reconstruction of Europe in the wake of the Second World War.[24]

While tariffs on goods are still a form of taxation, tariffs are less direct than post war taxes on the populace. Other constituents—such as ally nations of the victims and the aggressor, other regional parties, and international trade organizations—could also establish short-term favorable trade policies that would help the victims recover. Trade has the added benefit of being relational and potentially reconciliatory. Nations that cooperate with each other through trade are more likely to eventually see their former enemy as a new partner because they share common economic interests.

David Miller, a prolific author on social justice and an Official Fellow in Social and Political Theory at Nuffield College in Oxford, expands the collective responsibility argument in two significant ways. First, he argues that collective responsibility is inheritable; in other words, responsibility for reparations extends to future generations. Second, the victims' right to compensation also extends to future generations. Like Walzer, Miller contends that if a nation (as a collective) can be held responsible for its bad behavior, so, too, the individuals who make up that nation can be accountable. Miller defends national collective responsibility because nations are like a collective moral agent. They engage in "cooperative practices" from which they derive benefits, and they see themselves as members of a single community, which is best exemplified in their willingness to sacrifice to defend their community.[25]

Pope John Paul II makes a similar, although not identical, claim in his case for social sin. At first he seems to be arguing against a notion of collective responsibility: "Sin, in the proper sense, is always a personal act, since it is an act of freedom on the part of an individual person and not properly of a group or community.... Hence there is nothing so personal and untransferable in each individual as merit for virtue or responsibility for sin."[26] But he goes on to reject the idea that personal responsibility cannot be subsumed under collective guilt:

> Whenever the church speaks of situations of sin or when she condemns as social sins certain situations or the collective behavior of certain social groups, big or small, or even of whole nations and blocs of nations, she knows and she proclaims that such cases of social sin are the result of the accumulation and concentration of many personal sins. It is a case of the very personal sins of those who cause or support evil or who exploit it; of those who are in a position to avoid, eliminate or at least limit certain social evils but who fail to do so out of laziness, fear or the conspiracy of silence, through secret complicity or indifference; of those who take refuge in the supposed impossibility of changing the world and also of those who sidestep the effort and sacrifice required, producing specious reasons of higher order. The real responsibility, then, lies with individuals.[27]

Citizens are personally responsible for the sins of their nation. Benefits and burdens come with membership in any collective.

Miller extends the rights and responsibilities of membership intergenerationally by arguing that the right to receive or the duty to pay reparations is inheritable. In opposition to this claim, proponents of the "nonidentity problem" ask, "How can a person claim to be the victim of a wrong that took place prior to their own birth?" or conversely, "How can a person be held liable for actions that took place before they were born?"[28] For example, in questions regarding the legacy of slavery in the United States, some whites often object to the idea of reparations for descendants of slaves or even affirmative action programs by asking, "Why should I be penalized for something that was done centuries ago by someone else? I never owned a slave. Why should I be disadvantaged because of what others did in the past?"

Miller counters by noting that since one can inherit the benefits of national identity such as cumulative economic, social, political, and cultural benefits created by previous generations, as well as other material benefits and immaterial goods, including language, music, literature, and other hallmarks of culture, then one must also accept the liabilities, burdens, and responsibilities of national membership.[29] These obligations exist as long as the nation or collective identity exists. While the particular membership of a nation changes with each passing generation, as long as mechanisms for bequeathing the benefits of national membership exist, then so, too, the obligations also extend to future generations.

How Much Is Owed and How Should It Be Distributed?

No single calculation can determine what an unjust aggressor owes the victim of its crime. The debt is relative to the nature and severity of the crime and the ability of the aggressor to pay.[30] As the example of the Treaty of Versailles aptly illustrates, compensation agreements that cripple an aggressor so severely that the nation never returns to a functioning civil society only sow seeds of resentment and could lead to future wars. Compensation agreements need to be proportional: enough to make restitution more than a token gesture and enough to serve as a penalty that satisfies, at least in part, the victims of the crime, but not so severe that the vanquished never recover.

Bass rightly points out that reparations have their limits: "Economic reconstruction can only do so much," as no sum of money can compensate for the death of a loved one or for rape and torture; as such, "Reparations should be compensatory, not vindictive."[31] The penal dimension of post war compensation dictates that post war reparations should hurt, not in a tit-for-tat or eye-for-an-eye manner, but because (1) the crime of war ought not to pay; (2) the behavior, and ideally the motivating attitudes, of the perpetrator should change as a result (a kind of conversion); and (3) others in the future who might consider similar actions should see the reparations as a deterrent.

The Australia Stolen Generations Inquiry, formed to address the forced removal of aboriginal and Torres Strait Islanders from their families by government and church agencies between 1869 and 1969, provides one example of how reparations could be distributed. The Inquiry recommended the formation of a National Compensation Fund, managed by an indigenous majority. The Inquiry recommended the procedures for distributing funds "should be culturally appropriate, expeditious and non-confrontational. The principles include widest possible publicity; free legal advice and representation for claimants; no limitation period; independent decision making including participation of Indigenous people; minimum formality; not bound by rules of evidence; and cultural appropriateness."[32] Clearly, the animus of this procedure was to make the process as easy as possible for the victim/claimant, with the burden of proof falling on the perpetrator.

While such open and unobstructed compensation procedures could easily lead to abuse, corruption, and a slate of false claims, this is part of the price for having done wrong. We do not mean to suggest that such abuses are justified ("two wrongs don't make a right"), rather only to illustrate that reparations require a reversal of power. Those who once were dominant are now in a submissive/vulnerable position. Since perfect justice is not achievable, in this phase those most culpable should shoulder the burden of the injustices. The victims have suffered enough.

The philosophical and political literature on reparations has a tendency to focus on intra-nation conflicts and not international affairs. The literature also tends to collapse reconciliation under reparations, making acknowledgment and apology a condition of reparations. The strength of this approach is that it maintains the link between the two. Its weakness is that it collapses the two together, as if they were the same thing. Part of the confusion is due to the competing rationales for reparations. Reparations are justified as a requirement of reparatory justice, compensatory justice, restorative justice, distributive justice, and penal justice, but these aims are not mutually exclusive and share significant overlap. Theological literature has a tendency to emphasize reconciliation while underemphasizing the punitive dimension of reparations (see previous chapter). However, we reject the either/or paradigm in favor of a both/and approach. Reparations are both punitive and reconciliatory.

In short, reparations are both instrumental to and constitutive of post war reconciliation, reconstruction, and justice. While reparations have a notorious history, they can also serve as a powerful disincentive for aggression. By forcing the architects and profiteers of unjust aggressions to compensate their victims, and by constructing reparation agreements in a way that does not unduly burden those who were not "materially linked to the aggression in a morally culpable way," the crime of aggression can be, in part, properly punished and effectively discouraged in the future.

WAR CRIMES TRIALS

War crimes trials are about accountability. If war always involves crimes, then there must be criminals who must be brought to justice. The credibility of just war theory depends upon legitimately prosecuted war crimes trials. If the use of deadly force is justified under certain restrictions, then when deadly force is used unjustly, those who have broken the rules must be punished; otherwise, just war theory is a dog without teeth.

War crimes trials are nothing new in military affairs. As long as rules have governed war, there have been war crimes. While the crimes typically take place *ad bellum* or *in bello*, war crimes trials are usually convened *post bellum*. War crimes trials are a key component of *jus post bellum* in that they endeavor to end war well by holding accountable those who violate the norms and standards of just war theory. Six questions shape the debate on war crimes trials: What are war crimes? Who should be held responsible? Why are war crimes trials important? When should they be held? Where should they be held? How ought they be conducted? We address these questions in two clusters.

What Are War Crimes? Who Is Responsible? Why Are War Crimes Trials Necessary?

Traditionally, just war theory has addressed war crimes under its two long-standing categories: *ad bellum* (crimes against peace or aggression) and *in bello* (for example, intentionally targeting civilians, use of torture, killing POWs). *Jus ad bellum* crimes include unjust aggression or what Nuremburg prosecutors called "crimes against peace," such as "planning, preparing, initiating and waging" a war of aggression, genocide, and crimes against humanity.[33] *Jus ad bellum* war crimes trials are absolutely essential to post war justice because they "strip away the veneer of statehood to reveal human beings making choices."[34] States, like corporations or any collective entity, do not commit crimes. People acting in the name of the state make decisions, give orders, and act in ways that are criminal. As such, the architects of an unjust aggression ought to bear the greatest punishment. Political leaders, as opposed to military leaders, are usually the ones prosecuted for *ad bellum* crimes. Prosecution of *jus ad bellum* crimes must determine those most responsible for the crimes— distinguishing between those who orchestrated them from those who were mere pawns.

In theory, all crimes of unjust aggression ought to be vigorously prosecuted. Failure to prosecute war crimes is a form of passive endorsement and violates the just cause principle. As Davida Kellogg contends,

> If in fact the only acceptable reason for going to war is ... to do justice—then stopping short of trying and punishing those most responsible for war crimes and crimes against humanity which either led to the war or were committed in its prosecution may be likened to declaring "checkmate," and then denying to take your opponent's king. It makes no strategic sense, since the purpose for which war was undertaken is never achieved. It makes no legal sense, since the criminal activities the war was undertaken to rectify or curtail are allowed to continue unchecked. What is worse, it makes no legal sense since justice is not done for the victims of atrocities in such an outcome to war. Declining to do full justice for those who have been most grievously wronged by aggression ... leads to the perpetration of further moral injustice on both the victims of war crimes and on innocents.... Sweeping these injustices under the dusty rug of history, whether to keep a fragile peace or in a foredoomed effort at reconciliation, only continues their abusive treatment as non-persons who do not even register on the radar screen of international justice.[35]

A dose of realism is needed to temper this idealism. First, there is the very real possibility that the war of aggression was or is popular among the citizenry of the aggressive nation or that they interpret the action as a just war. Furthermore, sometimes the political leaders of an aggressive nation "in spite of their moral decrepitude, retain considerable popular legitimacy,"[36] as was the case with Somali faction leader Mohammad Farah Aidid (1992-1993) and again with Bosnian Serb leaders Ratko Mladic and Radovan Karadzic (1994-1995).

Second, sometimes full or perfect justice must be sacrificed on the altar of peace. War is frequently ended by negotiating with the architects of the unjust aggression. They often demand immunity as part of the peace settlement. Such compromises, while imperfect, are a proportionate response because without immunity the architects of the aggression have no incentive to seek an end to the conflict and may prolong the violence in the hope of victory. If the aim of a just war is peace, then granting immunity along with other conditions may in fact be the best solution. Such a scenario is not merely theoretical, as the case of Slobodan Milosevic in Bosnia illustrates. "But," as Bass stipulates, "the fact that sometimes one must reluctantly sell out justice for the sake of peace does not mean that there should never be justice."[37] In contradiction to the adage, "Justice delayed is justice denied," sometimes war criminals must be engaged and prosecution of their crimes delayed in the name of the greater good: peace. Nevertheless, the crimes ought not to be ignored or excused, for the aim of a just war is not simply peace at any cost, but a just peace. Making a deal with the devil is not the same as excusing the devil's behavior. As Orend concludes, "Justice delayed need not be justice denied—a trial will be held but only after the political community has progressed enough to absorb its impact.... The point here is simply that the principle itself—of calling those most responsible for the aggression to task for their crimes—must be respected as an essential aspect of justice after war."[38] This is a matter of balancing principle and practice, rectifying the ideal with the real.

Jus in bello crimes include such acts as disproportionate uses of force, failure to discriminate between soldiers and civilians, or engaging in inherently immoral acts (rape, torture, using civilians or POWs as shields, and so on). On a practical level, prosecution and punishment of *in bello* war criminals is necessary for *post bellum* justice simply because it "gets the thugs off the streets." It is also a basic demand of justice. Whereas political leaders are usually held accountable in cases of aggression, military leadership and soldiers are typically the ones responsible for *in bello* crimes.[39] As noted in the previous chapter, soldiers are "not responsible for the overall justice of the wars they fight";[40] they are, however, responsible for their own behavior in battle, which leads to the question, "How responsible are they?"

The two most common defenses for war crimes committed by soldiers in the field are the heat-of-battle defense and the following-orders defense. The former contends that in the frenzy of battle (which can extend to the entire war period), soldiers may lack *mens rea* (guilty mind, or more fully, *actus non facit reum nisi mens sit rea*, "the act does not make a person guilty unless the mind be also guilty"). In order for an act to be considered a crime, one must intentionally choose to do the wrong. The heat-of-battle defense contends that soldiers are whipped into such fervor that they no longer really know what they are doing; in essence they've lost their mind. This defense was proffered by the defendants in the infamous My Lai massacre during the Vietnam War. Commanding officers can be held partly responsible for situations of battle frenzy if they intentionally helped to create the crazed environment. In most situations of battle frenzy, however, there are soldiers who do not succumb and are able to keep their wits about them, which casts a shadow of doubt on the legitimacy of this claim. The heat-of-battle defense is at best a mitigating factor, but not an excuse.[41]

The following-orders defense was also used by defendants in the My Lai massacre as well as by Nazi soldiers accused of killing innocents. This defense typically comes in two forms. First, soldiers claim to be not responsible for unjust actions because to disobey the order would have resulted in some kind of penalty (demotion, ridicule, being ostracized, physical abuse or even their own death). While there are accounts of Nazi commanding officers who shot disobedient subordinates, this extreme case appears to be the only one in which following an obviously unjust order might be defensible. But as Orend observes, "There is always some penalty for disobedience, but not any old penalty will suffice as an excuse.... It counts *only as an excuse or mitigation in punishment,* and never as a justification for a verdict of innocence."[42]

Second, soldiers claim that their training conditions them not to ask questions. Certainly military training calls for and drills obedience. It is crucial to battlefield success. But as Walzer notes, "Soldiers can never be transformed into mere instruments of war. The trigger is always part of the gun, not part of the man. If they are not machines that can just be turned off, they are also not machines that can just be turned on.... It is a mistake to treat soldiers as if they were automatons who make no judgments at all."[43] One of the hallmarks of professional military training is the capacity and moral courage to defy unjust orders.

Commanding officers, by virtue of their rank, experience, and training, should be held to a higher level of responsibility than lower-ranking soldiers in the field.[44] The question of holding commanding officers responsible for the behavior of their subordinates is contentious because rarely is the commanding officer the one actually pulling the trigger. How can one be held responsible for an action that one did not commit? David Luban, who teaches philosophy and law at Georgetown University, argues that the military command structure itself is what makes it possible to hold commanding officers responsible for their subordinates' behavior. Officers can be held responsible in at least three ways: (1) as accessories to the crimes committed by their soldiers when they fail to prevent or punish, (2) for dereliction of duty whereby the failure to punish or prevent is a self-standing crime of the officer, and (3) for vicarious liability, wherein the commanding officer can be convicted of the soldiers' crimes, "as though the soldier were a mere extension of the commander rather than an independent intervening decision maker."[45]

While the third standard is the most radical, it is centuries old and widely upheld. The principle dates back to the fifteenth-century French king Charles VII and is part of the American Articles of War of 1775; it was also used to convict General Yamashita for massacres in the Philippines (1945), and is part of the current International Criminal Court statutes.[46] Commanding officers enjoy tremendous power. They shape the course of battle, control considerable deadly force, and have soldiers at their command. With this power comes monumental responsibility, or as Luban poetically phrases it, "Vicarious liability for the commander is, in a sense, the army's price of admission to the sphere of Athena."[48] In accepting their commissions, officers accept the liability inherent in leadership.

Modern Mercenaries

The use of private security forces by the U.S. State Department and the Central Intelligence Agency complicates the notion of holding combatants responsible for in bello war crimes. In the wars in Iraq and Afghanistan, private security guards from Blackwater International (now called Xe Services) were used to provide security and participated, along with C.I.A. agents and Special Forces, in snatch-and-grab raids to capture suspected insurgents or members of Al-Qaida. While Blackwater was originally hired to provide defensive security to U.S. installations, as time progressed it took on a more aggressive role.

The role of Blackwater in Iraq came to international attention when five Blackwater guards opened fire in Nisour Square in Baghdad in 2007, leaving seventeen Iraqi dead and twenty wounded. While the guards claimed they acted in self-defense, investigators concluded they were unprovoked and fired indiscriminately on civilians. Blackwater contractors operated in a legal limbo. Since they were not military personnel, they did not fall under military law. They were immune from prosecution under Iraqi law due to an immunity agreement signed by the U.S.-installed Coalition Provisional Authority of Iraq (the interim governing body of Iraq at the time). In addition, because the alleged crime took place outside the United States, the applicability of U.S. law to the case was questionable.

Eventually the case was brought before a U.S. federal judge, who dismissed the case, citing "reckless violation of the defendants' constitutional rights."[47] The U.S. government is appealing this ruling.

The use of private security forces (sometimes called mercenaries) confounds traditional thinking about prosecution for in bello war crimes. Most mechanisms of military accountability are tied to an explicit command structure and have detailed procedures of due process under either military or civilian law. When private security forces are permitted to operate in a war zone on behalf of a nation state, they must be held accountable to some kind of legal process.

While most scholars and jurists readily identify *ad bellum* and *in bello* crimes, very few identify *post bellum* crimes. If there are *ad bellum* and *in bello* crimes, then there must also be *post bellum* crimes. A failure to meet *post bellum* responsibilities, such as a refusal to pay reparations, the failure to address the needs of refugees and other victims of conflict, a refusal to hand over those indicted for war crimes and crimes against humanity, and a refusal to meet the restoration obligations (such as security, political reform, economic recovery, social rehabilitation, and ecological cleanup, which we explore in great detail in chapter 6) all represent a failure to end war justly.

Throughout we have been arguing that just war theory requires the development of a systematic set of *jus post bellum* criteria that ought to be codified and ratified by the international community in a manner similar to the present *ad bellum* and *in bello* standards. A just war can be fought justly or unjustly; likewise, a just war can be ended justly or unjustly. In those instances when a war is ended unjustly, those who engaged and fought the war must be held accountable. War leaves a wake of destruction. It wreaks havoc on people, cultures, the environment, and social, political, and economic infrastructures. Those who engage in war must be held responsible for the effects of their actions.

The rationale for war crimes trials is multivalent. First, as Bass suggested, trials "strip away the veneer of statehood"[49] to reveal that decisions to wage war or pursue certain courses of action are not made by "the state" or by "the military," but by individuals who can and should be held accountable for their choices and actions. Second, trials serve as a deterrent. Robust and consistent prosecution of war criminals signals to all that there are in fact rules of war (hence the credibility of just war theory depends on war crimes trials) and that human rights violations will be taken seriously and will be upheld by the global community.

Third, consistent prosecution of war crimes provides a "war termination benefit" in that it provides a framework and potential mechanism (for example, the International Criminal Court or ad hoc tribunals) for how to end a conflict.[50] Fourth, trials work to remove brutes from the political scene, which aids in the construction of a peaceful society. Seeking a just peace is hard when those bent on dominance or fueled by hatred are allowed to walk free. Fifth, trials serve an "expressive function," signaling that the war is over and that law and order, not vengeance, have won the day.[51] Finally, as noted in the previous chapter, trials can aid in reconciling enemies. When the most heinous acts of war are brought into the light of day and those most responsible are punished, then victims may derive a sense of healing and a nation may move forward to a just peace.

When and Where Should War Crimes Trials Be Held? How Should They Be Conducted?

In the post war period, victors face the temptation to prosecute only *jus ad bellum* crimes, thereby avoiding the ugly reality that all sides commit crimes *in bello*. In order to avoid claims of victors' justice, the prosecution of all war crimes is best left to an independent third party such as an international war crimes tribunal or a third-party state. Deciding when and where to hold war crimes trials depends in large part on the context. A war-ravaged nation may not have the facilities for such proceedings, but holding them in the victor's nation or in a nation seen as sympathetic to the victors taints the process. And, as noted above, sometimes arraigning political leaders is delayed because they enjoy popular support or in order to facilitate a peace deal, but there should be no statute of limitations on war crimes, just as there is none for crimes against humanity.

Post war trials must not only pursue justice, but must ensure that the process appears just. The standards for how the trials should be conducted include the norms of any fair trial and of due process. The accused must have competent legal representation, the right to cross-examine witnesses and experts, and access to all evidence; the rules of the proceeding must be known to all, the judge and jury must be fair and impartial, and the proceeding should be as transparent as possible.

Since the trials at Nuremburg and Tokyo at the close of World War II, the custom for prosecuting war crimes has been to form ad hoc tribunals, as was done in response to atrocities committed in Bosnia (1992-1995) and Rwanda (1994), both of which tried key political leaders, including the president of Serbia/

Yugoslavia Slobodan Milosevic and Rwandan prime minister Jean Kambanda. Special courts and tribunals were also set up to address crimes committed in Sierra Leone, Lebanon, East Timor, Cambodia, and Iraq.[52] In 2002 a permanent tribunal, the International Criminal Court (ICC), was established in the Hague, Netherlands, to prosecute individuals for genocide, crimes against humanity, war crimes, and the crime of aggression. The ICC also has mechanisms for paying reparations. While the viability and effectiveness of the ICC is still questionable, due in large part to the United States' desire to have immunity for its soldiers, the ICC has opened cases investigating crimes committed in Uganda, the Democratic Republic of the Congo, the Central African Republic, and Sudan.[53]

There is a difference between war crimes trials and punishment for war crimes. War crimes trials, even when they fail to fully punish perpetrators of war crimes and human rights abuses, still serve post war justice. They counter Cicero's claim that "laws are silent when arms are raised" or Sherman's defense that "war is hell."[54] The aim of a just war is the *tranquillitas ordinis*. There can be no tranquility without order, no order without law.

CONCLUSION

Our discussion has focused on compensation and war crimes trials as two primary examples of post war punishment. Both share significant overlap with other aspects of post war justice, especially reconciliation (chapter 4) and post war reconstruction (chapter 6). One form of post war punishment that we have not addressed is the use of sanctions. While sanctions are sometimes used to pressure states to change their behaviors or even to encourage internal revolt or regime change and thus are seen as a means to an end, sanctions can also be construed as a form of punishment. Sanctions that severely cripple the civilian population, such as those used against Iraq (1991-2003), are rightly condemned as disproportionate and indiscriminate. But there are also so-called "smart sanctions" that target the guilty political and military leaders (as well as arms dealers) by freezing their bank accounts, prohibiting international travel, and banning all arms trades to the offending country. Sanctions can be an effective punitive measure.

Throughout, this analysis has raised the question of "who is responsible?" In most cases the clearest answer is the principal architects of the aggression and the military leaders who ordered crimes to be committed as well as the soldiers who carried out those orders. In other words, guilt falls upon those who are materially linked to the crime. But guilt can extend further, especially in a functioning democracy. Miller's argument for collective responsibility challenges the notion that citizens are immune from responsibility for the actions of their government and military. Certainly citizens are immune from prosecution for war crimes and are not directly responsible if their government leaders choose to wage an unjust war. So, how can citizens in a democracy be held morally liable for the actions of their government?

Walzer takes up this line of questioning by theorizing about a "perfect democracy," which he describes as "a small community where all the citizens are fully and accurately informed about public business, where all of them participate, argue, vote on matters of communal interest, and where they all take turns holding public office."[55] He goes on to speculate that if this ideal fictional community were to wage an unjust war against its neighbor, then the blame would fall in proportion to the support each citizen gave to the effort, with those who voted for the war bearing the greatest responsibility and those who voted against it and refused to cooperate as blameless. Walzer's "perfect democracy" is not purely speculative, however. He engages in this thought experiment as a way to discern the responsibility of ordinary Americans for the Vietnam War. In 1977 he wrote,

> We can now drop the myth of perfection and paint a more realistic picture.... [Our state is] governed at a great distance from its ordinary citizens by powerful and often arrogant officials.... Political participation is occasional, intermittent, limited in its effects, and it is mediated by a system for the distribution of news which is partially controlled by those distant officials.... When a state like this commits itself to a campaign of aggression, its citizens (or many of them) are

likely to go along, as Americans did during the Vietnam war, arguing the war may after all be just; that it is not possible for them to be sure whether it just or not; that their leaders know best and tell them this or that, which sounds plausible enough; and that nothing they can do will make much difference anyway.[56]

Walzer concludes that such rationalizing is understandable, but "reflects badly on the society ... these people are or may be blameworthy, not for aggressive war, but for bad faith as citizens."[57]

We resurrect his argument in the years following the U.S. invasions of Iraq and Afghanistan in order to ask, What are the responsibilities of the American public for the war on terror? While many just war theorists found the U.S. invasion of Afghanistan immediately after the September 11, 2001, bombings to be justified, the invasion of Iraq is troublesome, as are other aspects of the war on terror, including the use of torture, extraordinary renditions, "detainees" in Guantanamo Bay, and the use of drone aircraft and cluster munitions. Walzer's description of an alienated, uninformed, and apathetic citizenry rings prophetic.

Orend adapts his argument to the contemporary context by asking,

> If citizens choose not to seek out such information, preferring either to "zone out" in front of the TV, or to endorse the war out of unreflective patriotism, then they are blameworthy, though *not* of the full charge of aggressive war. What they are guilty of ... is "bad faith as citizens." The information about the war's injustice is available.... It is critically important to do what one can to prevent serious harm (especially when it is being done in one's name).[58]

Orend goes on to call this bad faith a "searing indictment of the democracy in which it occurs," indicating a poor system of education, weak media outlets, a dysfunctional political system, and poor character and moral immaturity on the part of the people. We would add, it also indicates a failure on the part of churches, church leadership, and all people of goodwill. Christianity has long upheld that there are sins of commission and sins of omission. Failure to be an informed and engaged citizen is not merely "bad faith," it is also a sin of omission. Religious communities are more than social clubs or places of spiritual palliative care. They are supposed to be prophetic places that remind us of our ethical heritage and the moral commitments inherent to religious life. They are places where we are supposed to be challenged. The lack of robust, persistent, and widespread condemnation of the invasion of Iraq represents a serious moral failure of the Christian communities and in particular the leadership of the church.

Throughout this book we argue that how a war ends is as important a moral consideration as why it is waged and how it is fought. Unjust wars in particular place a heavy burden on their architects and, if waged by a democracy, upon its people. Membership has its privileges and its obligations. As we outline what *jus post bellum* entails, one might quickly counter, "But this is expensive, too hard, and unreasonable." The costs incurred are the penance for having committed the sin of war.

6

THE RESTORATION PHASE

"I don't trust anyone anymore," he said. "This is what the war has taught me, not to trust."[1]

The principal aim of a just war is not the *status quo ante bellum*. Rather, it seeks to put into place at least a "minimally just state," one that respects human rights and behaves in a manner that allows it to be seen as legitimate in the eyes of its own people and internationally. It should create a sustainable political, economic, social, and ecological environment that allows its citizens to flourish. A just war ends with the creation of conditions that permit citizens to pursue a life that is meaningful and dignified.

But who is most responsible for post war restoration? At least initially, for both practical and moral reasons, the victor bears the greatest burden.[2] Security and policing are typically the most pressing concerns. Since the victor is already in place and equipped to handle security, the task falls to it, at least in the immediate aftermath. Morally the so-called Pottery Barn principle—"you broke it, you bought it"—applies. While just cause may permit the invasion of another nation (of course, while satisfying and adhering to each of the other *ad bellum* criteria), right intent carries with it the obligation to reconstruct. Just reconstruction should not be a unilateral effort, but should involve local, regional, and international partners. As Brian Orend notes, "The war winner should not have problems attracting such outside aid *if* the war itself was just.... Nor should the international community hesitate to provide such aid, since it is not just a matter of charity but also of improving the peace and security of themselves and their own people."[3] While states are often apprehensive to provide aid in the wake of an unjust or unpopular war because it could be seen as an endorsement of the war effort, failure to aid in reconstruction efforts most often further penalizes citizens, the primary victims of war.[4]

Just reconstruction aims at restoring sovereignty to the vanquished, a process best measured in years, if not decades (and certainly not in weeks or months). *Post bellum* responsibilities are implicit in the *ad bellum* criteria. Reconstruction is neither a gift or a donation, nor is it optional. It is a constitutive dimension of just cause and right intent, as well as a necessary investment for peace and security in the short and long terms. *Post bellum* obligations of reconstruction are not appendices to *jus ad bellum* and *jus in bello*, they are concomitant duties. We explore the restoration phase by focusing on five principal concerns: security and policing, political reform, economic recovery, social rehabilitation, and ecological cleanup.

SECURITY AND POLICING

Concerning post war Iraq, Bishop Thomas G. Wenski observed in 2006, "Stability remains elusive and rebuilding efforts are uneven, inadequate and frequently undermined by the lack of security."[5] Indeed, persons interviewed by Anne Nivat in both Iraq and Afghanistan reported that, more than anything, "a lack of security" left them with "an absence of faith in the future." Shaheeda Hussein, a forty-eight-year-old Afghan mother, offered these somber reflections: "People hoped that, thanks to the Americans, the Taliban would disappear, that the new strongmen of the country would bring us peace, stability, and prosperity and would rebuild our country. Yet I've never felt so unsafe."[6] Security is a precondition for everything included under the principle of restoration, and it ought to be one of the first things pursued under the wider umbrella of *jus post bellum*. "Victors," writes former rear admiral Louis Iasiello, "have a moral obligation to ensure the security and stabilization of the defeated society."[7]

According to Catholic moral theologian Kenneth Himes, OFM,

"An expansion of the principle of restoration" would entail "the work of securing domestic peace through protection of civil liberties and human rights, as well as helping to organize police and judicial institutions so that the necessary social space is created for men and women to begin the work of restoring public life."[8] Before roads can be rebuilt, electric services restored, and crops planted and harvested, an immediate priority is the provision of stability and security. Indeed, a secure peace that protects civil liberties and human rights should magnify the probability of success of other tasks necessary for restoring public life. Security is a necessary condition for stability and development, and, as Himes suggests, police and judicial institutions can play an important role in the equation. These are areas, however, that very few theological ethicists have explored in any depth. Until recently, policing, for example, has been something of a gap in Christian social ethics. As Edward LeRoy Long Jr. has noted, "One can go through the indices of book after book in the field and find no entries for either law enforcement or police work. In comparison with the immense amount of thinking about the problem of war and the moral issues surrounding military service, this lacuna is telling."[9]

The Rule of Law

Providing for effective military and police security for the defeated country is one of the ingredients in Orend's recipe for achieving the goal of a minimally just society. "Most experts suggest a two-stage approach here: the successful 'attack and overthrow' war divisions be replaced by other divisions specifically trained in post-combat peace-keeping and nation-building."[10] Here he notes that ratios are crucial, referencing research that shows the need for approximately twenty soldiers per thousand residents to secure and stabilize post war populations. This shows the locals "strong—not hesitant—intentions to protect them and to provide a secure backdrop for the development of law and legitimacy, to say nothing of the economy and the re-birth of a peaceful and regular pace of life."[11]

In the literature of political science, international relations, and human rights, a number of scholars highlight the "rule of law" as an important component of post conflict security, peacebuilding, and development. According to Irish international human rights legal scholar Vivienne O'Connor, "The rule of law is recognized as an inherent element in ensuring long-term sustainable peace, economic and political development in post-conflict states."[12]

The police and judicial institutions that Himes mentions above are two components of the rule of law; however, political scientist and international peacebuilding scholar Rama Mani rightly adds a third prong: prisons.[13] Each of these three institutions is interdependent. In her view, the police have a "key role ... to perform in the transition from conflict to peace."[14] Without police there would be no one to apprehend criminals for trial and possible imprisonment. "The police force is responsible for upholding and enforcing the law," writes Mani, "and is the most publicly visible pillar of the rule of law to citizens in their daily life."[15] Graham Day, another international peacekeeping scholar and practitioner, agrees. Once the fighting stops, "The efficacy of the military dramatically diminishes ... [and] the need for civilian peace-building tools—the agencies of law and order: the police, judiciary, penal system, and body of law—increases."[16]

To establish the space for construction and implementation of the rule of law, Day suggests the development of a rapid-deployment police or "blue force" consisting of civilian police from the region and internationally. He elaborates, "From the time of the signing of the cease-fire agreement, the blue force would be responsible for public order, routine police work, the arrest of war criminals, security for refugees, and most important, starting the process of vetting, restructuring, and training the local police."[17] While most scholars would include all of this under "peacebuilding," Day names this dimension "policekeeping."[18] In a post conflict country, the transition to a just peace (Day refers to "democracy") proceeds in three phases: order, law and order, and finally, law and order with justice.[19] Policekeeping, as Day envisions it, "begins in the immediate aftermath of hostilities and continues in diminishing measure until governance has been fully transferred to local authorities."[20] The goal, however, is not merely a return to the *status quo ante* or some minimal conditions of order. The third phase of law and order with justice appears congruent with Himes's understanding of restoration as involving a just peace, where civil liberties and human rights flourish.

Positive versus Negative Peacekeeping

Along these lines, Mani distinguishes "positive peace," which includes justice and human rights along with order and security, from "negative peace," which is merely maintaining and enforcing law and order. Indeed, she worries about too much focus on enforcing the law and maintaining order, where the police are seen primarily as law *enforcers* and as the coercive arm of the state. She posits that if "the rule of law is treated primarily as a mechanism to restore order and security and to maintain and enforce negative peace ... the police may backslide towards the use of excessive force."[21] For this reason, she recommends that instead of using the term "police force" we should refer to the police with a more positive, peacebuilding twist. She writes that in Ireland, "The police are called *Garda Siochána* or the guardians of the peace; in Spain, the term is the *Guardia Civil*, roughly, the guardians of civility."[22] The policekeeping that Day proposes seems consonant with Mani's focus on positive peace for the rule of law and police. With regard to the use of force, for example, Day points out that the policekeeping approach would have a higher degree of respect for strict rules of engagement due to the policekeeping rather than the military orientation.[23]

Mani's concerns about the police, however, are not necessarily with the international or regional police that Day sees as doing most of the law and order work at the front end of the post conflict situation. Rather, Mani is worried about the restored or rebuilt police of the defeated or post conflict nation, especially if the police were abusive before or during the conflict, or if they are inept, corrupt, or simply devastated and thus impotent in its aftermath. As international law scholar Hurst Hannum puts it, "In many countries, incompetent or inadequate police forces, biased or corrupt courts, [and] inhumane prisons not only perpetuate human rights violations but also undermine attempts to introduce stability and accountability to newly formed governments."[24]

For these reasons, Mani makes a number of suggestions for reforming the police institution.[25] A crucial step involves delinking the military and the police in the transition from conflict to peace, especially since in many countries the two institutions are closely merged prior to or during the hostilities.[26] Also she expresses some reservations about allowing new recruits to come from demobilized, unemployed soldiers, or rehiring police who were implicated in earlier abuses.[27] She emphasizes, moreover, that police need training in human rights and some sort of "exercises that bring police and communities closer to each other, so that the police's genuine commitment to generating and upholding the rule of law is made evident to a fearful, distrustful public."[28] In this connection, she mentions community policing as a possible model, but she goes on to note that there is no consensus on what community policing is, and that it has had mixed results as in, for instance, Haiti. Nevertheless, the participation of local populations with the police is a key element, which Day and Freeman say is "paramount."[29]

Just as Christian social ethicists have neglected the topic of policing until recently, political scientists, while apparently more familiar with aspects of policing, do not delve into it in depth. However, a brief examination of the literature of criminology, especially with regard to models of policing, reveals a great deal of support for the kind of police that Mani and Day have in mind for restoring a just post conflict rule of law. Within this literature, several different models of policing are found. In his book *The Ethics of Policing*, John Kleinig, a philosopher specializing in criminal justice ethics, identifies a spectrum of policing models circulating among philosophers, sociologists, and criminologists that purport to offer a normative framework for policing.[30] The two main models at opposite ends of the spectrum are the crimefighter model and the social peacekeeper model.

The primary paradigm of policing that developed and prevailed among police institutions within the United States during much of the twentieth century was the crime-fighter model. As Kleinig notes, it is often referred to as the law enforcement or military model. According to Joycelyn Pollock-Byrne, police take "very seriously" their role as crime fighters, so much so that this forms and shapes their self-understanding.[31] Indeed, when referring to "real" police work, law enforcement officers generally have in mind crime fighting. Within this vision of policing, the use of force occupies a central position, for police officers believe they must be armed and ready to do battle with crime and criminals.

Obviously, the political refrain in recent decades about winning "the war on crime" is consonant with the crime-fighter approach, which is why Kleinig and others regard it as synonymous with a military model for policing. "The conception of the police as a quasi-military institution with a war-like mission," observes Egon Bittner, "plays an important part in the structuring of police work in modern American departments."[32] Not only do American police tend to regard themselves as crime fighters in the war on crime, but as Jerome Skolnick and James Fyfe observe, the "military metaphor also colors the public's expectations of the police."[33] The film and television industries often perpetuate this false impression of police work. Indeed, Peter Scharf and Arnold Binder name these media depictions "the mythology of police work," especially with regard to viewing the gun as "the primary symbol of law enforcement," the "tool of the trade," and the "culturally defined essence of police work."[34]

Because both institutions "are instruments of force," the analogy often is assumed to exist between the police and the military.[35] The use of force in policing, as in the military, is regarded as the "essential" or "inherent" ingredient in the profession, which is why a number of criminologists highlight that the police often are referred to as a law *enforcement* agency or as a police *force*.[36] Accordingly, this view of police as coercion specialists assumes "the *primacy* of force in coping with crime and criminals."[37] This model, therefore, reckons the use of force as the key characteristic of policing or, put differently, it regards coercive power as the raison d'être of policing—the sort of activity about which Mani expresses concern.

Criminologists warn that the crime-fighter or military model of policing may be the soil from which sprout the weeds of police brutality and excessive force. One group of criminologists observes, the "belief that being a law enforcement officer is akin to the work of a soldier on the frontlines ... [and] this pervasive sense that their mission is a dangerous one cannot help but affect the way that police officers deal with the public."[38] For one thing, the military or crime-fighter model alienates the police from the public—an us-versus-them attitude—possibly leading to the dehumanization of the very people the police are pledged to serve and protect. Everyone is viewed suspiciously and cynically as a potential "enemy," and a criminal suspect is especially regarded as such.

In turn, this makes it easier, according to Paul Chevigny, for police "to abuse those who are the enemy, easier even to kill or torture them."[39] According to Bittner, the "quasi-military model implicitly extends the stamp of legitimacy to methods that would not be acceptable on moral and legal grounds."[40] Likewise, Skolnick and Fyfe assert that a "causal connection" exists between "the idea that cops are like soldiers in wars on crime" and the use of excessive force.[41] As a fairly recent example, they claim that the Rodney King beating should be considered a reflection of the predominant crime-fighting philosophy of policing, which the Los Angeles Police Department has exemplified in recent decades. Indeed, they believe that the war model of policing constitutes "a major cause of police violence and the violation of citizens' rights," and it "encourages police violence of the type that victimized Rodney King."[42]

Kleinig agrees that the crime-fighter model cannot adequately rein in the use of force. "Unless and until police see themselves primarily as peacekeepers rather than as crime fighters," he writes, "firearms will tend to be used unnecessarily."[43] Therefore, he argues that an alternative approach is needed "that acknowledges the nonnegotiable force at police disposal without transforming it into the police raison d'être."[44] Instead of seeing the use of force as the primary characteristic or as the essence of policing, Kleinig regards the use of force more as an instrument of policing. In his view, the social peacekeeper model of policing encompasses better most of the responsibilities and tasks of the police in society (for example, directing traffic, aiding the injured at an accident, searching for lost persons, and so on), and in this model the fact that police are armed is merely "a contingent matter."[45] Thus, the use of force by police is "a last (albeit sometimes necessary) resort rather than their dominant modus operandi."[46] Kleinig suggests that had the Los Angeles police officers who participated in the beating of Rodney King understood themselves "primarily as social peacekeepers, for whom recourse to force constituted a last and regrettable option, events would almost certainly have turned out very differently."[47]

This social peacekeeper model is actually a return to the way policing was originally conceived and conducted in the nineteenth century in England and the United States, and it resonates well with recent calls for community policing that Mani briefly mentioned above. Many criminologists writing about community policing observe that it is both a philosophy and a strategy of policing, which is why it seems appropriate to locate it within the philosophical model of social peacekeeping as delineated by Kleinig.[48] One of the chief characteristics of community policing is that it involves a partnership between the police and the community. It seeks to foster a relationship of mutual trust, bonds of empathy, and a common purpose, rather than an adversarial us-versus-them mentality. Police and the citizens participate together and share a stake in the common good and welfare of their community. The police are part of the community and therefore work in cooperation with the community.

In addition, community policing programs promote the hiring of recruits who reflect or understand the diverse communities that they will serve. At the same time, as part of this partnership, community residents have a role to play. Through neighborhood watch programs, safe houses, and other community service organizations, citizens share responsibility with police for the quality of life and common good of their community. Police officers also are encouraged to become involved in community activities such as coaching sports teams or participating in town and neighborhood meetings. Community agencies partner with police and citizens in this model. Together they can explore and possibly implement creative solutions to local problems that may give rise to crime. Also, when someone commits a crime, he or she is treated as a fellow community member rather than some external enemy. In this model, therefore, if force is necessary to apprehend the suspect, it should be in accordance with strict criteria for the ethical use of force.

At first blush, these alternative models of policing may appear naively ineffective in a post war scenario. However, their success comes precisely because these approaches are markedly different, in substance and appearance, from military attempts at keeping the peace. They are a signal to the community that it is indeed no longer at war and that the post war period is a time of peace and reconstruction. This social peacekeeper or community model of policing appears consonant with the police that Day has in mind for policekeeping and Mani for policing the rule of law for a positive peace. We believe that these models are consonant with the kind of policy demanded by *jus post bellum* efforts at restoration.

POLITICAL REFORM

Political reform focuses on what to do about the power vacuum left in war's wake. According to Walzer and Orend, the answer depends on the type of regime that was responsible for the aggression, the severity of their actions in battle (for example, did they use WMDs or commit or attempt genocide) and the range of options presented by the cultural-political context. *Post bellum* political reform involves reform of military and political structures.

Militarily, the immediate post conflict period requires some type of quick demilitarization (such as buffer zones, curtailing military capabilities, or no-fly zones) similar to what the United States imposed on Iraq after its invasion of Kuwait in 1990-1991. Demilitarization might also be more extensive and include reorganizing military/police command structures and the education of military/police personnel. Minimally, demilitarization needs to be pursued to the point that the vanquished aggressor no longer poses an immediate threat to the nation it initially attacked or to its neighbors. But it cannot be pursued to the point that the vanquished become vulnerable to reprisal attacks from others or cannot maintain law and order within its own borders. This approach may require that the victors provide internal and external security to the vanquished aggressor (a costly endeavor in terms of lives and finances) until the vanquished can defend itself and establish law and order.[49]

Proportionality and prudence reign supreme in these efforts. The original crime of the unjust aggressor should not be glossed over; this crime needs to be punished for both principled reasons (namely justice) and for practical reasons. The aggressor demonstrated a willingness to attack others. In discerning an answer to the question, "To what extent should the aggressor be demilitarized?" the presumption should be in favor of leaving the aggressor militarily crippled, but not vulnerable.[50] During this period of protectorship, the victor must not only provide protection (internally and externally) for the vanquished, but must also assume responsibility for the reconstruction and maintenance of systems necessary for life (such as water, sewage treatment, health care, electricity, and so on). Finally, the victor should also work bilaterally or multilaterally in order to avoid charges of pursuing a victors' justice.

Political reform follows many of the same principles as military reform. The response needs to be proportional and prudential, and again the devil is in the details. Simply reinstating the same political powers that waged the war in the first place (*status quo ante bellum*) is undesirable and unjust, but triumph in battle does not confer upon the victor the right to restructure the vanquished in any way it sees fit. For example, following the Second World War, General Douglas MacArthur served as the civil administrator of post war Japan. In this position he managed key aspects of the transition, including writing a new constitution, restoration of the economy, and establishing programs for social transformation—accomplishments that some historians record as his greatest feat.

Similarly, in the aftermath of the 2003 invasion, Iraq faced a power vacuum with no constitution, judiciary, legislature, or executive. The United States assumed political power because it had military power. A provisional authority under U.S. leadership was established while a provisional constitution was adopted and a panel of Iraqi judges (independent from the United States) acted as a provisional judiciary in the trial, conviction, and execution of former president Saddam Hussein and other leading figures in his regime.

Gary Bass, drawing heavily on Walzer and Rawls, identifies sovereignty, territorial integrity, and political autonomy as key concerns of political reform. Since sovereignty is "the bedrock of international relations," victors must limit their occupation to the shortest possible period, but not end it prematurely—in other words, not before internal and external security are established and a functioning civil society is in place.[51] Furthermore, victors must exercise restraint. "Once the war is over, the enemy country must be seen in a radically different light. Its sovereignty must be respected.... Victorious states have no right to impose puppet regimes, or reconstruct a polity for the victor's economic, military, or political gain."[52]

This notion that former enemies must see each other "in a radically different light" colors the entire reconstruction phase. War places people in a relationship. Once the formal combat phase has ended, the relationship changes; it does not end. Recalling the biblical notion of justice as fidelity to the terms of relationship, post war justice requires an act of the will by both the victor and the vanquished. Justice demands that they make the effort to see their former enemy in a new light—no longer as a threat that needs to be destroyed or even as someone who is suspicious or untrustworthy, but as a people to whom they are bound, inextricably linked by the blood they have shed, which mirrors the biblical concept of covenant, an unbreakable bond that was ritually sealed in blood.

Orend finds Bass's approach to political restructuring overly cautious: "There should be a presumption *in favor of permitting rehabilitative measures* in the domestic political structure of the defeated aggressor. But such rehabilitation does need to be proportional to the degree of depravity inherent in the political structure itself," because, if the actions of the regime during the war or the nature of the regime at the war's end "is still so heinous that its continued existence poses a serious threat to international justice and human rights, then—and only then— may such a regime be forcibly dismantled and a new and more defensible regime established in its stead."[53] Orend adds the caveat, "But we should be quick to note, and emphasize, that such construction necessitates an additional commitment *on the part of* [the] *Victim and any Vindicators* to assist the new regime in [the] Aggressor [nation] with this enormous task of political restructuring."[54] This implies an act of the will by both warring parties. They must shift from an adversarial relationship to one in which they see themselves as partners in resolving a common problem, similar to the third principle of just peacemaking (see Introduction and chapter 1): cooperative conflict resolution that aims at getting adversaries to realize they have mutual interests in resolving their conflict nonviolently.

Orend is open to more permissive arguments in favor of regime change and other forms of "political therapy."[55] He agrees with Walzer that particularly heinous regimes (for example, Nazi Germany) warrant complete dismantling and represent exceptional cases.

> But comparatively minor renovations—like human rights education programs, police and military retraining programs, reform of the judiciary and bureaucracy into accountable institutions, external verification of subsequent election results, and the like—are permitted in *any* defeated aggressor, subject to need and proportionality.[56]

Nevertheless Orend does recognize that "forcible, forward-looking rehabilitation" is fraught with controversy, especially in instances where there was collusion between political and military apparatuses.[57]

Political reform touches upon a related and contentious issue: regime change and its cousin, "nation-building."[58] Several questions arise in this context. Is regime change ever justified, and if so, under what conditions? What are the obligations of the overthrowing party to the citizenry of the vanquished? When faced with a rogue, hostile, rights-violating nation, are other strategies (such as containment or sanctions) morally and practically preferable to military intervention? Who ought to orchestrate the formation of the replacement political structure?

The era of colonial expansion is rife with examples of regime change. As the European powers (such as Great Britain, Spain, France, and Portugal) expanded, they often forcibly replaced native ruling authorities with their own appointees and created political structures similar to their own. In this respect, post war reconstruction served as a moral cover story for neo-imperialism or colonialism.[59]

While "colonialism" is a term most often used pejoratively, some scholars, such as Niall Ferguson, point out that the Roman and British empires brought peace, economic prosperity, political stability, and technological advances to many parts of the world.[60] For example, many parts of the world where democracy, human rights, and constitutional law currently flourish are former British colonies (the United States, Canada, Australia, and India, for example). This is not to suggest these places are perfectly just, nor does it intend to make light of the atrocities committed during the colonial and neocolonial conquests, but only to illustrate that empires can bring some good with the bad.

Regime Change

Orend identifies two types of regime change: change intended from the start (*ad bellum*) and change required by the aftermath (*post bellum*). Addressing the former, he raises the question of whether regime change can ever be considered a just cause for going to war. His reply is that "the imposition of institutional therapy," one of his preferred terms for regime change, "on an aggressor is consistent with, even implied by ... rights vindication."[61] In other words, if the protection of human rights is a just cause for war, then aiming to overthrow a habitually rights-offending regime (not just stopping the violation of those rights) is permissible and perhaps obligatory.

The genocide in Sudan provides a gripping illustration of this case. An estimated four hundred thousand Sudanese (mostly black Africans) have been killed by the Khartoum regime and their partners, the *janjiweed* militias. The crisis has also created more than 2.5 million refugees. Can or should the international community intervene to stop the genocide by protecting the victims, or should the aim of military intervention be to topple the Khartoum regime and overthrow the sitting president, Omar al-Bashir, who has been charged with crimes against humanity? What is the moral response to the crisis in Darfur? Is it simply to protect the people from their genocidal government (and if so, for how long) or to enact regime change, topple the government, and assist in the creation of a new government that respects the rights of all citizens?

Although Orend's political realism may garner favor with hawkish Christian just war thinkers such as George Weigel, justifying regime change as a just cause for going to war is a far more hawkish stance than what contemporary Christian just war theorists hold (including the National Conference of Catholic Bishops). Orend anticipates criticism of his justification for *ad bellum* regime change by critiquing the purportedly less violent option of containment.

Regime Change versus Containment

Containment strategies do not seek to overthrow the offensive regime, but instead aim only to defang it through isolation or pressure for change by means of other, less explicitly violent measures, such as sanctions. For example, at the end of the first Gulf War, sanctions were imposed on Iraq as part of an effort to pressure the Hussein regime into backing off its aggressive stance toward its neighbors and to compensate Kuwait for damages done as a result of the invasion and occupation. This supposedly less violent alternative resulted in 350,000 to 500,000 civilian deaths as vital materials and medicines were prohibited because they also had the potential to be used in weapons systems.[62] Sanctions strengthened the hand of Hussein and the Baathist Party because as vital resources became scarce, Hussein and the Baathists used the resources to reward those who cooperated with them. Sanctions are not necessarily less violent than military action and can actually strengthen the hand of tyrants.

Orend strongly criticizes containment strategies over regime change. "Containment sacrifices justice for what it thinks is expediency."[63] But Orend criticizes with a sober view of the cost of regime change:

Rehabilitation is more costly and risky: *cost* in the form of overthrowing the regime and rebuilding the economy; and *risk* in the form of botching reconstruction.... [But] *containment has its own costs and risks*: the *cost* of enforcing containment, both financially and militarily; the risk that civilians will continue to suffer material deprivations and rights violations, perhaps even more so.[64]

Orend argues that regime change is expensive and perilous, but worth it.

> The rewards of good rehabilitation are *greater than* those of good containment, and so the greater risk can be reconceived as a more promising investment.... I do not deny that containment sometimes make great sense ... [but] containment's tools are dull and slow, whereas those of rehabilitation are sharper and quicker.[65]

Orend's critiques challenge pacifist and contemporary just war theorists alike. While containment strategies often appear as less violent alternatives to conflict, in practice they have strengthened the hand of despots and resulted in more civilian deaths than swift tactical military intervention might have done, thereby violating the principles of proportionality and discrimination. Sometimes military intervention is the less deadly alternative.

Post Bellum Regime Change

Turning to *post bellum* regime change, Orend notes, "The goal of justified post war regime change—whether permitted by rights or demanded by duties—is the timely construction of a minimally just political community."[66] The "minimally just political community" is his moral litmus test. It refers to a community that "makes every reasonable effort to: 1) avoid violating the rights of other minimally just communities; 2) gain recognition as being legitimate in the eyes of the international community and its own people; and 3) realizes the human rights of all its individual members."[67] In a more extensive exploration of the "minimally just state," he claims that the "main purpose of the state, in our era, is to do its part in realizing the human rights of its people," principally the rights to "physical security; material subsistence; personal freedom; elemental equality; and social recognition as a person and rights holder ... the things we all need to live minimally decent and tolerable lives in the modern world."[68] Orend's notion of the minimally just state is grounded in two additional rights that are granted to the state: political sovereignty and territorial integrity, the same conditions Bass identifies as necessary for just political reform.

Orend's understanding of the purpose of government and human rights differs significantly from the Christian tradition, and particularly that of Catholic social thought. In the Catholic social justice tradition, the purpose of government is not merely to secure human rights, but to pursue the common good.[69] In addition, Orend's understanding of human rights is primarily about individual rights, whereas the Christian tradition tends to stress more heavily social and cultural rights. Orend's minimally just state sets the bar much lower than the Christian tradition would adopt as the goal for *post bellum* regime change.

A Christian understanding of *post bellum* regime change would aim for a just and lasting peace, inclusive of robust human rights, political sovereignty, and territorial integrity as well as social, political, economic, religious, and cultural conditions that allow citizens to flourish, to pursue lives that are meaningful and worthy of creatures made in the image and likeness of God. Orend's minimally just state is a realistic, attainable, and proximate goal for *post bellum* regime change, while the Christian aim, although attractive, lofty, and worthwhile, can prove elusive, especially in the short term.

Some degree of political reform is almost always necessary *post bellum*, and it should be considered a normative part of a war's end. Orend, Walzer, and Bass disagree not on the substance of the reform, but on the degree. While Walzer and Bass are more cautious in calling for complete political reform (regime change), Orend is more permissive. The victor must fill the political power vacuum left in war's wake—at least initially, by assuming both military and political power—for both moral and practical reasons. Law and order must replace the anarchy of war as quickly as possible, which, practically, requires some force. Morally, victors in battle must assume responsibility for the consequences of their actions.

Proportionality, which is a guiding principle of political reform, requires prudence, a cardinal virtue in Western and Catholic traditions. In this sense, prudence does not mean "the modern conception of prudence," which, as Daniel Mark Nelson notes in his book *The Priority of Prudence*, "has departed from the classical notion" and instead reduces it to "self-interested calculation of costs and benefits," leading to an "undue caution."[70] Nor do we have in mind here "craftiness," which Aquinas includes as one of the "vices opposed to prudence, which have a resemblance thereto."[71] In addition, both Walzer and Nelson point out the influence of Machiavelli on how prudence is mistakenly understood today. Machiavelli divorced prudence from Christian morality and wedded it to power. He associated it with *virtu*, which has to do with the prince's use of power, and it involves strategies and techniques in battle (literally or in politics) given changing circumstances. This is a "worldly prudence," a prescriptive realism, whereby leaders do what they "have to do," what is "necessary." While many scholars argue that *The Prince* is a satire and that Machiavelli never intended it be taken seriously as a handbook for political leadership, nevertheless there is no shortage of "modern Machiavellis" who dream of "whispering in the ear of the prince," as Walzer puts it.[72] They focus on getting results in terms of "the national interest" through "the calculated application of force." In contrast to these flawed sorts of prudence, we understand prudence as the moral virtue that has to do with practical intellect, which involves the "skill of making right judgments about things to be done."[73] Proportionality, in our view, therefore needs this ability to size up a situation accurately; it is a "reading of the signs of the times" in order to act in a way that is most fitting.

The vanquished do not surrender their sovereignty, territorial integrity, or the right to self-determination. Minimally, the political, policing, and military structures of the vanquished aggressor need to be reformed to the extent that the conditions that led to the aggression are eliminated and new threats are removed, but not to the extent that they become vulnerable or are reduced to a puppet government. Maximally, the goal is a just and lasting peace inclusive of robust defense of human rights, a functioning and stable government pursuing the common good, and socio-economic conditions that allow the citizenry to flourish.

ECONOMIC RECOVERY

War is destructive by its very nature. It is also very expensive. In the previous chapter, punishment, compensation, and trade policies were cast largely as a means of reprimanding the unjust aggressor, but they are also part of the restoration effort. War interrupts normal commerce, manufacturing, transportation, and financial markets and forces a host of industries to shift their production efforts to accommodate the war effort. In the *post bellum* phase, steps need to be taken to retrofit the economy to a non-wartime model. If a conflict has waged for decades, then countries face the possibility of a workforce that knows no vocation other than soldiering. In such situations, vocational training is paramount for peace.

As Pope Paul VI noted decades ago, "Development is the new name for peace."[74] A concerted effort by governmental and nongovernmental agencies, international aid groups (for example, the World Bank, the International Money Fund [IMF]), and private industry must be courted to invest in infrastructure reconstruction and development, including roads, ports, rail lines, electrical grids, and vocational training. Such endeavors are necessary for post war peace. Private industry is legitimately apprehensive in investing in volatile areas, and an unskilled workforce physically and emotionally scarred by war is equally unattractive to investors. Therefore, other incentives are required to attract private investment in a post war economy. Reconstruction of the economy is absolutely essential. Work is a normal human activity essential for returning to a prewar life. Persons must feel they are sustaining themselves and contributing to the common good.

The Marshall Plan in post war Europe (officially called the European Recovery Program) and the post war economic recovery efforts in Japan (often called the "Japanese Miracle") stand as shining examples of post war recovery.[75] While some accounts of these efforts tend toward hyperbole, claiming the United States singlehandedly saved Europe and Japan from economic ruin, most historians agree that the programs were remarkably successful. For example, the United States spent $13 billion between 1947 and 1951 in Europe (approximately $100 billion in today's dollars), equivalent to approximately 5.4 percent of the U.S. GNP.[76] In Japan, the United States spent $500 million annually (from 1946 to 1949). The United States also insisted that Japan be included in the General Agreement on Tariffs and Trade (GATT, which later became the World Trade Organization) and that it enact major land reforms; the United States also oversaw the reconstruction of the industrial and finance sectors. These efforts resulted in the "miraculous" growth of the Japanese economy. Between 1950 and 1973, the Japanese GNP grew by an average of 10 percent annually. In 2008 Japan had the second largest national economy in the world.[77]

Money alone is not responsible for the success of these post war efforts. U.S. experts in management and production provided the intellectual capital needed to position Europe and Japan to emerge as economic leaders in a very short period. In both arenas the emerging economies took on the cultural characteristics of their people. Business literature is replete with analyses of the Japanese, European, and German economic models. These post war economic recovery programs were not a form of economic imperialism whereby the United States recast the local economies as miniature versions of the U.S. economy or turned them into puppet economies.

This points to a crucial factor in post war economic recovery: a willingness on the part of the victors to sacrifice for the economic recovery of the vanquished and to refrain from taking advantage of the weaker party. One of the chief obstacles to post war economic justice is getting victors, who have already paid a dear price, to (1) realize their sacrifices are not yet over, and (2) avoid the temptation to seek revenge through retaliatory measures (the desire "to make those bastards pay for what they have done"), but instead (3) invest in the reconstruction of the vanquished, their former enemy.

Equally important is the need for the vanquished to accept the help of its former enemy, which requires overcoming suspicion and fear built up during the combat period. As Orend notes,

> Success *did* come [to postwar Germany and Japan] at a huge cost in terms of time and treasure: it cost trillions of dollars; took trillions of "man-hours" in work and expertise; it took decades of real time; it took cooperation of most of the German and Japanese people; and, above all, it took the will of the United States to see it through.... Such is the magnitude of commitment needed by any party bent on implementing substantial post-war rehabilitation.[78]

These efforts in Europe and Japan reveal that post war commitments are expensive, but that the cost of doing nothing can be far worse. Unstable economies are fertile ground for extremism, militant fundamentalism, demagoguery, and political unrest. As World War I taught, such conditions can easily flare up again into full-scale war. In destroying the infrastructure of a nation and crippling its economy through war, even if one has justified reasons for doing so, a nation automatically assumes responsibility for the economic recovery of the vanquished. If the aim of a just war is the tranquility that comes from order, then the jobs, infrastructure, and banking and financial institutions needed to bring economic stability must be seen as concomitant duties implicit in the reasons cited for going to war in the first place.

SOCIAL REHABILITATION

Louis Iasiello, a retired admiral and a U.S. Navy chaplain, gives unusual attention to social rehabilitation and *post bellum* ethics. He identifies the need to safeguard the innocent and vulnerable and to pay attention to the transition of the military as two vital components to *post bellum* social rehabilitation. In particular, children, the elderly, the sick, and some groups of women who lack the ability to defend themselves in times of war are easily overlooked. Furthermore, the long-range psychological effects of war are especially damaging to children. Refugees and internally displaced populations pose additional burdens. Lacking shelter, sustenance, water, health care, and other basic human needs, they become easy targets for physical and sexual abuse, slavery and forced conscription in regular armies, militias, and guerrilla groups. They also can become the unintended targets of munitions left behind after the war (such as land mines or cluster bombs), an issue addressed below.[79]

The preferential option for the poor, a biblically based Judeo-Christian moral principle, provides the most vigorous moral argument for the defense of the innocent. This principle holds that social, political, and economic decisions and policies should be based primarily on how they impact the lives of the poor, weak, vulnerable, and those most alienated in society. Ideally armed forces should protect civilians; history, however, teaches that these vulnerable groups often bear the heaviest burdens of war. All post war restoration efforts ought to begin by addressing the needs of the weakest and most vulnerable.

Iasiello is also concerned with reintegrating soldiers into society:

> Combatants are not amoral agents or machines.... Warriors are persons—they are body-mind-spirit. They are complex moral agents who must live and fight within the context of military protocol and duty.... While warriors submit to the authority of their superiors, they never submit so completely that they surrender or forfeit their moral personhood.... Warriors are soldiers, marines, sailors, and airmen who must kill when legally ordered to do so, but must live with those decisions the rest of their lives.[80]

While the emotional destruction of war has always been painfully obvious, whether recognized as shell shock or battle fatigue, only recently has it received significant clinical attention as posttraumatic stress disorder. For example, in 2007 the U.S. Department of Defense found that 30 to 40 percent of soldiers returning from the 2003 Iraq War suffered from some form of psychological trauma and that the military, due to a lack of trained personnel and funding, was failing to provide basic mental health care for these soldiers.[81] Other studies report significant increases in divorce, suicide, and alcoholism among military personnel who saw combat duty in Iraq or Afghanistan.[82]

When a nation sends its citizens to war, it turns ordinary men and women into potential killers. In so doing, nations should assume the responsibility to assist warriors in their transition back to civilian life once the fighting has ended. This includes rehabilitation for physical injuries sustained in combat, as well as the care of emotional and psychological disabilities. Given all the evidence that soldiers returning from war need physical and emotional healing, we note the appropriateness of a medieval practice that encouraged soldiers coming home from war to make a retreat in order to repent for the sins of war and to heal from the psychological and spiritual damage inherent in combat. The

Penitentials, which were guidebooks for clergy to use in the sacrament of Confession during the medieval period, often required a period of penance for soldiers returning from war. According to the Penitential Ordinance following the battle of Hastings in 1066, "Anyone who knows that he has killed a man in a great battle is to do one year of penance for each man killed."[83] While we are not here necessarily calling for the exact retrieval of this practice, we do believe that some analogous healing practices ought to be a more regular option offered by churches as a way to help their members scarred by war. As the Most Reverend Timothy P. Broglio, archbishop for the military services of the United States, notes, "Christians bear a responsibility to those coming back from military service and to their families."[84] It is a duty incumbent upon the entire Christian community.

In addition to safeguarding the innocent and supporting the transition of the military, other more structured forms of social transformation are necessary, including educational and cultural reforms. In many wars, ruling authorities effectively employ propaganda based on prejudice to demonize the enemy and inculcate fear in their own citizens. Such propaganda can all too easily become part of the official education system or policies of the government. Education and cultural reform should include superficial changes, such as removing the insignias, statues, images, and slogans of a previous ruling party, and more systematic efforts (such as the de-Nazification of Germany and the de-Baathification programs in Iraq) that remove from public service bureaucrats sympathetic to the previous regime, launch reeducation campaigns for the general population, and rewrite school curricula and textbooks. These efforts aim at a cultural shift to challenge and dispel deeply and widely held prejudices and propaganda from previous ruling parties. Progress in these areas is generally slow because cultural shifts, which are hard to bring about, often take generations.

ENVIRONMENTAL CLEANUP

Our work in *post bellum* ethics began several years ago with an analysis of two new types of weapons: depleted uranium shells and cluster bombs. The nature of this new class of weaponry convinced us of the importance of developing *post bellum* criteria as part of just war theory.[85] These weapons of long-term destruction (WLTDs) extend the pernicious effects of war well into the future. Chemical, biological, and nuclear weapons, and antipersonnel land mines and cluster bombs claim victims decades and possibly centuries after the formal battle has ended. Two examples of WLTDs clearly illustrate this point: depleted uranium (DU) shells and land mines and cluster bombs.

Depleted Uranium

Despite its innocuous name, depleted uranium (DU) has a radioactive half-life of 4.5 billion years.[86] It is the by-product of the enrichment of natural uranium and maintains 60 percent of the radioactivity of natural uranium. It is highly valued by U.S. military because it is cheaper, more readily available, and more effective than its closest alternative, tungsten. As a by-product of manufacturing nuclear weapons and supplying nuclear energy, this low-level radioactive waste exists in abundance, and any DU used for military ordinances does not have to be stored in toxic waste dumps.

Due to its high density, DU shells can penetrate most kinds of armor, which enables the military to fire shells from greater and safer distances. DU ordinances have been used in Afghanistan, Bosnia, Iraq, Kosovo, Kuwait, Serbia, and Somalia. According to the Pentagon, over 320 tons of DU (944,000 rounds) were used in the 1991 Gulf War. Information on the use of DU shells in the 2003 Iraq and Afghanistan conflicts is sparse; it has been estimated that 100 to 200 tons were used by U.S. and U.K. forces.[87]

The long-term effects of DU raise serious moral questions. When a 120 mm DU shell strikes metal, the DU vaporizes and then settles as dust contaminating an area up to fifty meters. This dust can be inhaled, ingested, or enter the human body through open wounds. DU is even more deadly once it enters the food chain, where it gathers strength as it moves up and onto the kitchen table. While U.S. Army studies conclude that DU poses no significant health risks, the U.K. Atomic Energy Authority estimates that a half million people in Kuwait and Iraq could die due to the use of DU in the first Gulf War alone.

The health risks associated with DU include chromosomal damage, stillborn births, birth defects, renal collapse, infertility, leukemia, and a host of cancers. Following the 1991 Gulf War, for example, cancer rates in Iraq increased seven to ten times, and birth deformities increased four- to sixfold. In the Basra area, where DU shells were heavily used, stillborn births and congenital birth defects rose 250 percent between 1989 and 1999. It is hard to ignore the hypocrisy of the United States' use of DU in Iraq: after all, the United States invaded Iraq for violating U.N. sanctions and because of a perceived threat of weapons of mass destruction and then in the invasion used weapons sanctioned by the United Nations as WMDs.

Cluster Bombs and Land Mines

The second kind of WLTDs—cluster bombs and their close cousin, land mines—also extend the pernicious effects of war beyond the formal combat phase. Antipersonnel land mines are small, light, and cheap. Although they have been described as "the perfect soldier, ever vigilant," they cannot distinguish between soldiers and civilians and remain active until triggered, often decades after the fighting has ended. While "smart mines" (which self-destruct or self-deactivate after a set period) are available, most land mines are "dumb," meaning that they remain active until detonated. An estimated fifteen thousand to twenty thousand land-mine casualties take place every year, and most of those harmed are civilians. In addition, land mines seriously hamper post war reconstruction efforts by rendering swaths of land unusable, slowing relief efforts, delaying the return of war refugees, and killing livestock on which the rural poor depend. Landmines ostensibly continue the war until every mine has claimed a victim or been removed.[88]

Early versions of cluster bombs were used by the Soviets and Germans during World War II, and the U.S. military has employed them in almost every conflict from the Vietnam War on.[89] For example, according to a special report in *USA Today*, in its 2003 war against Iraq the United States used nearly 10,800 cluster munitions. [90] Approximately seventy countries currently possess cluster munitions in their arsenals, and these weapons have been used in some thirty-five countries and regions, including Georgia, Iraq, Kuwait, Afghanistan, Lebanon, Chechnya, the former Yugoslavia, Angola, Cambodia, and Vietnam.

Technically known as cluster bomb units or CBUs, these munitions are canisters that are dropped by aircraft or launched from land and sea by artillery, missiles, or rockets. [91] Inexpensive to manufacture, each canister contains up to 650 bomblets or submunitions, and at a certain point while over the target these are dispersed across a wide area. The bomblets sometimes come with a small parachute, so that they float toward their target. Often brightly colored, small, and coming in various shapes—resembling batteries, tennis balls, soda cans, or hockey pucks—each submunition, in turn, contains shrapnel, steel pellets, or ball bearings that are released when detonated in mid-air or on impact. Like a hand grenade, these metal fragments can kill or injure many enemy soldiers, especially when they are in mass formation. As dual-use devices, they are not only antipersonnel but are also designed to be antimateriel in that the shrapnel can penetrate and render inoperable enemy tanks, armored personnel carriers, and grounded aircraft. Some cluster munitions, moreover, contain an incendiary feature that causes fires if the submunition lands upon flammable materials or fuel. Cluster munitions thus are different from single warhead munitions designed to strike a single point. They could be likened to a shotgun blast as opposed to a bullet fired from a rifle.

Because cluster submunitions blanket a wide area, referred to as their "footprint"—which can be as large as two football fields, or approximately one square kilometer—opponents of these weapons warn of the increased likelihood of hitting civilians along with legitimate military targets, even without taking into account possible errant bombs. Human rights and religious groups accuse cluster munitions themselves of failing to distinguish between combatants and noncombatants, causing significant harm to civilians during conflicts. As Rob Nixon critically observes, to refer to these weapons as "cluster" bombs is actually a misnomer, given that what "distinguishes cluster bombs is less their clustering than the dispersal of their malign effects." [92]

Recall, moreover, that concern was also expressed about the lingering effects of cluster munitions even after hostilities have officially concluded. Many bomblets fail to explode on impact. First, submunitions may not detonate because they landed on a soft surface, such as sand, mud, weeds, water, or snow. These remain "live" and are a continuing threat. Second, there is the possibility of mechanical failure. Some bomblets simply fail to explode on initial impact. The latter, like those that land on soft surfaces, still pose an ongoing threat to unsuspecting civilians who later come into contact with them. Indeed, cluster submunitions had "dud" rates ranging from 5 percent to 30 percent in Kosovo and Afghanistan, depending on the particular type of cluster bomb and the conditions. In Kosovo, this meant that between fifteen thousand and ninety thousand unexploded bomblets remained on the ground.[93] Here the comparison with shotgun pellets breaks down, for these individual pellets themselves do not detonate, either on impact or later on. There are no "dud" shotgun pellets. Thus, as Virgil Wiebe puts it, many unexploded cluster bomblets are "de facto landmines" that continue to be "indiscriminate killers for decades to come."[94] In addition, remaining unexploded ordnance impacts the environment, interferes with the efforts of displaced civilians to return to their homes, and impedes farming, fishing, and other important social-economic matters.

During its conflict with Hezbollah in the summer of 2006, Israel launched some 2.6 million to 4 million submunitions into southern Lebanon, where unexploded remnants continue to litter the countryside and threaten civilian lives. The United Nations estimates that 1 million did not explode and that two-thirds were scattered in populated areas. A very high percentage—as much as 40 percent—of the bomblets used in Lebanon did not explode immediately and remained active on the ground, harming civilians and even experienced demolition experts after the conflict had ended.[95] Many landed on balconies, outside front doors, in trees and gardens, and some inside homes. These will hamper southern Lebanon's economic recovery for years to come, especially with regard to agriculture that produces olives, bananas, tobacco, and wheat. Similar protracted consequences may be found in the wake of other conflicts in recent decades.

In Laos, for instance, where bombing by the United States

ended in 1973, two or three Laotian civilians continue to be killed per month, with another six or seven injured, due to unexploded submunition ordnance left over from the Vietnam War.[96] The United States dropped 80 million cluster bomblets on Laos, with such a percentage failing to explode on impact that an estimated 8 million to 24 million unexploded submunitions remain scattered across the country.[97] Farmers still are not able to cultivate areas of land to grow rice due to the unexploded ordnance. Laotian farmer Phousavien Phetdonxay owns about twelve acres of land, but he cultivates only one because of safety concerns about unexploded ordnance. Rural areas and urban population centers can be drastically affected by cluster submunitions during hostilities and long after they have ended. In sum, cluster munitions wreak mass destruction when deployed as well as decades after the shooting putatively stops.

During and after recent armed conflicts—such as the U.S.-led wars in Afghanistan and Iraq, the hostilities between Israel and Hezbollah in southern Lebanon in 2006, and the fighting between Russia and Georgia (2008) in the southern Georgian province of Ossetia—graphic news accounts about persons injured or killed by cluster munitions have stirred world public opinion. In an article appearing in *Time* magazine in May 2003, Michael Weisskopf shared the story of an Iraqi family in Karbala. After hiding from two days of U.S. bombing, Jabar and her six-year-old daughter Duaa Raheem emerged from their house in order to fetch some water. A black plastic object shaped like a C-cell battery attached to a white ribbon roused Duaa's curiosity, so she grabbed it and took her discovery home to share with her two sisters, three-year-old Duha and eight-year-old Saja. On their kitchen floor, as she situated the device on her lap and twisted a screw, it exploded, sundering Duaa in half and also killing Duha and severely injuring Saja. The grief-stricken mother's bitter words are conveyed by Weisskopf: "We thought we were safe because the bombs had stopped," says Jabar, a thirty-year-old farmer's wife. "My daughters were stolen from me."[98]

Unfortunately, such incidents are all too common. According to a preliminary report released in November 2006 and followed up by another in May 2007 from Handicap International, an organization that campaigns against cluster bombs, 98 percent of the casualties caused by these munitions are civilians, with 27 percent of them children.[99]

For this reason, in May 2008 representatives of 107 governments gathered in Dublin, Ireland, to draft an international treaty, with over 90 signing it in Oslo, Norway, seven months later, categorically banning the production, use, and export of cluster munitions, as well as committing nations to destroy their stockpiles within eight years.[100] The Convention on Cluster Munitions was the fruit of a process that Norway initiated in February 2007 after talks about cluster munitions got bogged down at the United Nations' normal forum for discussion of such weapons, the Convention on Certain Conventional Weapons. As we write, thirty nations have now ratified it—with Norway, the Republic of Ireland, Sierra Leone, and the Holy See the first four to do so—paving the way for the Convention to take effect. As with the 1997 Ottawa Treaty banning land mines, the Convention reflects an emerging consensus during the last several years among nations, human rights groups, and religious organizations about the pernicious threat cluster bombs pose, in particular to innocent civilians.

On a practical level the use of WLTDs seriously hampers post war reconstruction efforts by rendering huge swaths of land unusable and blocking the return of refugees and the internally displaced. WLTDs challenge the just war theory to consider the countless future victims of war, most of whom are civilians and some of whom have not yet even been born, thereby extending the effect and moral responsibilities of war well beyond active combat. The principle of restoration requires that those who employ WLTDs be held responsible for post war cleanup efforts. Those who resort to WLTDs must return the environment (soil, water, and animal and plant life) to its prewar condition and make every effort to rehabilitate those affected by WLTDs. Restoration is a logical consequence of the aim of all just wars, namely a just peace. A nation cannot return to a state of affairs that encourages its citizens to flourish when its land remains unusable or when people are severely physically debilitated, plagued by cancers, or suffer chromosomal defects for generations. On practical grounds, such a requirement should dissuade the use of such weapons since the cleanup efforts are prohibitively expensive. The cost-benefit analysis of the use of WLTDs ought to accurately reflect the true cost of resorting to such weaponry, forcing military leaders to consider whether or not the effectiveness of WLTDs is worth the cleanup costs.

CONCLUSION

The restoration efforts outlined here are expensive and laborious. That is a good thing. Waging war is one of the most destructive and evil human activities. There is no such thing as a good war, only degrees of less evil wars. By burdening those who engage in war, whether for just cause or not, with security and policing, political reform, economic recovery, social rehabilitation, and environmental cleanup, the true cost of war would be revealed; perhaps the often feverish rush to war might be quelled. War is and ought to be expensive.

CONCLUSION

"New realities dictate that war should only be deemed just if the victor is completely committed to order, stability, economic prosperity, and political peace."[1]

Hamid is a forty-three-year-old Tajik who lives in Faizābād, the capital of the province of Badakshān in northern Afghanistan. He is an engineer. Back in 2003 when French journalist Anne Nivat visited him and his family in their house made out of baked clay bricks, Hamid admitted that he "is an angry man: angry at his government, which he considers weak and cowardly; angry at the international community, which is not making the right strategic choices in Afghanistan; and angry at his fellow citizens, who are not managing to reason any differently from what the recent historical situation has inculcated in them."[2] He expressed some hope for the future of his six-year-old daughter, wanting her to go to school and to find work in the field of her choosing. His nineteen-year-old nephew, Uman, however, muttered, "As soon as I've finished school, I'll leave this goddamned country, which has had nothing but wars and has no future."[3]

Mohamed Moussa, who resides in al-Hilla, about sixty miles south of Baghdad, described to British reporter Robert Fisk how on March 31, 2003, silvery objects "like small grapefruit" fell from white canisters onto his neighborhood. "If it hadn't exploded and you touched it, it went off immediately," he said. "They exploded in the air and on the ground, and we still have some in our home, unexploded." On that day cluster submunitions killed 38 and injured 156 civilians in al-Hilla. And their remnant unexploded "duds" continued to possess "the power to rend a community's social, economic, and environmental fabric."[4]

Eugene Cherry deployed to Iraq in 2004 as a medic for the

U.S. Army. In an interview with Kansas City freelance writer Emiliano Huet-Vaughn, he described his assignment: "I had recovery missions where I'd go out to a site where guys got burnt so bad you could still smell their flesh—still charred, still burning and smoking when you get there."[5] After his return to Fort Drum, New York, in June 2005, Cherry said, "There's many times I've drunk myself to sleep because I can't fall asleep, and the meds they gave me didn't help." He exhibits the characteristic symptoms of post-traumatic stress disorder, and he's not alone. According to a Pentagon survey released in May 2007 one-third of soldiers and Marines in high levels of combat in Iraq reported depression, generalized anxiety, or post-traumatic stress—with a number of government and media reports indicating that mental health departments within the military and the Department of Veterans Affairs health-care systems have been too underfunded and understaffed to meet the needs of the returning soldiers.[6]

As we conclude this book, these three vignettes of the lingering and pernicious effects of war remind us that what we are proposing affects real people. Our use of this word "proposing" is intentional and important. Traditional just war theory assumes that moral responsibilities dissipate with the smoke of the battlefield. A more comprehensive just war theory appropriate for the twenty-first century, however, should consider not only events preceding combat and behavior on the battlefield but the long-term effects of war as well. We hope that readers agree that the four chief considerations or categories—just cause, reconciliation, punishment, and restoration—that we have examined are general areas that need to be addressed for any possibility of post war justice. Still, this is a proposal. Even as these four criteria are beginning to gain some traction in discussions about what to do in the wake of war, we invite others to develop and further refine what we have suggested. Even if these categories and their criteria are not necessarily employed in exactly the same terms, hopefully future work on *jus post bellum* will more or less interface in ways inspired by or consonant with what we have set forth.

Similarly, while we expect a fair amount of agreement on the general level of these four categories or considerations, we acknowledge that there exists legitimate room for differences of opinion with regard to their concrete applications on the ground. What we are proposing is akin to a template. It does not claim to provide a one-size-fits-all solution to each and every post war situation or society, especially since there will be unique features in any given conflict and country.

In making this point, we are more or less following the moral methodology of the U.S. Catholic bishops in their statements on social-ethical issues such as war, economics, immigration, or the environment. As Charles Curran has noted in connection with the 1983 pastoral letter *The Challenge of Peace*, the bishops employ the traditional Catholic distinction between universal moral principles and their application to concrete cases.[7] Citing the Second Vatican Council's *Gaudium et Spes* on "how to relate principles to concrete issues," the bishops admit that their treatment of "many concrete questions concerning the arms race, contemporary warfare, weapons systems, and negotiating strategies" do not "carry the same moral authority as our statement of universal moral principles and formal Church teachings."[8] Differences of judgment are permitted regarding applications of principles to issues that, as Curran puts it, "by their very nature are so complex and specific that one cannot achieve a certitude that excludes the possibility of error."[9] Such is also the case with what we have written here. Indeed, we ourselves, as two ethicists, might not necessarily agree 100 percent on every concrete application and recommendation we have offered in the preceding pages!

There are, however, some concrete judgments that leave little, if any, room for dispute. According to Catholic theologian Richard Gaillardetz, a number of concrete moral teachings by the bishops, such as "the immorality of directly targeting civilians in an act of war or the prohibition of certain reproductive technologies like in vitro fertilization," fall under the category of authoritative doctrine, about which there should be agreement, rather than the categories of prudential admonitions and provisional application of church doctrine, in which there is more room for disagreement.[10]

Indeed, *Gaudium et Spes* prohibited certain concrete acts of war. Most well known is its negative judgment of total warfare tactics that intend the destruction of civilian population centers:

"Any act of war aimed indiscriminately at the destruction of entire cities or of extensive areas along with their population is a crime against God and man himself. It merits unequivocal and unhesitating condemnation."[11] *Gaudium et Spes* also includes physical and psychological torture and "arbitrary imprisonment" in the list of intrinsically evil acts that can never be morally justified regardless of circumstances, and that also include genocide, abortion, and euthanasia.[12]

While the examples that are given fit under the purview of *jus in bello*, we believe that it is possible for such judgments to be made under *jus ad bellum* and *jus post bellum*.[13] After all, during the Vietnam War, in their "Resolution on Southeast Asia" in November 1971, the bishops finally determined that a "speedy ending of this war is a moral imperative of the highest priority," and they based their judgment upon a concrete application of the *jus ad bellum* criterion of proportionality: "At this point in history it seems clear to us that whatever good we hope to achieve through continued involvement in this war is now outweighed by the destruction of human life and of moral values which it inflicts."[14] Of course, and as we noted in the last chapter, the key in such applications of general principles to concrete cases is the moral virtue of prudence.

Finally, we want to remind readers that this is a proposal that emerges from and extends the Christian just war tradition. There are, to be sure, efforts under way in other disciplines to address post war justice. Indeed, we view these contributions to be an important sign of the times today. *Gaudium et Spes* called upon the church to read the "signs of the times" and to address them in light of the gospel.[15]

In their examination of this methodology, M. C. Vanhengel, O.P., and J. Peters, O.C.D., observed that for the expression "signs of the times" to be truly significant and not theologically trivial, two elements are necessary: first, there must be an accumulation of facts that point in the same direction, and, second, this trajectory must be generally acknowledged by others.[16] We see such signs in the progress that has been made to promote further attention to practices of just peacemaking, that seek to prevent war by addressing its root causes. Just as just war ethicists have supported work in that direction, so too should they be persuaded to turn their attention to preventing further wars by addressing justice in the aftermath of war. We think *jus post bellum* thereby helps to close the just peacemaking and just war loop.

Another sign of the times is the recent focus on the "responsibility to protect" (R2P), which encompasses three areas of responsibility: (1) the responsibility to prevent violent conflict from happening (which we view as coinciding with the just peacemaking paradigm); (2) the responsibility to react to and stop egregious crimes against humanity, such as genocide; and (3) the responsibility to rebuild in the wake of such atrocities.[17] We see *jus post bellum* as correlating with this third phase of R2P. Other signs of the times include the several treatments of *jus post bellum* from other disciplines, including philosophy, political science, and international law. Missing from these discussions has been a theological voice, which is rather curious, given how just war thought is significantly indebted to the Christian tradition.

Our hope is that our account of *jus post bellum* not only adds to the current interdisciplinary conversation that is already under way, but that it also becomes a lasting and integral component of Christian theological reflection on just war. As Christians, we believe we owe this to Hamid, his young daughter, and his nephew. We have a duty also to Mohamed Moussa. And we indeed are our brother's keeper when it comes to returning soldiers like Eugene Cherry. For them and countless others, Ezekiel's ancient words about false prophets "saying 'Peace!' when there was no peace" ring true. Destruction, displacement, illness, and death—these evils sadly continue to accompany war, including putatively just wars, in these initial decades of the twenty-first century. "Victory" may be declared by presidents and other leaders, yet no just peace is to be found for the people caught in the wake of today's conflicts.

Yet as Christians we believe in Ezekiel's metaphorical message of hope for Israel's resurrection, or restoration, as the New Jerusalem, which is vividly portrayed by the image of a plain filled with dry bones being transformed into a habitat teeming with new life and shalom (Ez 37:1-14). This is a commission that we have inherited as a new community brought into being through the life, death, and resurrection of Jesus Christ. According to Hugo Slim, a British ethicist and policy director at the Centre for Humanitarian Dialogue, Jesus Christ is a source of hope and comfort before, during, and after times of trouble: "In the gospel, he seeks to call people away from disaster before it happens, to be with them as they suffer and to remake lives anew after they have been shattered."[18]

If Christians are going to continue to view armed intervention as sometimes regrettably justified—whether we call it "just war" or "legitimate defense" or "the responsibility to protect"— there needs to be not only criteria to help warrant such forceful actions (*jus ad bellum*) and criteria to govern conduct during these interventions (*jus in bello*), but also criteria to guide us in establishing a just and lasting peace (*jus post bellum*) after the smoke clears.

NOTES

Introduction: Just War and Just Peace

[1] Anne Nivat, *The Wake of War: Encounters with the People of Iraq and Afghanistan* (Boston: Beacon Press, 2005), xiii.

[2] Ibid., 149.

[3] Ibid., 284.

[4] Donald Senior, C.P., *Jesus: A Gospel Portrait*, rev. ed. (Mahwah, NJ: Paulist Press, 1992), 50.

[5] Ibid., 86.

[6] National Conference of Catholic Bishops (NCCB), *The Challenge of Peace: God's Promise and Our Response* (Washington, DC: United States Catholic Conference, 1983), par. 333. This moral obligation for Christians, as well as for people of goodwill, to seek peace and an end to war is highlighted also in Second Vatican Council, "Pastoral Constitution on the Church in the Modern World" (*Gaudium et Spes*), in *The Documents of Vatican II*, ed. Walter M. Abbot, S.J. (Piscataway, NJ: New Century Publishers, 1966), no. 82; and *Catechism of the Catholic Church* (New York: Image/Doubleday, 1995), par. 2308.

[7] This connection between the liturgy—in particular, the Eucharist—and peace is mentioned in NCCB, *Challenge of Peace*, par. 295. Similarly, at the end of its chapter on war and peace, the *Compendium of the Social Doctrine of the Church* says, "In particular, the Eucharistic celebration, 'the source and summit of the Christian life,' is a limitless wellspring for all authentic Christian commitment to peace" (Pontifical Council for Justice and Peace, *Compendium of the Social Doctrine of the Church* [Washington, DC: United States Conference of Catholic Bishops, 2004], par. 519). Also, the next-to-last footnote (#1102), which is by far the longest of the footnotes in that chapter, highlights the emphasis on peace that runs throughout the Mass. For more on Christian worship as a starting point for addressing the moral issue of war, see Tobias Winright, "The Liturgy as a Basis for Catholic Identity, Just War Theory, and the Presumption against War," in *Catholic Identity and the Laity*, College Theology Society Annual Vol. 54, ed. Tim Muldoon (Maryknoll, NY: Orbis Books, 2009), 134-51; and Gerald Schlabach, "Breaking Bread: Peace and War," in *The Blackwell Companion to Christian Ethics*, ed. Stanley Hauerwas and Samuel Wells (Malden, MA: Blackwell, 2006), 360-74.

[8]NCCB, *Challenge of Peace*, par. 295.

[9]*Gaudium et Spes*, no. 78.

[10]Ibid.; NCCB, *Challenge of Peace*, par. 78.

[11]Charles Reed, *Just War?* (New York: Church Publishing, 2004), 32.

[12]Glen Stassen, ed., *Just Peacemaking: The New Paradigm for the Ethics of Peace and War*, rev. ed. (Cleveland: Pilgrim Press, 2008).

[13]Pope Paul VI, 1972 World Day for Peace address, available at the Vatican web page, http://www.vatican.va/holy_father/paul_vi/messages/peace/index/htm.

[14]John Howard Yoder, "How Many Ways Are There to Think Morally about War?" *Journal of Law and Religion* 11, no. 1 (1994-95): 107.

[15]Michael Joseph Smith, "Strengthen the United Nations and International Efforts for Cooperation and Human Rights," in *Just Peacemaking: The New Paradigm for the Ethics of Peace and War*, rev. ed., ed. Glen Stassen (Cleveland: Pilgrim Press, 2008), 166.

[16]See, for example, the various essays included in Semegnish Asfaw, Guillermo Kerber, and Peter Weiderud, eds., *The Responsibility to Protect: Ethical and Theological Reflections* (Geneva: World Council of Churches, 2005). R2P consists of three major prongs: the responsibility to prevent; the responsibility to react; and the responsibility to rebuild. From a just war perspective, the responsibility to rebuild corresponds with *jus post bellum*.

[17]For a recent book that offers a constructive account of just war as requiring communal disciplines, practices, and virtues, see Daniel M. Bell Jr., *Just War as Christian Discipleship* (Grand Rapids: Brazos Press, 2009).

[18]Mark J. Allman, *Who Would Jesus Kill? War, Peace, and the Christian Tradition* (Winona, MN: Anselm Academic, 2008), 223-25; Tobias Winright, "Just Cause and Preemptive Strikes in the War on Terrorism: Insights from a Just-Policing Perspective," *Journal of the Society of Christian Ethics* 26, no. 2 (Fall/Winter 2006): 157-81.

[19]Wesley K. Clark and Kal Raustiala, "Why Terrorists Aren't Soldiers," *New York Times*, August 8, 2007, http://www.nytimes.com/2007/08/08/opinion/08clark.html; Seth G. Jones and Martin C. Libicki, *How Terrorist Groups End: Lessons for Countering al Qa'ida* (Santa Monica, CA: RAND Corporation, 2008).

[20]Allman, *Who Would Jesus Kill?* 261-62, and Allman, "Reconstruction Needed to Atone for Our Crime in Iraq," *Eagle-Tribune*, North Andover, MA, August 3, 2007, A15; Winright, "Just Cause and Preemptive Strikes," 174.

[21]Chris J. Dolan, *In War We Trust: The Bush Doctrine and the Pursuit of Just War* (Aldershot, UK: Ashgate Publishing, 2005), 2, 22.

[22]Peter Steinfels, "Churches and Ethicists Loudly Oppose the Proposed War on Iraq, But Deaf Ears Are Many," *New York Times*, September 28, 2002, http://query.nytimes.com/gst/fullpage.html?res=9802E5D61638F93BA1575AC0A9649C8B63.

[23]NCCB, *Challenge of Peace*, pars. 80-110.

[24]Darrel Mollendorf, a philosopher at San Diego State University, argues in

addition for the need to develop *jus ex bello*, a "set of considerations that govern whether a war, once begun, should be brought to an end and if so how," and which he regards as "a middle phase doctrine, and therefore distinguishable from *jus post bellum*" (Darrel Mollendorf, "Jus ex Bello," *Journal of Political Philosophy* 16, no. 2 [2008]: 123, 131).

[25]Bishop Thomas G. Wenski, "Toward a Responsible Transition in Iraq," http://www.usccb.org/comm/archives/2006/06-006.shtml, accessed June 19, 2007. For a follow-up letter by Bishop William S. Skylstad, president of the United States Conference of Catholic Bishops, see "Call for Dialogue and Action on Responsible Transition in Iraq," http://www.usccb.org/sdwp/international/iraqresponsibletransition.pdf, accessed June 19, 2007.

[26]United States Conference of Catholic Bishops, *Forming Consciences for Faithful Citizenship: A Call to Political Responsibility from the Catholic Bishops of the United States* (Washington, DC: United States Conference of Catholic Bishops, 2007), 20-21, http://www.usccb.org/bishops/FCStatement.pdf.

[27]NCCB, *Challenge of Peace*, par. 86.

[28]Ibid., par. 95.

[29]Serena K. Sharma, "Reconsidering the Jus ad Bellum/Jus in Bello Distinction," in *Jus Post Bellum: Towards a Law of Transition from Conflict to Peace*, ed. Carsten Stahn and Jann K. Kleffner (The Hague: T M C Asser Press, 2008), 13.

[30]Ibid., 30.

[31]Michael Schuck, "When the Shooting Stops: Missing Elements in Just War Theory," *Christian Century* 111, no. 30 (October 26, 1994): 982-83. Mark Allman, a former student of Schuck, followed up on this matter with "Postwar Justice," *America* 193, no. 11 (October 17, 2005): 9-13. The two of us subsequently pursued this subject further in Mark Allman and Tobias Winright, "*Jus Post Bellum*: Extending the Just War Theory," in *Faith in Public Life*, College Theology Society Annual 53, ed. William J. Collinge (Maryknoll, NY: Orbis Books, 2008), 241-64.

[32]NCCB, *Challenge of Peace*, pars. 8-9; see also pars. 10-12.

[33]Charles E. Curran, "The Moral Methodology of the Bishops' Pastoral," in *Catholics and Nuclear War: A Commentary on The Challenge of Peace*, ed. Philip J. Murnion (New York: Crossroad, 1983), 55.

[34]John Howard Yoder, *When War Is Unjust: Being Honest in Just-War Thinking*, 2nd ed. (Maryknoll, NY: Orbis Books, 1996), 5.

Chapter 1: The Just War Tradition

[1]John Howard Yoder, "Just-War Tradition: Is It Credible?" *Christian Century* 108, no. 9 (March 13, 1991): 296 (emphasis in original).

[2]John Howard Yoder, *When War Is Unjust: Being Honest in Just-War Thinking*, 2nd ed. (Maryknoll, NY: Orbis Books, 1996), 2.

[3]Serena K. Sharma, "Reconsidering the Jus ad Bellum/Jus in Bello Distinc-

tion," in *Jus Post Bellum: Towards a Law of Transition from Conflict to Peace*, ed. Carsten Stahn and Jann K. Kleffner (The Hague: T M C Asser Press, 2008), 22; also, Brian Orend, *"Jus Post Bellum*: A Just War Theory Perspective," in *Jus Post Bellum: Towards a Law of Transition from Conflict to Peace*, ed. Carsten Stahn and Jann K. Kleffner (The Hague: T M C Asser Press/Cambridge University Press, 2008), 31-32.

⁴For a description and critique of the just war as checklist approach, see Daniel M. Bell Jr., *Just War as Christian Discipleship: Recentering the Tradition in the Church Rather Than the State* (Grand Rapids: Brazos Press, 2009), 71-83.

⁵David L. Clough and Brian Stiltner, *Faith and Force: A Christian Debate about War* (Washington, DC: Georgetown University Press, 2007), 7.

⁶For a more secular/philosophical survey of the just war tradition, see Brian Orend, "A Sweeping History of Just War Theory," in *The Morality of War* (Peterborough, Ontario: Broadview, 2006), 9-30.

⁷Gregory M. Reichberg, Henrik Syse, and Endre Begby, eds., *The Ethics of War: Classic and Contemporary Readings* (Malden, MA: Blackwell Publishing, 2006), 18-19, where the editors cite the *Statesman* passage as 307e-308a; see 19-30 for relevant excerpts from some of Plato's works. For more excerpts on war from Plato's *Republic* and *Laws*, see Arthur F. Holmes, ed., *War and Christian Ethics: Classic and Contemporary Readings on the Morality of War*, 2nd ed. (Grand Rapids: Baker Academic, 2005), 13-23.

⁸Roland H. Bainton, *Christian Attitudes toward War and Peace: A Historical Survey and Critical Reevaluation* (Nashville: Abingdon Press, 1960), 37. Of course, as Bainton notes, Plato had in mind here conflicts between Greek cities, which were more akin to duels or feuds, and not wars between Greeks and barbarians, in which these rules were not expected to be followed.

⁹Reichberg et al., *Ethics of War*, 19.

¹⁰Bell, *Just War as Christian Discipleship*, 25; Bainton, *Christian Attitudes toward War and Peace*, 39. We are relying here on Bell's brief account of Aristotle's thought on just war. For relevant excerpts from Aristotle's works, see Reichberg et al., *Ethics of War*, 31-46.

¹¹Aristotle, *Politics*, trans. Trevor J. Saunders (New York: Penguin, 1981), 79.

¹²Cicero, *De Officiis* 1:11-12, trans. W. Miller, in the Loeb Classical Library (Cambridge, MA: Harvard University Press, 1913), available in Holmes, *War and Christian Ethics*, 29-30. Unlike his Greek predecessors, Cicero held that the dictates of morality concerning war should not apply only to fellow Greeks or Romans but in principle to all people. For more relevant excerpts from Cicero, see Reichberg et al., *Ethics of War*, 51-59.

¹³Cicero, *De Republica* 3, trans. C. W. Keyes, in the Loeb Classical Library (Cambridge, MA: Harvard University Press, 1988), available in Holmes, *War and Christian Ethics*, 24-25.

¹⁴John Howard Yoder, *Nevertheless: The Varieties and Shortcomings of Religious Pacifism* (Scottdale, PA: Herald Press, 1971), 9-10.

[15]Stanley Hauerwas, *Dispatches from the Front: Theological Engagements with the Secular* (Durham, NC: Duke University Press, 1994), 131.

[16]Tobias Winright, "Pacifism in Roman Catholicism," in *The Encyclopedia of Religion and War*, ed. Gabriel Palmer-Fernandez (New York: Berkshire/ Routledge, 2004), 379-84.

[17]We find the work of Walter Wink on the subject of "Jesus' Third Way" persuasive on the gospel texts about nonviolent engagement. See, for example, Walter Wink, *Engaging the Powers: Discernment and Resistance in a World of Domination* (Minneapolis: Fortress Press, 1992), 175-93, and *Jesus and Nonviolence: A Third Way* (Minneapolis: Augsburg Fortress, 2003). Of course, not everyone agrees with Wink's understanding of these passages. See, for example, Richard A. Horsley, "Ethics and Exegesis: 'Love Your Enemies' and the Doctrine of Nonviolence," in *The Love of Enemy and Nonretaliation in the New Testament*, ed. Willard M. Swartley (Louisville, KY: Westminster/John Knox Press, 1992), 72-101, followed by responses and counterresponses between Wink and Horsely in the same volume.

[18]James Turner Johnson, *The Quest for Peace: Three Moral Traditions in Western Cultural History* (Princeton, NJ: Princeton University Press, 1987), 19; see Bell, *Just War as Christian Discipleship*, 24-25.

[19]Bell, *Just War as Christian Discipleship*, 25.

[20]Clough and Stiltner, *Faith and Force*, 52-59. For relevant excerpts from Ambrose, see Reichberg et al., *Ethics of War*, 67-69.

[21]Bainton, *Christian Attitudes toward War and Peace*, 90.

[22]Clough and Stiltner, *Faith and Force*, 53.

[23]William T. Cavanaugh, *Torture and Eucharist: Theology, Politics, and the Body of Christ* (Oxford, UK: Blackwell Publishers, 1998), 244. For Ambrose's letter to Theodosius, see Holmes, *War and Christian Ethics*, 55-60.

[24]For this brief account of Augustine's thought, we are relying on Bell, *Just War as Christian Discipleship*, 27-32.

[25]Augustine, Letter 189, trans. J. G. Cunningham, in *The Nicene and Post-Nicene Fathers*, 1st series, 1 (Buffalo, NY: The Christian Literature Company, 1886); reproduced in Holmes, *War and Christian Ethics*, 62-63.

[26]For a fair treatment of Augustine here, see Bell, *Just War as Christian Discipleship*, 28-31.

[27]Augustine, Letter 47, in *Nicene and Post-Nicene Fathers*, 1st ser., vol. 1, ed. Philip Schaff (Peabody, MA: Hendrickson, 1994), 293.

[28]Augustine, "Questions on the Heptateuch," bk. 6, chap. 10, in Louis J. Swift, ed. and trans., *The Early Fathers on War and Military Service* (Wilmington, DE: Michael Glazer, 1983), 138.

[29]Augustine, *Augustine: Political Writings*, ed. E. M. Atkins and R. J. Dodaro (New York: Cambridge University Press, 2001), 135.

[30]Ibid., 38. Of course, Augustine's approach to dealing with heretical groups such as the Donatists, in our view, is not congruent with this vision of restorative justice we are seeking to retrieve from him.

[31]Augustine, Letter 189, in Holmes, *War and Christian Ethics*, 63.

[32]Ibid.

[33]Augustine, *Reply to Faustus the Manichean*, bk. 22, chap. 74, trans. R. Stothert, in *The Nicene and Post-Nicene Fathers*, 1st series, vol. 4 (Edinburgh: T&T Clark, 1886-88), 69-76; reproduced in Holmes, *War and Christian Ethics*, 64.

[34]Augustine, "Letter 229," in *The Political Writings of St. Augustine*, ed. Henry Paolucci (Chicago: Regnery Gateway, 1962), 183.

[35]Bell, *Just War as Christian Discipleship*, 41-42.

[36]Ibid., 44-45; see also Joseph J. Fahey, *War and the Christian Conscience: Where Do You Stand?* (Maryknoll, NY: Orbis Books, 2005), 91-93; Mark J. Allman, *Who Would Jesus Kill? War, Peace, and the Christian Tradition* (Winona, MN: Anselm Academic, 2008), 171.

[37]Bell, *Just War as Christian Discipleship*, 45-46; Fahey, *War and the Christian Conscience*, 93-95; and Allman, *Who Would Jesus Kill?* 85-87.

[38]Thomas Aquinas, *Summa Theologica*, trans. Fathers of the English Dominican Province (Westminster, MD: Christian Classics, 1981), II-II, Q. 40, Art. 1. For this section on Aquinas, we are also relying on Fahey, *War and the Christian Conscience*, 96-99; Clough and Stiltner, *Faith and Force*, 55-56; Allman, *Who Would Jesus Kill?* 171-76; and Bell, *Just War as Christian Discipleship*, 46-48.

[39]Aquinas, *Summa Theologica*, II-II, Q. 64, Art. 7.

[40]Fahey, *War and the Christian Conscience*, 101; Bell, *Just War as Christian Discipleship*, 48-53.

[41]Fahey, *War and the Christian Conscience*, 101, 168-69.

[42]Bell, *Just War as Christian Discipleship*, 55.

[43]Ibid., 56.

[44]David Clough and Brian Stiltner, "On the Importance of a Drawn Sword: Christian Thinking about Preemptive War—and Its Modern Outworking," *Journal of the Society of Christian Ethics* 27, no. 2 (Fall/Winter 2007): 254-55.

[45]Clough and Stiltner, *Faith and Force*, 57.

[46]Sharma, "Reconsidering the Jus ad Bellum/Jus in Bello Distinction," 18.

[47]Second Vatican Council, "*Gaudium et Spes*: Pastoral Constitution on the Church in the Modern World," in *Catholic Social Thought: The Documentary Heritage*, ed. David J. O'Brien and Thomas A. Shannon (Maryknoll, NY: Orbis Books, 1992), no. 78.

[48]National Conference of Catholic Bishops, *The Challenge of Peace: God's Promise and Our Response* (Washington, DC: United States Catholic Conference, 1983), par. 16.

[49]Yoder, *When War Is Unjust*, 93.

[50]Drew Christiansen, S.J., "After Sept. 11: Catholic Teaching on Peace and War," *Origins* 32, no. 3 (May 30, 2002): 36. For the U.S. bishops' references to this presumption for peace and against harm or war, see *Challenge of Peace*, pars. 70, 80, 83, and 120.

[51]Clough and Stiltner, *Faith and Force*, 58.

⁵²For more in this area, see Allman, *Who Would Jesus Kill?* 69-97 and 125-54; Fahey, *War and the Christian Conscience*, 29-69 and 115-47; and Lisa Sowle Cahill, *Love Your Enemies: Discipleship, Pacifism, and Just War Theory* (Minneapolis: Fortress Press, 1994), 119-48.

⁵³Sharma, "Reconsidering the Jus ad Bellum/Jus in Bello Distinction," 10.

⁵⁴Orend, *"Jus Post Bellum*: A Just War Theory Perspective," 33.

⁵⁵NCCB, *Challenge of Peace*, pars. 84-110.

⁵⁶John Paul II, "Principles Underlying a Stance toward Unjust Aggressors," *Origins* 22, no. 34 (January 28, 1993): 587.

⁵⁷*Catechism of the Catholic Church* (New York: Image/Doubleday, 1995), par. 2309; Pontifical Council for Justice and Peace, *Compendium of the Social Doctrine of the Church* (Washington, DC: United States Conference of Catholic Bishops, 2004), pars. 500 and 504.

⁵⁸*Catechism*, par. 2308.

⁵⁹William L. Portier, "Are We Really Serious When We Ask God to Deliver Us from War? The Catechism and the Challenge of Pope John Paul II," *Communio* 23, no. 1 (Spring 1996): 48, citing *Catechism*, par. 2309.

⁶⁰Ibid., 55.

⁶¹Benedict XVI, "The Human Person, the Heart of Peace," World Day of Peace Message 2007, par. 14, http://www.vatican.va/holy_father/benedict_xvi/messages/peace/documents/hf_ben-xvi_mes_20061208_xl-world-day-peace_en.html.

⁶²Ibid., par. 16.

⁶³Ibid., n. 7.

⁶⁴*Catechism*, par. 2309.

⁶⁵Quoted in Daniel C. Maguire, *The Horrors We Bless: Rethinking the Just-War Legacy* (Minneapolis: Fortress Press, 2007), 30-31.

⁶⁶NCCB, *Challenge of Peace*, pars. 89-90.

⁶⁷*Catechism*, par. 2309.

⁶⁸Yoder, "Just-War Tradition," 296.

⁶⁹NCCB, *Challenge of Peace*, par. 95.

⁷⁰Louis V. Iasiello, *"Jus Post Bellum*: The Moral Responsibilities of Victors in War," *Naval War College Review* 57, nos. 3/4 (Summer/Autumn 2004): 33, 37.

⁷¹Helmut David Baer and Joseph E. Capizzi, "Just War Theory and the Problem of International Politics: On the Central Role of Just Intention," *Journal of the Society of Christian Ethics* 26, no. 1 (2006): 170.

⁷²Ibid.

⁷³Ibid., 171.

⁷⁴Ibid. Baer and Capizzi draw on Theodore R. Weber, *Modern War and the Pursuit of Peace* (New York: Council on Religion and International Affairs, 1968); Weber, "Vengeance Denied, Politics Affirmed: The Reconciling Criterion of Just Intention," *Societas Ethica Jahresherict/Annual* (2000): 170-76; and Weber, *Politics in the Order of Salvation: New Directions in Wesleyan Political Ethics* (Nashville: Abingdon Press, 2001).

[75]*Catechism*, par. 2309.

[76]NCCB, *Challenge of Peace*, par. 98.

[77]*Catechism*, par. 2309.

[78]We refer to "smart" sanctions here because during the 1990s we learned in Iraq that sanctions are not necessarily discriminate and nonviolent. See Joseph E. Capizzi and Tobias Winright, "The 'Slow War' Against Iraq: A Moral Analysis," *Josephinum Journal of Theology* 8, no. 1 (Winter/Spring 2001): 27-42.

[79]Clough and Stiltner, *Faith and Force*, 61.

[80]*Catechism*, par. 2309.

[81]Allman, *Who Would Jesus Kill?* 199.

[82]NCCB, *Challenge of Peace*, par. 100; see National Conference of Catholic Bishops, *Resolution on Southeast Asia* (Washington, DC: NCCB, 1971).

[83]NCCB, *Challenge of Peace*, par. 93.

[84]For example, see Orend, "War," in *Stanford Encyclopedia of Philosophy*, ed. Edward Zalta (July 2005), http://plato.stanford.edu/entries/war/, and *The Morality of War* (Peterborough, Ontario: Broadview Press, 2006), 105-39. See also Yoder, *When War Is Unjust*, 154-60.

[85]As Oliver O'Donovan notes, the word "direct" has to do with intent, so the difference between intended and unintended damage is equivalent to the difference between direct and indirect damage. See Oliver O'Donovan, *The Just War Revisited* (Cambridge: Cambridge University Press, 2003), 43.

[86]*Gaudium et Spes*, no. 80; cited in the *Catechism*, par. 2314.

[87]*Catechism*, par. 2269.

[88]For recent treatments of double effect, see John Berkman, "How Important Is the Doctrine of Double Effect for Moral Theology? Contextualizing the Controversy," *Christian Bioethics* 3, no. 2 (1997): 89-114; and T. A. Cavanaugh, *Double Effect Reasoning: Doing Good and Avoiding Evil* (New York: Oxford University Press, 2006).

[89]John C. Ford, "The Morality of Obliteration Bombing," *Theological Studies* 5, no. 3 (September 1944): 289.

[90]Ibid., 263.

[91]Ibid., 264-65.

[92]Ibid., 269.

[93]O'Donovan, *Just War Revisited*, 45.

[94]*Catechism*, par. 2269.

[95]For recent works that treat these particular matters of double effect, see William C. Mattison III, *Introducing Moral Theology: True Happiness and the Virtues* (Grand Rapids: Brazos Press, 2008), 171-77; and Brian Wicker, "Double Effect," *New Blackfriars* 90, no. 1028 (July 2009): 449-57.

[96]Tom Jackson, "Depraved Heart Murder," *Common Dreams News Center*, July 5, 2001, http://www.commondreams.org/views01/0705-01.htm.

[97]Aquinas, *Summa Theologica*, II-II, Q. 64, Art. 7.

[98]Ibid., II-II, Q. 64, Art. 2, and at least five other places, according to LeRoy B. Walters, "Five Classic Just-War Theories: A Study in the Thought of Thomas

Aquinas, Vitoria, Suarez, Gentili, and Grotius" (PhD diss., Yale University, 1971), 160ff.

[99]Thomas Aquinas, *On Evil*, ed. Brian Davies, trans. R. Regan (New York: Oxford University Press, 2003), 1.3.15.

[100]See Orend, "War," and Allman, *Who Would Jesus Kill?* 204.

[101]See John Kleinig, *The Ethics of Policing* (Cambridge: Cambridge University Press, 1996), 107; Edward A. Malloy, C.S.C., *The Ethics of Law Enforcement and Criminal Punishment* (Lanham, MD: University Press of America, 1982), 20; and Tobias L. Winright, "The Challenge of Policing: An Analysis in Christian Social Ethics" (PhD diss., University of Notre Dame, 2002), 320-27.

[102]G. E. M. Anscombe, "Medalist's Address: Action, Intention and 'Double Effect,'" in *Proceedings of the American Catholic Philosophical Association 56*, ed. Daniel O. Dahlstrom et al. (Washington, DC: American Catholic Philosophical Association, 1982), 24-25.

[103]Iasiello, "*Jus Post Bellum*," 34.

[104]For example, Allman, "Just War Theory: A Third Way," and "Challenges to and Adaptations of the Just War Theory," in *Who Would Jesus Kill?* 158-268; Fahey, "Just War," in *War and the Christian Conscience*, 70-114; and Maguire, "The Strength and Weaknesses of Just-War Theory," in *Horrors We Bless*, 24-64.

[105]Maguire, *Horrors We Bless*, 21, 62-63.

[106]John Courtney Murray, S.J., "Remarks on the Moral Problem of War," *Theological Studies* 20, no. 1 (March 1959): 53-54.

[107]Yoder, "Just-War Tradition," 298.

[108]John Howard Yoder, *The Original Revolution: Essays on Christian Pacifism* (Scottdale, PA: Herald Press, 1971), 131-32.

[109]Ibid., 132.

[110]Eric Marcelo O. Genilo, *John Cuthbert Ford, SJ: Moral Theologian at the End of the Manualist Era* (Washington, DC: Georgetown University Press, 2007), 1-2; Yoder, *When War Is Unjust*, 41. Ford's article is mentioned, quoted, or anthologized in several articles and books, more so in recent decades than when it was published. See Bainton, *Christian Attitudes toward War and Peace*, 233, 248; Fahey, *War and the Christian Conscience*, 103-4; J. Bryan Hehir, "The Lessons of World War II: War Must Be Limited," *Commonweal* 122, no. 14 (August 18, 1995): 9-10; John R. Popiden, "An American Catholic Moralist and World War II: John Ford on Obliteration Bombing," *Irish Theological Quarterly* 56, no. 1 (Winter 1990): 1-19; and Michael Walzer, *Just and Unjust Wars: A Moral Argument with Historical Illustrations*, 4th ed. (New York: Basic Books, 2006), 151-53, 344.

[111]James W. Douglass, "The Morality of Thermonuclear Deterrence: Can We Resolve the Conflict between Absolute Principle and Strategic Necessity?" *Worldview* 7, no. 9 (October 1964): 4-5.

[112]J. Bryan Hehir, "Kosovo: A War of Values and the Values of War," *America* 180, no. 17 (May 15, 1999), 7-12.

[113]Ford, "Morality of Obliteration Bombing," 267.

[114]Yoder, "Just-War Tradition," 297. For a recent book that offers a Christian theological account of just war that includes attention to individual and communal practices and virtues for embodying this tradition in a way that has teeth, see Bell, *Just War as Christian Discipleship*. Also, see Tobias Winright, "The Liturgy as a Basis for Catholic Identity, Just War Theory, and the Presumption against War," in *Catholic Identity and the Laity*, College Theology Society Annual Vol. 54, ed. Tim Muldoon (Maryknoll, NY: Orbis Books, 2009), 134-51.

[115]Clough and Stiltner, *Faith and Force*, 50.

[116]Adrian Pabst, "Can There Be a Just War without a Just Peace?" *New Blackfriars* 88, no. 1018 (November 2007): 723.

[117]Paul Ramsey, *Speak Up for Just War or Pacifism: A Critique of the United Methodist Bishops' Letter "In Defense of Creation"* (University Park: Pennsylvania State University Press, 1988), 82; see also Ramsey, *The Just War: Force and Political Responsibility* (New York: Charles Scribner's Sons, 1968), 142-43; Ramsey, *Basic Christian Ethics* (1950; repr. Louisville, KY: Westminster/John Knox Press, 1993), 165, 169-71; Ramsey, *War and the Christian Conscience: How Shall Modern War Be Conducted Justly?* (Durham, NC: Duke University Press, 1961), xvi-xvii.

[118]Ramsey, *Speak Up for Just War or Pacifism*, 72.

[119]Ramsey, *Just War*, 142-43.

[120]Hugo Slim, *Killing Civilians: Method, Madness, and Morality in War* (New York: Columbia University Press, 2008), 9-10.

[121]Yoder, *When War Is Unjust*, 28.

[122]Ramsey, *Just War*, 143-44.

[123]Ibid., 144.

[124]Baer and Capizzi, "Just War Theory and the Problem of International Politics," 170.

[125]John Kelsay makes this claim in "How to Refine and Improve Just War Criteria," in David R. Smock, *Religious Perspectives on War: Christian, Muslim and Jewish Attitudes toward Force after the Gulf War* (Washington, DC: U.S. Institute for Peace Press, 1992), 28-29.

[126]Yoder, "Just-War Tradition," 296; and John Howard Yoder, *The Priestly Kingdom: Social Ethics as Gospel* (Notre Dame, IN: University of Notre Dame Press, 1984), 35.

[127]Glen Stassen, ed., *Just Peacemaking: The New Paradigm for the Ethics of Peace and War*, new ed. (Cleveland: Pilgrim Press, 2008).

[128]Michael Walzer, *Arguing about War* (New Haven, CT: Yale University Press, 2004), xi. Like Yoder, Walzer notes that some criticize just war theory for focusing attention "on the immediate issues at stake before the war begins—in the case of the recent Iraq war, for example, on inspections, disarmament, hidden weapons, and so on—and then, upon engagement, on the conduct of war, battle by battle; and so it avoids larger questions. . . ."

[129]Maureen O'Connell, "*Jus Ante Bellum*: Faith-Based Diplomacy as an

Emergent Trajectory of the Just War Tradition," presented at the 2007 Annual Convention of the CTSA, summarized by Brian Berry in the *CTSA Proceedings* 62 (2007): 124.

[130]Orend, "*Jus Post Bellum*: A Just War Theory Perspective," 36.

[131]Sharma, "Reconsidering the Jus ad Bellum/Jus in Bello Distinction," 29.

Chapter 2: *Jus Post Bellum*

[1]Augustine, Letter 189, to Boniface, in *Augustine: Political Writings*, trans. M. W. Tkacz and D. Kries (Indianapolis: Hackett, 1994), 220.

[2]Aristotle, *Nichomachean Ethics* (1177b6), in *The Complete Works of Aristotle*, vol. 2 (Princeton, NJ: Princeton University Press, 1985), 1861.

[3]Frederick H. Russell, *The Just War in the Middle Ages* (Cambridge: Cambridge University Press, 1975, 1977), 4-5; quoted in Paul Christopher, *The Ethics of War and Peace: An Introduction to Legal and Moral Issues*, 2nd ed. (Upper Saddle River, NJ: Prentice Hall, 1994), 10.

[4]Quoted in Louis V. Iasiello, "*Jus Post Bellum*: The Moral Responsibilities of Victors in War," *Naval War College Review* 62, nos. 3/4 (Summer/Autumn 2004): 41. See relevant excerpt from Plato's *The Republic* in Arthur F. Holmes, ed., *War and Christian Ethics: Classic and Contemporary Readings on the Morality of War* (Grand Rapids: Baker Academic, 2005), 17-18.

[5]Iasiello, "*Jus Post Bellum*," 41.

[6]N. G. L. Hammond, *Alexander the Great: King, Commander, and Statesman* (Park Ridge, NJ: Noyes Press, 1980), 78, 81; quoted in Christopher, *Ethics of War and Peace*, 11.

[7]Roland H. Bainton, *Christian Attitudes toward War and Peace: A Historical Survey and Critical Reevaluation* (Nashville: Abingdon Press, 1960), 28.

[8]Russell, *Just War in the Middle Ages*, 7-8. Also see Bainton, *Christian Attitudes toward War and Peace*, 18; Daniel M. Bell Jr., *Just War as Christian Discipleship: Recentering the Tradition in the Church Rather Than the State* (Grand Rapids: Brazos Press, 2009), 26.

[9]Cicero, *De Officiis* 1:11-12, trans. W. Miller, in the Loeb Classical Library (Cambridge, MA: Harvard University Press, 1913), available in Holmes, *War and Christian Ethics*, 29-30.

[10]Bainton, *Christian Attitudes toward War and Peace*, 23.

[11]Ibid., 38.

[12]See Chalmers Johnson, *Blowback* (New York: Henry Holt, 2000), and Carl Boggs, *Imperial Delusions: American Militarism and Endless War* (Lanham, MD: Rowman and Littlefield, 2005), xiii, 13, 45-46.

[13]Augustine, *The City of God*, trans. Gerald G. Walsh et al. (Garden City, NY: Image Books, 1958), 452.

[14]Augustine, *Augustine: Political Writings*, ed. E. M. Atkins and R. J. Dodaro (New York: Cambridge University Press, 2001), 125.

[15]Bainton, *Christian Attitudes toward War and Peace*, 97.

¹⁶Francisco de Vitoria, *De Indiis et de Iure Belli Relectiones*, second reflection, in Holmes, *War and Christian Ethics*, 118; also available in Gregory Reichberg, Henrik Syse, and Endre Begby, eds., *The Ethics of War: Classic and Contemporary Readings* (Malden, MA: Blackwell Publishing, 2006), 315, 332. See Stephen C. Neff, "Conflict Termination and Peace-making in the Law of Nations: A Historical Perspective," in *Jus Post Bellum: Towards a Law of Transition from Conflict to Peace*, ed. Carsten Stahn and Jann K. Kleffner (The Hague: T M C Asser Press, 2008), 79.

¹⁷Bell, *Just War as Christian Discipleship*, 51.

¹⁸Vitoria, *De Indiis et de Iure Belli Relectiones*, in Reichberg et al., *Ethics of War*, 330-32.

¹⁹Bell, *Just War as Christian Discipleship*, 52-53.

²⁰Francisco Suarez, *The Three Theological Virtues: On Charity*, disputation 13, "On War," in Holmes, *War and Christian Ethics*, 219.

²¹Ibid., 220-23; also see Reichberg et al., *Ethics of War*, 362-64.

²²Carsten Stahn, "*Jus Post Bellum*: Mapping the Discipline(s)," in *Jus Post Bellum: Towards a Law of Transition from Conflict to Peace*, ed. Carsten Stahn and Jann K. Kleffner (The Hague: T M C Asser Press, 2008), 94.

²³Oliver O'Donovan, *The Just War Revisited* (Cambridge: Cambridge University Press, 2003), 109-10.

²⁴Serena K. Sharma, "Reconsidering the Jus ad Bellum/Jus in Bello Distinction," in *Jus Post Bellum: Towards a Law of Transition from Conflict to Peace*, ed. Carsten Stahn and Jann K. Kleffner (The Hague: T M C Asser Press, 2008), 15.

²⁵John Locke, *Second Treatise on Civil Government*, in Holmes, *War and Christian Ethics*, 252-62, 265-69.

²⁶Brian Orend, "Kant's Ethics of War and Peace," *Journal of Military Ethics* 3, no. 2 (2004): 161. For examples of how Kant has not tended to be treated as a just war thinker, see Bainton, *Christian Attitudes toward War and Peace*, 181-82, and Holmes, *War and Christian Ethics*, 273-74.

²⁷Orend, "Kant's Ethics of War and Peace," 176.

²⁸Immanuel Kant, *The Metaphysics of Morals* (1797), in Reichberg et al., *Ethics of War*, 538.

²⁹Stahn, "*Jus Post Bellum*: Mapping the Discipline(s)," 94.

³⁰Orend, "Kant's Ethics of War and Peace," 174.

³¹Brian Orend, "Kant's Just War Theory," *Journal of the History of Philosophy* (1999): 323-53. See also Brian Orend, "*Jus Post Bellum*: A Just War Theory Perspective," in Stahn and Kleffner, *Jus Post Bellum*, 34-35.

³²Immanuel Kant, *Perpetual Peace* (1795), in Reichberg et al., *Ethics of War*, 521.

³³Stahn, "*Jus Post Bellum*: Mapping the Discipline(s)," 94.

³⁴Michael Walzer, *Arguing about War* (New Haven, CT: Yale University Press, 2004), 161.

[35]Carsten Stahn, "The Future of Jus Post Bellum," in Stahn and Kleffner, *Jus Post Bellum*, 231.

[36]In particular, see the collection of essays from the workshop, "The Ethics of Postconflict Reconstruction and Statebuilding sponsored by the Center for International Studies," University of Oxford (June 26, 2008), published in *Ethics and International Affairs* 23, no. 2 (Summer 2009); "The Ethics of Exit: The Morality of Withdrawal from Iraq," Fordham Center on Religion and Culture, Fordham University (March 21, 2005), http://www.fordham.edu/academics/programs_at_fordham_/center_on_religion_a/fordham_center_on_re/the_ethics_of_exit/; and the Society for Applied Philosophy Annual Meeting, University of Manchester (July 4-6, 2008), http://www.appliedphil.org/AnnualConference2008.shtml.

[37]Orend, *"Jus Post Bellum*: A Just War Theory Perspective," 34. See also Brian Orend, *War and International Justice: A Kantian Perspective* (Waterloo, Ontario: Wilfrid Laurier University Press, 2000), and *The Morality of War* (Peterborough, Ontario: Broadview Press, 2006), 19-20.

[38]Orend, *"Jus Post Bellum*: A Just War Theory Perspective," 38.

[39]Ibid., 39. See also *Morality of War*, 160-222.

[40]Orend, *"Jus Post Bellum*: A Just War Theory Perspective," 40-41.

[41]Ibid., 42.

[42]Ibid., 43.

[43]Ibid., 38.

[44]Ibid.

[45]Gary J. Bass, *"Jus Post Bellum," Philosophy and Public Affairs* 32, no. 4 (2004): 384.

[46]Ibid., 386.

[47]Ibid., 392.

[48]Ibid., 387. See Michael Walzer, *Just and Unjust Wars: A Moral Argument with Historical Illustrations*, 3rd edition (New York: Basic Books, 2000), 123; John Rawls, *The Law of Peoples* (Cambridge, MA: Harvard University Press, 1999).

[49]Bass, *"Jus Post Bellum,"* 389.

[50]Ibid., 389-90.

[51]Ibid., 390.

[52]Ibid., 392.

[53]Ibid., 393.

[54]Ibid., 395.

[55]Ibid., 396.

[56]Ibid., 397.

[57]Ibid., 399.

[58]Ibid., 403.

[59]Ibid., 401.

[60]Ibid., 403.

[61]Ibid., 412.

[62]Doug McCready, "Ending the War Right: *Jus Post Bellum* and the Just War Tradition," *Journal of Military Ethics* 8, no. 1 (2009): 68.

[63]Mark Evans, "Balancing Peace, Justice and Sovereignty in *Jus Post Bellum*: The Case of 'Just Occupation,'" *Millennium: Journal of International Studies* 36, no. 3 (2008): 533-54.

[64]Mark Evans, "Moral Responsibilities and the Conflicting Demands of *Jus Post Bellum*," *Ethics and International Affairs* 23, no. 2 (Summer 2009): 155.

[65]Ibid., 157.

[66]Ibid.

[67]Ibid., 160.

[68]Ibid., 161-62.

[69]Michael Walzer, "Just and Unjust Occupations," *Dissent* 51 (2004): 61-63; and E. Patterson, "*Jus Post Bellum* and International Conflict: Order, Justice and Reconstruction," in *Rethinking the Just War Tradition*, ed. M. W. Brough et al. (Albany: State University of New York Press, 2007), 35-52.

[70]James Turner Johnson, "*Jus Post Bellum* and Counterinsurgency," *Journal of Military Ethics* 7, no. 3 (2008): 215-30; and Alex J. Bellamy, "The Responsibilities of Victory: *Jus Post Bellum* and the Just War," *Review of International Studies* 34, no. 4 (2008): 601-25.

[71]Darrel Mollendorf, "*Jus ex Bello*," *Journal of Political Philosophy* 16, no. 2 (2008): 123, 131.

[72]Adrian Pabst, "Can There Be a Just War without a Just Peace?" *New Blackfriars* 88, no. 1018 (November 2007): 730. Pabst has in his sights Michael Walzer and John Rawls, but we suspect he would extend this criticism to the recent work of others such as Orend and Bass.

[73]Ibid., 732.

[74]Ibid., 738.

[75]Ibid.

[76]Ibid., 723.

[77]Ibid., 724-25.

[78]Ibid., 730.

[79]Iasiello, "*Jus Post Bellum*," 39.

[80]Stahn, "*Jus Post Bellum*: Mapping the Discipline(s)," 94.

[81]Helmut David Baer and Joseph E. Capizzi, "Just War Theory and the Problem of International Politics: On the Central Role of Just Intention," *Journal of the Society of Christian Ethics* 26, no. 1 (Spring/Summer 2006): 164. See also Theodore Weber, "Vengeance Denied, Politics Affirmed: The Reconciling Criterion of Just Intention," *Societas Ethica Jahresherict/Annual* (2000): 170-76.

[82]Baer and Capizzi, "Just War Theory and the Problem of International Politics," 164.

[83]Ibid.

[84]Ibid., 171.

[85]Bell, *Just War as Christian Discipleship*, 167.

[86]Ibid.

[87]Bishop Thomas G. Wenski, "Toward a Responsible Transition in Iraq," http://www.usccb.org/comm/archives/2006/06-006.shtml (accessed June 19, 2007).

[88]"Bishops Back Obama Afghanistan Strategy," *National Catholic Reporter*, December 21, 2009, http://ncronline.org/news/peace/bishops-back-obama-afghanistan-strategy.

[89]Orend, *"Jus Post Bellum*: A Just War Theory Perspective," 38.

Chapter 3: The Just Cause Principle

[1]National Conference of Catholic Bishops, "The Harvest of Justice Is Sown in Peace: A Reflection of the National Conference of Catholic Bishops on the Tenth Anniversary of *The Challenge of Peace*" (issued on November 17, 1993), in *Peacemaking: Moral and Policy Changes for a New World*, ed. Gerard F. Powers, Drew Christiansen, S.J., and Robert T. Hennemeyer (Washington, DC: United States Catholic Conference, 1994), 320.

[2]Annalisa Koeman, "A Realistic and Effective Constraint on the Resort to Force? Pre-commitment to *Jus in bello* and *Jus post bellum* as Part of the Criterion of Right Intention," *Journal of Military Ethics* 6, no 3 (2007): 204.

[3]Brian Orend, *"Jus Post Bellum,"* *Journal of Social Philosophy* 31, no. 1 (Spring 2000): 128; Orend, "Justice after War," *Ethics and International Affairs* 61, no. 1 (2002): 46; Orend, "Kant's Just War Theory," *Journal of the History of Philosophy* 37, no. 2 (April 1999): 346; and Orend, *The Morality of War* (Peterborough, Ontario: Broadview Press, 2006), 32-50, 162-66.

[4]Augustine, *Reply to Faustus the Manichean*, vol. 4, bk. 22, par. 75, in *A Select Library of the Nicene and Post-Nicene Fathers of the Christian Church*, ed. Philip Schaff (Grand Rapids: Ferdmans Publishing, 1979), 368.

[5]Although there are differences between the "classical just war tradition" and the "contemporary just war tradition" with regard to what constitutes just cause, such differences do not diminish or significantly affect our logical extension of the just cause principle into *jus post bellum*. For more on the differences between the classical and contemporary versions of just war theory, see "War and Peace: Parallel Traditions," in *Just War, Lasting Peace: What Christian Traditions Can Teach Us*, ed. John Kleiderer et al. (Maryknoll, NY: Orbis Books, 2006), 17-30.

[6]Michael Walzer, *Just and Unjust Wars: A Moral Argument with Historical Illustrations* (New York: Basic Books, 2000), 119-21. See also Orend, *"Jus post bellum,"* 122-23; and "Justice after War," 45.

[7]Orend identifies a "minimally just state" as the objective of a just war. He describes it as a community that "does all it reasonably can to: 1) gain recognition as being legitimate in the eyes of its own people and the international community;

2) adhere to basic rules of international justice and good international citizenship, notably non-aggression; and 3) satisfy the human rights of its individual members." These ideas are addressed in greater detail in chap. 6 of this book in the section "Political Reform."

[8]Gary J. Bass, "*Jus Post Bellum*," *Philosophy and Public Affairs* 32, no. 4 (Fall 2004): 386.

[9]Orend, "Justice after War," 46; see also Orend's *Morality of War*, 163.

[10]Orend, "Justice after War," 46.

[11]Walzer, *Just and Unjust Wars*, 109-24, 263-68; Orend, "Justice after War," 46; Orend, "*Jus Post Bellum:* A Just War Theory Perspective," in *Jus Post Bellum: Towards a Law of Transition from Conflict to Peace*, ed. Carsten Stahn and Jann K. Kleffner (The Hague: T M C Asser Press/Cambridge University Press, 2008), 31-32, 39; and Orend, *Morality of War*, 163-64. Both Walzer and Orend use the Allied forces' insistence in an unconditional surrender at the close of World War II to illustrate their point and show that this insistence was more rhetoric than reality.

[12]Koeman, "Realistic and Effective Constraint on the Resort to Force?" 214n4.

[13]Walzer, *Just and Unjust Wars*, 304.

[14]Ibid., 39-40, 127-28, and 138; and Orend, *Morality of War*, 107-10.

[15]Orend, *Morality of War*, 109 (emphasis in original).

[16]Russell B. Connors Jr. and Patrick T. McCormick, *Character, Choices and Community: The Three Faces of Christian Ethics* (Mahwah, NJ: Paulist Press, 1998), 130-32; Richard C. Sparks, *Contemporary Christian Morality: Real Questions, Candid Responses* (New York: Crossroad, 1996), 16-18.

[17]Orend, *Morality of War*, 48 (emphasis in original).

[18]Other images he uses to describe just cause *ad bellum* include: it is like "*the crucial opening note that sets the tone for all that follows*," and like surgery, whereby radical measures (active combat) are undertaken with just cause and require significant postoperative recovery and therapy (*Morality of War*, 49, 162, and 165).

[19]Ibid., 162 (emphasis in original).

[20]Ibid., 195 (emphasis in original).

[21]Ibid., 48 (emphasis in original).

[22]Ibid., 49.

[23]Ibid., 162.

[24]John Langan, "An Imperfectly Just War," *Commonweal* 118, no. 11 (June 1, 1991): 361-65. Also available in *War in the Twentieth Century: Sources in Theological Ethics*, ed. Richard Brian Miller (Louisville, KY: Westminster/John Knox Press, 1992).

[25]John J. DiIulio, "Another War President?" *America*, December 21, 2009, http://www.americamagazine.org/content/article.cfm?article_id=12059&comments=1.

[26]Orend, *Morality of War*, 195.

[27]Walzer, *Just and Unjust Wars*, 251-68, and *Arguing about War* (New Haven, CT: Yale University Press, 2004), 33-50.

[28]James T. Bretzke, *A Morally Complex World: Engaging Contemporary Moral Theology* (Collegeville, MN: Liturgical Press, 2004), 75.

[29]Immanuel Kant, "Perpetual Peace: A Philosophical Sketch," in *Kant: Political Writings*, ed. H. Reiss (Cambridge: Cambridge University Press, 1999), 105.

Chapter 4: The Reconciliation Phase

[1]Archbishop Desmond Tutu, quoted in Rachel Kerr and Eirin Mobekk, *Peace and Justice: Seeking Accountability after War* (Cambridge, UK: Polity Press, 2007), 5.

[2]John Paul II, "No Peace without Justice, No Justice without Forgiveness," World Day of Peace Message, no. 15 (January 1, 2002), http://www.vatican.va/holy_father/john_paul_ii/messages/peace/documents/hf_jp-ii_mes_20011211_xxxv-world-day-for-peace_en.html.

[3]Mark Allman, "Postwar Justice," *America* 193, no. 11 (October 17, 2005): 11.

[4]Kerr and Mobekk, *Peace and Justice*, 6.

[5]Davida Kellogg, "*Jus Post Bellum*: The Importance of War Crimes Trials," *Parameters* 32, no. 3 (September 22, 2002): 93. See also Anthony Ellis, "What Should We Do with War Criminals?" in *War Crimes and Collective Wrongdoing, A Reader*, ed. A. Jokic (Cambridge: Blackwell, 2001), 97-111.

[6]For more on reconciliation, see Andrew Rigby, "Forgiveness and Reconciliation in *Jus Post Bellum*," in *Just War Theory: A Reappraisal*, ed. Mark Evans (New York: Palgrave MacMillan, 2005), 177-200; Walter Wink, *When the Powers Fall: Reconciliation in the Healing of Nations* (Minneapolis: Fortress Press, 1998); and James Turner Johnson, "War Crimes and Reconciliation after Conflict," in his *Morality and Contemporary Warfare* (New Haven, CT: Yale University Press, 1999), 191-218.

[7]Wink, *When the Powers Fall*, 16.

[8]William Bole, "Forgiveness: A Radical New Factor," *America* 188, no. 14 (April 21, 2003): 18.

[9]Ibid. Highly recommended, especially in connection with post-war dealings by the United States with Germany and Japan following World War II, is Donald W. Shriver Jr., *An Ethic for Enemies: Forgiveness in Politics* (New York: Oxford University Press, 1997).

[10]Wink, *When the Powers Fall*, 14-16.

[11]Trudy Govier, "War's Aftermath," in *War: Essays in Political Philosophy*, ed. Larry May (Cambridge: Cambridge University Press, 2008), 230.

[12]Ibid., 237-38.

[13]Center for Restorative Justice, "What Is Restorative Justice?" (Boston: Suf-

folk University, July 5, 2010), http://www.suffolk.edu/research/6953.html.

[14]John Donahue, "Biblical Perspectives on Justice," in *The Faith That Does Justice*, ed. John Haughey (Mahwah, NJ: Paulist Press, 1977), 69.

[15]John Paul II, "No Peace without Justice," no. 2 (emphasis in original).

[16]Ibid., no. 3 (emphasis in original).

[17]For more on social trust, see Govier, "War's Aftermath," 234-37, and Trudy Govier and Wilhelm Verwoerd, "Trust and the Problem of National Reconciliation," *Philosophy of the Social Sciences* 32, no. 2 (2002): 178-205.

[18]Samuel Eliot Morison, *The Oxford History of the American People* (New York: Oxford University Press, 1965), 700; quoted in Louis Iasiello, "*Jus Post Bellum*: The Moral Responsibilities of Victors in War," *Naval War College Review* 57, nos. 3/4 (Summer/Autumn 2004): 38.

[19]Iasiello, "*Jus Post Bellum*," 38.

[20]Michael Schuck, "When the Shooting Stops: Missing Elements in Just War Theory," *Christian Century* 111, no. 30 (October 26, 1994): 982-83.

[21]Allman, "Postwar Justice," 11.

[22]Wink, *When the Powers Fall*, 34.

[23]Kerr and Mobekk, *Peace and Justice*, 5.

[24]Robert J. Schreiter, *Reconciliation* (Maryknoll, NY: Orbis Books, 1992), 71. Quoted in Wink, *When the Powers Fall*, 21.

[25]Wink, *When the Powers Fall*, 34.

[26]Govier, "War's Aftermath," 235.

[27]Ibid., 237; see also Kerr and Mobekk, *Peace and Justice*, 134-35.

[28]Wink, *When the Powers Fall*, 53.

[29]Govier, "War's Aftermath," 242.

[30]Wink, *When the Powers Fall*, 56.

[31]Ibid.

[32]There are many examples of collective apologies, including the United Church of Canada's apology to the Native Americans of Canada; Japanese Prime Minister Tomiichi Murayama's attempt to get Parliament to formally apologize to Asian countries that were victims of Japanese aggression; and the U.S. Fellowship of Reconciliation's collection of over eight thousand signatures on a petition apologizing for the bombings of Hiroshima and Nagasaki. See Wink, *When the Powers Fall*, 54-59, for these and several other collective apologies.

[33]Daniel Philpott, "Lessons in Mercy: Justice and Reconciliation in the Aftermath of Atrocities," *America* 200, no. 14 (May 4, 2009): 14.

[34]Pontifical Council for Justice and Peace, *Compendium of the Social Doctrine of the Church* (Washington, DC: United States Conference of Catholic Bishops, 2004), no. 518 (emphasis in original).

[35]Kerr and Mobekk, *Peace and Justice*, 136.

[36]John Howard Yoder, *He Came Preaching Peace* (Scottdale, PA: Herald Press, 1985), 34.

[37]Ibid.

[38]Wink, *When the Powers Fall*, 34.

[39]Kerr and Mobekk, *Peace and Justice*, 139.

[40]Ibid., 140.

[41]Examples include Namibia, Haiti, and Brazil. See Wink, *When the Powers Fall*, 33-50.

Chapter 5: The Punishment Phase

[1]Bernard Boxill, "The Morality of Reparation," in *Today's Moral Problems*, 2nd ed., ed. Richard A. Wasserstrom (New York: Macmillan, 1979), 258.

[2]Judith Shklar convincingly argues that what is characterized as "acts of God" are often actually forms of injustice. For example, deaths resulting from an earthquake are often seen as an unfortunate consequence of a natural disaster for which no one is to blame; in fact, however, poor building standards, government corruption, and faulty building inspections can be contributing factors to the death toll. Thus, what initially looks like a misfortune is actually an injustice. See Judith Shklar, *The Faces of Injustice* (New Haven, CT: Yale University Press, 1990).

[3]Boxill, "Morality of Reparation," 259.

[4]Haig Khatchadourian, "Compensation and Reparation as Forms of Compensatory Justice," *Metaphilosophy* 37, nos. 3-4 (July 2006): 430-31.

[5]Ibid., 441-42.

[6]Ibid., 433.

[7]Ernesto Verdeja, "A Normative Theory of Reparations in Transitional Democracies," in *Genocide's Aftermath: Responsibility and Repair*, ed. Claudia Card and Armen T. Marsoobian (Malden, MA: Blackwell, 2007), 171.

[8]Ibid., 172.

[9]Ibid., 176.

[10]Ibid., 177

[11]Erica Goode and Stephen Farrell, "Iraqis Unite to Restore Minority Representation Law," *New York Times*, October 6, 2008, http://www.nytimes.com/2008/10/07/world/middleeast/07iraq.html.

[12]See Verdeja, "Normative Theory of Reparations in Transitional Democracies," 175-76; and Chris Cunneen, "Reparations and Restorative Justice: Responding to the Gross Violation of Human Rights," in *Restorative Justice and Civil Society*, ed. Heather Strang and John Braithwaite (Cambridge: Cambridge University Press, 2001), 86-87.

[13]Verdeja, "Normative Theory of Reparations in Transitional Democracies," 178 (emphasis in original).

[14]Ibid., 179.

[15]Ibid. (emphasis in original).

[16]Ibid., 180 (emphasis in original).

[17]Ibid. (emphasis in original).

[18]Ibid., 181.

¹⁹Ibid.

²⁰Gary Bass, *"Jus Post Bellum,"* *Philosophy and Public Affairs* 32, no. 4 (Fall 2004): 408.

²¹Michael Walzer, *Just and Unjust Wars: A Moral Argument with Historical Illustrations,* 4th ed. (New York: Basic Books, 2006), 297. In making his argument for collectivist responsibility Walzer quotes J. Glenn Gray, who wrote eloquently in his World War II memoir about the responsibilities of citizen and soldier in times of war: "He is bound to reflect that his nation has given him refuge and sustenance, provided him with whatever education and property he calls his own. He belongs and will always belong to it in some sense no matter where he goes or how hard he seeks to alter his inheritance. The crimes, therefore, that his nation or one of its units commits cannot be indifferent to him. He shares the guilt as he shares the satisfaction in the generous deeds and worthy products of nation or army. Even if he did not consciously will them and was unable to prevent them, he cannot wholly escape responsibility for collective deeds" (*The Warriors: Reflections on Men in Battle* [New York: HarperCollins, 1967], 196-97).

²²Walzer, *Just and Unjust Wars,* 297.

²³Brian Orend, *The Morality of War* (Peterborough, Ontario: Broadview Press, 2006), 167 (emphasis in original); see also Orend's "Justice after War," *Ethics and International Affairs* 61, no. 1 (2002): 49.

²⁴The Network of Spiritual Progressives, "An Ethical Way to End the War in Iraq: Generosity Beats Domination as a Strategy for Homeland Security," and "What Is the NSP's Global Marshall Plan?" http://www.spiritualprogressives. org/, accessed June 15, 2007.

²⁵David Miller, *National Responsibility and Global Justice* (Oxford: Oxford University Press, 2007), 119, 131. See also Miller's "Collective Responsibility and International Inequality," in *Rawls's Law of Peoples: A Realistic Utopia?* ed. R. Martin and D. Reidy (Oxford: Blackwell, 2006), and Kok-Chor Tan, "National Responsibility, Reparations and Distributive Justice," *Critical Review of International Social and Political Philosophy* 11, no. 4 (December 2008): 449-64.

²⁶Pope John Paul II, *Reconciliatio et Paenitentia* (Reconciliation and Penance), no. 16, http://www.vatican.va/holy_father/john_paul_ii/apost_exhortations/ documents/hf_jp-ii_exh_02121984_reconciliatio-et-paenitentia_en.html.

²⁷Ibid.

²⁸See Melinda Roberts, "The Nonidentity Problem," *The Stanford Encyclopedia of Philosophy,* ed. Edward N. Zalta, http://plato.stanford.edu/entries/ nonidentity-problem/, accessed July 21, 2009.

²⁹Miller, *National Responsibility and Global Justice,* 161. See also Tan, "National Responsibility, Reparations and Distributive Justice," 452-53.

³⁰Orend, "Justice after War," 48-49.

³¹Bass, *"Jus Post Bellum,"* 409.

³²Cunneen, "Reparations and Restorative Justice," 94.

³³Walzer, *Just and Unjust Wars,* 292-301. See also Orend, "Justice after War," 53.

[34]Bass, "*Jus Post Bellum*," 404.

[35]Davida Kellogg, "*Jus Post Bellum*: The Importance of War Crimes Trials," *Parameters* 32, no. 3 (September 22, 2002): 88-89.

[36]Orend, *Morality of War*, 174.

[37]Bass, "*Jus Post Bellum*," 406.

[38]Orend, *Morality of War*, 174.

[39]See Larry May, *War Crimes and Just War* (Cambridge: Cambridge University Press, 2007), 235-300.

[40]Walzer, *Just and Unjust Wars*, 304.

[41]Ibid., 306-9, and Orend, *Morality of War*, 178.

[42]Orend, *Morality of War*, 179 (emphasis in original).

[43]Walzer, *Just and Unjust Wars*, 312.

[44]See Walzer, *Just and Unjust Wars*, 316; Orend, "Justice after War," 54; and May, *War Crimes and Just War*, 257-300.

[45]David Luban, "War Crimes: The Law of Hell," in *War: Essays in Political Philosophy*, ed. Larry May (Cambridge: Cambridge University Press, 2008), 282.

[46]Ibid., 282-83. See also Walzer, *Just and Unjust Wars*, 316-22, and Orend, *Morality of War*, 177-79.

[47]Charlie Savage, "Judge Drops Charges from Blackwater Deaths in Iraq," *New York Times*, January 1, 2010, and James Risen and Mark Mazzeti, "Blackwater Guards Tied to Secret Raids by the C.I.A.," *New York Times*, December 11, 2009.

[48]Luban, "War Crimes," 284.

[49]Bass, "*Jus Post Bellum*," 404.

[50]Orend, *Morality of War*, 172.

[51]Luban, "War Crimes," 286-87. To illustrate this idea he quotes Robert Jackson, the U.S. prosecutor at Nuremburg: "That four great nations, flushed with victory and stung with injury, stay the hand of vengeance and voluntarily submit their captive enemies to the judgment of the law, is one of the most significant tributes the Power ever has paid to Reason."

[52]Global Public Forum, "International Criminal Tribunal and Special Courts," http://www.globalpolicy.org/international-justice/international-criminal tribunals-and-special-courts.html; Suzannah Linton, "Cambodia, East Timor and Sierra Leone: Experiments in International Justice," *Criminal Law Forum* 12 (2001): 185-246. For more on the various kinds of post war justice mechanisms, including ad hoc international criminal tribunals, the International Criminal Court, "internationalized" courts, domestic trials, truth commissions, and traditional informal justice mechanisms, see Rachel Kerr and Eirin Mobekk, *Peace and Justice: Seeking Accountability after War* (Cambridge, UK: Polity Press, 2007); see also Garraway, "The Relevance of *Jus Post Bellum*: A Practitioner's Perspective," in *Jus Post Bellum: Towards a Law of Transition from Conflict to Peace*, ed. Carsten Stahn and Jann K. Kleffner (The Hague: T M C Asser Press, 2008),159-61; Mark Freeman and Dražan Djuki, "*Jus Post Bellum* and

Transitional Justice," in *Jus Post Bellum: Towards a Law of Transition from Conflict to Peace*, ed. Carsten Stahn and Jann K. Kleffner (The Hague: T M C Asser Press, 2008), 213-27.

[53]Current information regarding cases before the ICC is available at http://www.icc-cpi.int/.

[54]Cicero, *Pro Milone* 11. Quoted in Luban, "War Crimes," 266.

[55]Walzer, *Just and Unjust Wars*, 297. He prefaces this by saying, "Democracy is a way of distributing responsibility. . . . But that doesn't mean that all adult citizens share equally in the blame we assign for aggressive war. . . . Even in a perfect democracy, it cannot be said that every citizen is the author of every state policy, though every one of them can rightly be called to account."

[56]Ibid., 301.

[57]Ibid., 301-2.

[58]Orend, *Morality of War*, 177.

Chapter 6: The Restoration Phase

[1]Huso Kova, quoted in Chris Hedges, *War Is a Force That Gives Us Meaning* (New York: Anchor Books, 2002), 121.

[2]See James Robbin, *America's Role in Nation-Building: From Germany to Iraq* (Washington, DC: RAND, 2003).

[3]Brian Orend, *The Morality of War* (Peterborough, Ontario: Broadview Press, 2006), 210.

[4]Ibid.

[5]Thomas G. Wenski, "Toward a Responsible Transition in Iraq," United States Conference of Catholic Bishops, January 12, 2006, 1, http://www.usccb.org/comm/archives/2006/06-006.shtml.

[6]Anne Nivat, *The Wake of War: Encounters with the People of Iraq and Afghanistan* (Boston: Beacon Press, 2005), 91.

[7]Louis V. Iasiello, "*Jus Post Bellum*: The Moral Responsibilities of Victors in War," *Naval War College Review* 57, nos. 3/4 (Summer/Autumn 2004): 42.

[8]Kenneth Himes, "Intervention, Just War, and U.S. National Security," *Theological Studies* 65, no. 1 (March 2004): 156; see also Gary Bass, "*Jus Post Bellum*," *Philosophy and Public Affairs* 32, no. 4 (Fall 2004): 408, 412; Brian Orend, "*Jus Post Bellum*: A Just War Theory Perspective," in *Jus Post Bellum: Towards a Law of Transition from Conflict to Peace*, ed. Carsten Stahn and Jann K. Kleffner (The Hague: T M C Asser Press, 2008), 125-26.

[9]Edward LeRoy Long Jr., *Facing Terrorism: Responding as Christians* (Louisville, KY: Westminster John Knox Press, 2004); see 50-54, 81-85, at 83.

[10]Orend, "*Jus Post Bellum*: A Just War Theory Perspective," 45.

[11]Ibid., 45-46.

[12]Vivienne O'Connor, "Rule of Law and Human Rights Protections through Criminal Law Reform: Model Codes for Post-conflict Criminal Justice," *International Peacekeeping* 13, no. 4 (December 2006): 517. Similarly, international

law scholar Hurst Hannum writes, "No one would dispute that long-term capacity building and establishing the rule of law are essential to sustainable peace" (Hannum, "Peace versus Justice: Creating Rights as Well as Order Out of Chaos," *International Peacekeeping* 13, no. 4 [December 2006]: 590). See also Rama Mani, "Restoring Justice in the Aftermath of Conflict: Bridging the Gap between Theory and Practice," in *International Justice*, ed. Tony Coates (Burlington, VT: Ashgate Publishing, 2000), 264-69; and Iasiello, *"Jus Post Bellum,"* 39, 42.

[13]Rama Mani, *Beyond Retribution: Seeking Justice in the Shadows of War* (Cambridge: Polity Press, 2002), 56. See also Leslie Vinjamuri, "Order and Justice in Iraq," *Survival* 45, no. 4 (Winter 2003-2004): 136, 138.

[14]Rama Mani, "Contextualizing Police Reform: Security, the Rule of Law and Post-Conflict Peacebuilding," in *Peacebuilding and Police Reform*, ed. Tor Tanke Holme (London and Portland, OR: Frank Cass, 2000), 10.

[15]Mani, *Beyond Retribution*, 57. See also Rama Mani, "Balancing Peace with Justice in the Aftermath of Violent Conflict," *Development* 48, no. 3 (2005): 27.

[16]Graham Day, "After War, Send Blue Force," *Christian Science Monitor*, May 30, 2001, 11.

[17]Ibid.

[18]Graham Day, "'Policekeeping' Critical to Rebuilding Iraq," *Mondial* (May 2003): 3-4; and Graham Day and Christopher Freeman, "Policekeeping Is the Key: Rebuilding the Internal Security Architecture of Postwar Iraq," *International Affairs* 79, no. 2 (2003): 299-313. For a helpful grid of definitions for peacekeeping, peacebuilding, and so on, see Roland Paris, *At War's End: Building Peace after Civil Conflict* (Cambridge: Cambridge University Press, 2004), 38-39.

[19]Day, "'Policekeeping' Critical to Rebuilding Iraq," 4; Day and Freeman, "Policekeeping Is the Key," 305, attributing this insight to Michael Dziedzic in *Policing the New World Disorder: Peace Operations and Public Security* (Washington, DC: National Defense University Press, 1998), see also Iasiello, *"Jus Post Bellum,"* 42-43, where he mentions phases, starting with "protectorship" during the initial stage of providing immediate security; and Robert W. Williams and Dan Caldwell, *"Jus Post Bellum*: Just War Theory and the Principles of Just Peace," *International Studies Perspectives* 7, no. 4 (2006): 318, where they write, "The victor must, in the first place, restore order . . . [which is] an essential foundation for the restoration of human rights."

[20]Graham Day and Christopher Freeman, "Operationalizing the Responsibility to Protect—The Policekeeping Approach," *Global Governance* 11, no. 2 (April/June 2005): 142.

[21]Mani, "Balancing Peace with Justice in the Aftermath of Violent Conflict," 30; see also Mani, "Contextualizing Police Reform," 10, 17.

[22]Mani, "Contextualizing Police Reform," 12.

[23]Day and Freeman, "Policekeeping Is the Key," 304-5.

[24]Hannum, "Peace versus Justice," 589. See also Rama Mani, "Rebuilding

an Inclusive Political Community after War," *Security Dialogue* 36, no. 4 (December 2005): 515.

[25]Reforming state institutions, including the police, is referred to as vetting or lustration, which political scientist Jens Meierhenrich argues "must factor in considerations of justice after war, or *jus post bellum*" (Jens Meierhenrich, "The Ethics of Lustration," *Ethics & International Affairs* 20, no. 1 [April 2006]: 102).

[26]Mani, *Beyond Retribution*, 58.

[27]Ibid., 61-62.

[28]Ibid., 63; also, Mani, "Balancing Peace with Justice in the Aftermath of Violent Conflict," 29-30; and "Contextualizing Police Reform," 20, 26.

[29]Day and Freeman, "Policekeeping Is the Key," 309.

[30]John Kleinig, *The Ethics of Policing* (Cambridge: Cambridge University Press, 1996), 24. Similarly, David H. Bayley writes, "The 1990s are a watershed period in policing because very different paradigms are competing for the hearts and minds of police officers" (*Police for the Future* [New York: Oxford University Press, 1994], 119). For more on models of policing considered from a Christian theological and ethical perspective, see Tobias L. Winright, "The Challenge of Policing: An Analysis in Christian Social Ethics" (PhD diss., University of Notre Dame, 2002); and Winright, "Community Policing as a Paradigm for International Relations," in *Just Policing, Not War: An Alternative Response to World Violence*, ed. Gerald W. Schlabach (Collegeville, MN: Liturgical Press, 2007), 130-52.

[31]Joycelyn M. Pollock-Byrne, *Ethics in Crime and Justice: Dilemmas and Decisions* (Pacific Grove, CA: Brooks/Cole, 1989), 73. See Kleinig, *Ethics of Policing*, 24-25, 283, see n31.

[32]Egon Bittner, *The Functions of the Police in Modern Society* (Cambridge, MA: Oelgeschlager, Gunn and Hain, 1980), 52. Of course, as Michael S. Sherry makes clear, the military metaphor has impacted "every realm of American life—politics and foreign policy, economics and technology, culture and social relations" (*In the Shadow of War: The United States Since the 1930s* [New Haven, CT: Yale University Press, 1995], x). For a book written for a popular audience that casts policing through a military lens, see Charles W. Sasser, *Shoot to Kill: Cops Who Have Used Deadly Force* (New York: Simon and Schuster, 1994), vii, xv, 12, 233.

[33]Jerome H. Skolnick and James J. Fyfe, *Above the Law: Police and Excessive Use of Force* (New York: Free Press, 1993), 113. See Kleinig, *Ethics of Policing*, 283n31.

[34]Peter Scharf and Arnold Binder, *The Badge and the Bullet: Police Use of Deadly Force* (New York: Praeger, 1983), 31, 32, 38.

[35]Bittner, *Functions of the Police in Modern Society*, 53.

[36]Vance McLaughlin, *Police and the Use of Force: The Savannah Study* (Westport, CT: Praeger, 1992), 1. Interestingly, McLaughlin acknowledges that police "seldom use force" in the "vast majority of police-citizen contacts," but

he believes that force is central and "remains an ongoing concern for both police and public" (2). See also Scharf and Binder, *Badge and the Bullet*, 38.

[37]Stuart A. Scheingold, *The Politics of Law and Order: Street Crime and Public Policy* (New York: Longman, 1984), 101-2. In this vein, David Bayley asserts that "the defining task [in policing] is the application of physical force within a community" (*Patterns of Policing: A Comparative Analysis* [New Brunswick, NJ: Rutgers University Press, 1985], 37). Similarly, McLaughlin writes, "[Police] routinely use force to carry out their role as enforcers—the use of force is inherent in the profession" (*Police and the Use of Force*, 1).

[38]Victor Kappeler, Mark Blumberg, and Gary Potter, *The Mythology of Crime and Criminal Justice* (Prospect Heights, IL: Waveland Press, 1993), 131.

[39]Paul Chevigny, *Edge of the Knife: Police Violence in the Americas* (New York: New Press, 1995), 255-56. See also Scheingold, *The Politics of Law and Order*, 101; and Skolnick and Fyfe, *Above the Law*, 114.

[40]Bittner, *Functions of the Police in Modern Society*, 47-49. See also Kleinig, *Ethics of Policing*, 24; and Joseph Betz, "Police Violence," in *Moral Issues in Police Work*, ed. Frederick A. Elliston and Michael Feldberg (Totowa, NJ: Rowman & Allanheld, 1985), 181-82. When police view the public as a whole cynically and suspiciously, according to Christopher Daskalos, "the chances of police misuse of force are greatly increased" and the temptation to use excessive force is "exacerbated" (Christopher Daskalos, "Current Issues in Policing," in *The Past, Present, and Future of Criminal Justice*, ed. Brendan Maguire and Polly F. Radosh [Dix Hills, NY: General Hall, 1996], 67).

[41]Skolnick and Fyfe, *Above the Law*, xviii. To be sure, it would be helpful and more persuasive if empirical data supporting such a causal link could be provided.

[42]Ibid., 12-13, 115-16. The 1991 report of the Christopher Commission (Independent Commission on the Los Angeles Police Department) corroborates this view when it suggests "a strongly enforcement-oriented agency can enhance the proclivity of aggressive officers to engage in proactive exercises that include uses of excessive force" (cited in William A. Geller and Hans Toch, "Understanding and Controlling Police Abuse of Force," in *Police Violence: Understanding and Controlling Police Abuse of Force*, ed. William A. Geller and Hans Toch [New Haven, CT: Yale University Press, 1996], 295).

[43]Kleinig, *Ethics of Policing*, 117.

[44]Ibid., 27.

[45]Ibid., 293; see n3.

[46]Ibid., 29.

[47]Ibid., 96.

[48]For more on community policing, see Robert R. Friedmann, *Community Policing: Comparative Perspectives and Prospects* (New York: St. Martin's Press, 1992); Gene Stephens, "Peace in the 'Hood,'" in *Controversial Issues in Policing*, ed. James D. Sewell (Needham Heights, MA: Allyn & Bacon, 1999), 189-205; Gene Stephens, "The Future of Policing: From a War Model to a Peace Model,"

in Maguire and Radosh, *Past, Present, and Future of Criminal Justice*, 77-93; Steven R. Donziger, ed., *The Real War on Crime: The Report of the National Criminal Justice Commission* (New York: HarperCollins Publishers, 1996), esp. chap. 7, "Toward a New Model of Policing"; Office of Community Oriented Policing Services (COPS), U.S. Department of Justice, "What Is Community Policing?" A critical assessment of community policing may be found in William G. Doerner, "War on Crime," in *Controversial Issues in Policing*, ed. James D. Sewell (Needham Heights, MA: Allyn & Bacon, 1999).

[49]See Brian Orend, "Justice after War," *Ethics and International Affairs* 61, no. 1 (2002): 49-50.

[50]See Orend, *Morality of War*, 168-69.

[51]Bass, "*Jus Post Bellum*," 387.

[52]Ibid., 390.

[53]Orend, "Justice after War," 51.

[54]Orend, *Morality of War*, 169 (emphasis in original).

[55]Ibid., 170.

[56]Orend, "Justice after War," 51.

[57]Orend, *Morality of War*, 168-70.

[58]See Robert S. Litwak, *Regime Change: U.S. Strategy through the Prism of 9/11* (Washington, DC: Woodrow Wilson Press, 2007); available through Johns Hopkins University Press (Baltimore, MD).

[59]Orend, *Morality of War*, 190-91.

[60]Niall Ferguson, *Empire: The Rise and Demise of the British World Order and the Lessons for Global Power* (New York: Basic Books, 2002), and *Colossus: The Rise and Fall of the American Empire* (New York: Basic Books, 2004). See also Orend, *Morality of War*, 190-92.

[61]Orend, *Morality of War*, 212.

[62]David Cortright, "A Hard Look at Iraq Sanctions," *Nation*, December 3, 2001, http://www.thenation.com/doc/20011203/cortright. For an ethical evaluation of sanctions from a just war perspective, see Joseph E. Capizzi and Tobias Winright, "The 'Slow War' Against Iraq: A Moral Analysis," *Josephinum Journal of Theology* 8, no. 1 (Winter/Spring 2001): 27-42.

[63]Orend, *Morality of War*, 213-14.

[64]Ibid., 215 (emphasis in original).

[65]Ibid., 216-17 (emphasis in original).

[66]Ibid., 197.

[67]Ibid.

[68]Ibid., 33. See 33-37 for the extended discussion of the "minimally just state."

[69]The Catholic bishops at the Second Vatican Council defined the common good as: "the sum total of social conditions which allow people, either as groups or as individuals, to reach their fulfillment more fully and more easily" (*Gaudium et Spes*, no. 26, in *The Documents of Vatican II*, ed. Walter M. Abbot, S.J. [Piscataway, NJ: New Century Publishers, 1966]); see also *Catechism of the*

Catholic Church (New York: Image/Doubleday), pars. 1905-1912.

[70]Daniel Mark Nelson, *The Priority of Prudence: Virtue and Natural Law in Thomas Aquinas and the Implications for Modern Ethics* (University Park: Pennsylvania State University Press, 1992), ix, 78.

[71]Thomas Aquinas, *Summa Theologica*, trans. Fathers of the English Dominican Province, vol. 3 (New York: Benziger Bros., 1948), IIa-IIae, Q. 55.

[72]Michael Walzer, *Arguing about War* (New Haven, CT: Yale University Press, 2004), 6; Nelson, *Priority of Prudence*, ix. For more on *The Prince* as satire, see Garrett Mattingly, "Machiavelli's *Prince*: Political Science or Political Satire?" *American Scholar* (1958): 482-91.

[73]Paul J. Wadell, *Happiness and the Christian Moral Life: An Introduction to Christian Ethics* (Lanham, MD: Rowman & Littlefield Publishers, 2008), xiii, 166, 183. See Albert R. Jonsen and Stephen Toulmin, *The Abuse of Casuistry: A History of Moral Reasoning* (Berkeley: University of California Press, 1988), 130-31.

[74]Pope Paul VI, *Populorum Progressio*, nos. 76, 87.

[75]See Greg Behrman, *The Most Noble Adventure: The Marshall Plan and the Time When America Helped Save Europe* (New York: Free Press, 2007); Aaron Forsberg, *America and the Japanese Miracle: The Cold War Context of Japan's Postwar Economic Revival, 1950-1960* (Chapel Hill: University of North Carolina Press, 2000); and John W. Dower, *Embracing Defeat: Japan in the Wake of World War II* (New York: W. W. Norton and Co., 1999).

[76]Behrman, *Most Notable Adventure*, 4-5.

[77]Diana Lin, "Japanese Economic Takeoff," http://www.iun.edu/~hisdcl/h207_2002/jecontakeoff.htm.

[78]Orend, *Morality of War*, 194-95.

[79]Iasiello, "*Jus Post Bellum*," 39.

[80]Ibid., 45.

[81]Defense Health Board Task Force on Mental Health, "An Achievable Vision: Report of the Department of Defense Task Force on Mental Health," http://www.ha.osd.mil/dhb/mhtf/MHTF-Report-Final.pdf (accessed June 15, 2007). See also Charles Hoge et al., "Combat Duty in Iraq and Afghanistan, Mental Health Problems, and Barriers to Care," *New England Journal of Medicine* 351 (July 1, 2004): 13-22.

[82]Greg Zoraya, "Soldiers' Divorce Rates Up Sharply," *USA Today*, June 7, 2005; http://www.usatoday.com/news/nation/2005-06-07-soldier-divorces_x.htm; Jia-Rui Chong, "Percentage of Veterans with Mental Health Problems Jumps Dramatically," *Los Angeles Times*, July 16, 2009, http://latimesblogs.latimes.com/booster_shots/2009/07/veterans-mental-health-veterans-affairs-study-.html; Polly Curtis, "Iraq Veterans Suffer Stress and Alcoholism," *Guardian*, August 3, 2007, http://www.guardian.co.uk/uk/2007/aug/03/health.military.

[83]Quoted in Joseph J. Fahey, *War and the Christian Conscience: Where Do You Stand?* (Maryknoll, NY: Orbis Books, 2005), 92.

[84]Timothy P. Broglio, "Soldiers Home: Our Duty to Returning Veterans," *America* 201, no. 12 (November 2, 2009): 21-22.

[85] Mark Allman, "Postwar Justice," *America* 193, no. 11 (October 17, 2005): 9-13; and Tobias Winright, "Compunction over Cluster Bombs," *Cresset* 70, no. 1 (September 2006): 45-47.

[86] This section on depleted uranium is taken from Allman, "Postwar Justice."

[87] Dan Fahey, "The Use of Depleted Uranium in the 2003 Iraq War: An Initial Assessment of Information and Policies," http://www.wise-uranium.org/pdf/duiq03.pdf.

[88] Mark J. Allman, *Who Would Jesus Kill? War, Peace, and the Christian Tradition* (Winona, MN: Anselm Academic, 2008), 231-32.

[89] Virgil Wiebe, "Footprints of Death: Cluster Bombs as Indiscriminate Weapons under International Humanitarian Law," *Michigan Journal of International Law* 22, no. 1 (2000): 91. Rob Nixon asserts that the United States has used cluster bombs in more conflicts than any other nation; see Rob Nixon, "Of Land Mines and Cluster Bombs," *Cultural Critique* 67, no. 3 (Fall 2007): 164.

[90] Paul Wiseman, "Special Report: Cluster Bombs Kill in Iraq, Even after Shelling Ends," *USA Today*, December 11, 2003, 1a; Nixon, "Of Land Mines and Cluster Bombs," 166.

[91] For the details on cluster munitions, we are drawing from Barbara Hilkert Andolsen, "'The Vision Still Has Its Time': A Social-Ethical Cryptanalysis of the Signs of the Times," *Proceedings of the Annual Convention of the Catholic Theological Society of America* 57 (2002): 45-46; Thomas J. Herthel, "On the Chopping Block: Cluster Munitions and the Law of War," *Air Force Law Review* 51, no. 1 (2001): 234-35; Nixon, "Of Land Mines and Cluster Bombs," 168; Claire Schaeffer-Duffy, "War's Lethal Leftovers," *National Catholic Reporter*, August 2, 2002, 7-9; Wiebe, "Footprints of Death," 89-90, 111; Virgil Wiebe and Titus Peachey, "War's Insidious Litter: Cluster Bombs," *Christian Science Monitor*, June 9, 1999, 11; and Wiseman, "Cluster Bombs Kill in Iraq," 1a, 6a-7a.

[92] Nixon, "Of Land Mines and Cluster Bombs," 165.

[93] Schaeffer-Duffy, "War's Lethal Leftovers," 8; Wiebe, "Footprints of Death," 95-96.

[94] Wiebe, "Footprints of Death," 87; Nixon, "Of Land Mines and Cluster Bombs," 172.

[95] Donald Steinberg, "U.S. Should Ban Bomblets and Get on the Right Side of History," *Christian Science Monitor*, July 30, 2007, 9; Curt Goering, "A Call to Abolish Cluster Bombs," *Christian Science Monitor*, October 23, 2006, 9; Lucy Fielder, "Injuries in Lebanon Revive Bid to Ban Cluster Bombs," *Christian Science Monitor*, November 7, 2006, 11.

[96] Wiseman, "Cluster Bombs Kill in Iraq," 10a.

[97] Ibid.; Wiebe, "Footprints of Death," 92, gives slightly higher estimates of between 9 and 27 million unexploded submunitions.

[98] Michael Weisskopf, "The Bombs That Keep on Killing," *Time*, May 12,

2003, 43. This section on cluster munitions is based on Tobias Winright, "The Morality of Cluster Munitions," *Studies in Christian Ethics* 22, no. 3 (August 2009): 357-81, which offers an ethical critique—employing the *jus in bello* criteria of discrimination, proportionality, and the framework of double-effect reasoning—of the design and use of these weapons.

[99]Fielder, "Injuries in Lebanon," 11. The two reports, "Fatal Footprint: The Global Impact of Cluster Munitions" (November 2006), and "Global Impact: The Fatal Footprint of Cluster Munitions on People and Communities" (May 2007), appear on Handicap International's website, http://www.handicap-international.org.uk/.

[100]An English text of the Convention on Cluster Munitions is available at http://www.clustermunitionsdublin.ie/pdf/ENGLISHfinaltext.pdf.

Conclusion

[1]George A. Lopez, "Just? Unjust?" *Sojourners* 33, no. 5 (May 2004): 24.

[2]Anne Nivat, *The Wake of War: Encounters with the People of Iraq and Afghanistan* (Boston: Beacon Press, 2005), 176.

[3]Ibid., 180.

[4]Rob Nixon, "Of Land Mines and Cluster Bombs," *Cultural Critique* 67, no. 3 (Fall 2007): 166-67, citing Robert Fisk, "Wailing Children, the Wounded, the Dead," *Independent*, April 3, 2003, 13.

[5]Emiliano Huet-Vaughn, "Returning Soldiers' Mental Health Neglected," *National Catholic Reporter*, May 25, 2007, 7-8. Also see Bobby Muller, "A Broken Contract: Returning Service Members Deserve Better," *America* 196, no. 19 (May 28, 2007): 9-10, 12.

[6]Huet-Vaughn, "Returning Soldiers' Mental Health Neglected," 7.

[7]Charles E. Curran, "The Moral Methodology of the Bishops' Pastoral," in *Catholics and Nuclear War: A Commentary on* The Challenge of Peace, ed. Philip J. Murnion (New York: Crossroad, 1983), 53-54.

[8]National Conference of Catholic Bishops, *The Challenge of Peace: God's Promise and Our Response* (Washington, DC: United States Catholic Conference, 1983), pars. 8-9; see also pars. 10-12. See also National Conference of Catholic Bishops, *Economic Justice for All: Pastoral Letter on Catholic Social Teaching and the U.S. Economy* (Washington, DC: United States Catholic Conference, 1986), par. 134. The bishops cite the Second Vatican Council, *Gaudium et Spes*, in *The Documents of Vatican II*, ed. Walter M. Abbott, S.J. (Piscataway, NJ: New Century Publishers, 1966), no. 1, fn. 2.

[9]Curran, "Moral Methodology of the Bishops' Pastoral," 55.

[10]Richard R. Gaillardetz, *By What Authority? A Primer on Scripture, the Magisterium, and the Sense of the Faithful* (Collegeville, MN: Liturgical Press, 2003), 99-100.

[11]*Gaudium et Spes*, no. 90.

[12]Ibid., no. 27.

[13]John L. Allen Jr., *The Future Church: How Ten Trends Are Revolutionizing the Catholic Church* (New York: Doubleday, 2009), 130.

[14]National Conference of Catholic Bishops, "Resolution on Southeast Asia" (November 1971), in *Quest for Justice: A Compendium of Statements of the United States Catholic Bishops on the Political and Social Order 1966-1980*, ed. J. Brian Benestad and Francis J. Butler (Washington, DC: United States Catholic Conference, 1981), 78.

[15]*Gaudium et Spes*, no. 4.

[16]M. C. Vanhengel, O.P., and J. Peters, O.C.D., "Signs of the Times," *Concilium* 25 (Ramsey, NJ: Paulist Press, 1967): 145.

[17]Gareth Evans, "The Responsibility to Protect: Moving towards a Shared Consensus," in *The Responsibility to Protect: Ethical and Theological Reflections*, ed. Semegnish Asfaw et al. (Geneva: World Council of Churches, 2005), 5.

[18]Hugo Slim, "The Christian Responsibility to Protect," in Asfaw, *Responsibility to Protect*, 21.

SELECTED BIBLIOGRAPHY

Allman, Mark J. "Postwar Justice." *America* 193, no. 11 (October 17, 2005): 9-13.

———. *Who Would Jesus Kill? War, Peace, and the Christian Tradition.* Winona, MN: Anselm Academic, 2008.

———, and Tobias Winright. "*Jus Post Bellum*: Extending the Just War Theory." In *Faith and Public Life*, College Theology Society Annual Vol. 53. Edited by William J. Collinge, 241-64. Maryknoll, NY: Orbis Books, 2008.

Asfaw, Semegnish, Guillermo Kerber, and Peter Weiderud, eds. *The Responsibility to Protect: Ethical and Theological Reflections.* Geneva: World Council of Churches, 2005.

Baer, Helmut David, and Joseph E. Capizzi. "Just War Theory and the Problem of International Politics: On the Central Role of Just Intention." *Journal of the Society of Christian Ethics* 26, no. 1 (Spring/Summer 2006): 163-75.

Bainton, Roland H. *Christian Attitudes toward War and Peace: A Historical Survey and Critical Reevaluation.* Nashville: Abingdon Press, 1960.

Bass, Gary J. "*Jus Post Bellum.*" *Philosophy and Public Affairs* 32, no. 4 (Fall 2004): 384-412.

Bell, Daniel M., Jr. *Just War as Christian Discipleship: Recentering the Tradition in the Church Rather Than the State.* Grand Rapids: Brazos Press, 2009.

Bellamy, Alex J. "The Responsibilities of Victory: *Jus Post Bellum* and the Just War." *Review of International Studies* 34, no. 4 (2008): 601-25.

Benedict XVI. "The Human Person, the Heart of Peace." World Day of Peace Message 2007, http://www.vatican.va/holy_father/benedict_xvi/messages/peace/documents/hf_ben-xvi_mes_20061208_xl-world-day-peace_en.html.

Boxill, Bernard. "The Morality of Reparation." In *Today's Moral Problems*, 2nd ed. Edited by Richard A. Wasserstrom, 255-62. New York: MacMillan, 1979.

Caldwell, Dan. "*Jus Post Bellum*: Just War Theory and the Principles of Just Peace." *International Studies Perspectives* 7, no. 4 (2006): 309-20.

Capizzi, Joseph E., and Tobias Winright. "The 'Slow War' Against Iraq: A Moral Analysis." *Josephinum Journal of Theology* 8, no. 1 (Winter/Spring 2001): 27-42.

Cavanaugh, William T. *Torture and Eucharist: Theology, Politics, and the Body of Christ.* Oxford, UK: Blackwell Publishers, 1998.

Christiansen, Drew. "After Sept. 11: Catholic Teaching on Peace and War." *Origins* 32, no. 3 (May 30, 2002): 33, 35-40.

Clough, David L., and Brian Stiltner. *Faith and Force: A Christian Debate about War*. Washington, DC: Georgetown University Press, 2007.

Cunneen, Chris. "Reparations and Restorative Justice: Responding to the Gross Violation of Human Rights." In *Restorative Justice and Civil Society*. Edited by Heather Strang and John Braithwaite, 83-98. Cambridge: Cambridge University Press, 2001.

Day, Graham. "After War, Send Blue Force." *Christian Science Monitor*, May 30, 2001, 11.

———. "'Policekeeping' Critical to Rebuilding Iraq." *Mondial* (May 2003): 3-4.

———, and Christopher Freeman. "Operationalizing the Responsibility to Protect—The Policekeeping Approach." *Global Governance* 11, no. 2 (April/June 2005): 139-42.

———. "Policekeeping Is the Key: Rebuilding the Internal Security Architecture of Postwar Iraq." *International Affairs* 79, no. 2 (2003): 299-313.

Dolan, Chris J. *In War We Trust: The Bush Doctrine and the Pursuit of Just War*. Aldershot, UK: Ashgate Publishing, 2005.

Evans, Mark. "Balancing Peace, Justice and Sovereignty in *Jus Post Bellum*: The Case of 'Just Occupation.'" *Millennium: Journal of International Studies* 36, no. 3 (2008): 533-54.

———. *Just War Theory: A Reappraisal*. New York: Palgrave/Macmillan, 2005.

———. "Moral Responsibilities and the Conflicting Demands of *Jus Post Bellum*." *Ethics and International Affairs* 23, no. 2 (Summer 2009): 147-64.

Fahey, Joseph J. *War and the Christian Conscience: Where Do You Stand?* Maryknoll, NY: Orbis Books, 2005.

Gheciu, Alexandra, and Jennifer Welsh, eds. *Postwar Justice and the Responsibility to Rebuild*. A Special Section of *Ethics and International Affairs* 23, no. 2 (Summer 2009).

Govier, Trudy. "War's Aftermath." In *War: Essays in Political Philosophy*. Edited by Larry May, 229-48. Cambridge: Cambridge University Press, 2008.

Hehir, J. Bryan. "Kosovo: A War of Values and the Values of War." *America* 180, no. 17 (May 15, 1999): 7-12.

Himes, Kenneth. "Intervention, Just War, and U.S. National Security." *Theological Studies* 65, no. 1 (March 2004): 141-57.

Iasiello, Louis V. "*Jus Post Bellum*: The Moral Responsibilities of Victors in War." *Naval War College Review* 57, nos. 3/4 (Summer/Autumn 2004): 11-15.

John Paul II. "No Peace Without Justice, No Justice Without Forgiveness." World Day of Peace Message 2002. http://www.vatican.va/holy_father/john_paul_ii/messages/peace/documents/hf_jp-ii_mes_20011211_xxxv-world-day-for-peace_en.html.

————. "Principles Underlying a Stance toward Unjust Aggressors." *Origins* 22, no. 34 (January 28, 1993): 583-87.

Johnson, James Turner. *Morality and Contemporary Warfare*. New Haven, CT: Yale University Press, 1999.

————. *The Quest for Peace: Three Moral Traditions in Western Cultural History*. Princeton, NJ: Princeton University Press, 1987.

Kellogg, Davida. "*Jus Post Bellum*: The Importance of War Crimes Trials." *Parameters* 32, no. 3 (September 22, 2002): 87-100.

Khatchadourian, Haig. "Compensation and Reparation as Forms of Compensatory Justice." *Metaphilosophy* 37, nos. 3-4 (July 2006): 429-48.

Kleinig, John. *The Ethics of Policing*. Cambridge: Cambridge University Press, 1996.

Koeman, Annalisa. "A Realistic and Effective Constraint on the Resort to Force? Pre-commitment to *Jus in bello* and *Jus post bellum* as Part of the Criterion of Right Intention." *Journal of Military Ethics* 6, no. 3 (2007): 198-220.

Langan, John. "An Imperfectly Just War." *Commonweal* 118, no. 11 (June 1, 1991): 361-65. Also available in *War in the Twentieth Century: Sources in Theological Ethics*. Edited by Richard Brian Miller. Louisville, KY: Westminster/John Knox Press, 1992.

Luban, David. "War Crimes: The Law of Hell." In *War: Essays in Political Philosophy*. Edited by Larry May, 266-88. Cambridge: Cambridge University Press, 2008.

Maguire, Daniel C. *The Horrors We Bless: Rethinking the Just-War Legacy*. Minneapolis: Fortress Press, 2007.

Mani, Rama. "Balancing Peace with Justice in the Aftermath of Violent Conflict." *Development* 48, no. 3 (2005): 25-34.

————. *Beyond Retribution: Seeking Justice in the Shadows of War*. Cambridge: Polity Press, 2002.

————. "Contextualizing Police Reform: Security, the Rule of Law and Post-Conflict Peacebuilding." In *Peacebuilding and Police Reform*. Edited by Tor Tanke Holme, 9-26. London: Frank Cass, 2000.

————. "Restoring Justice in the Aftermath of Conflict: Bridging the Gap between Theory and Practice." In *International Justice*. Edited by Tony Coates, 264-99. Burlington, VT: Ashgate Publishing, 2000.

May, Larry, ed. *War: Essays in Political Philosophy*. Cambridge: Cambridge University Press, 2008.

————. *War Crimes and Just War*. Cambridge: Cambridge University Press, 2007.

McCready, Doug. "Ending the War Right: *Jus Post Bellum* and the Just War Tradition." *Journal of Military Ethics* 8, no. 1 (2009): 66-78.

Miller, David. *National Responsibility and Global Justice*. Oxford: Oxford University Press, 2007.

Mollendorf, Darrel. "Jus ex Bello." *Journal of Political Philosophy* 16, no. 2 (2008): 123-36.

National Conference of Catholic Bishops. *The Challenge of Peace: God's Promise and Our Response.* Washington, DC: United States Catholic Conference, 1983.

Nivat, Ann. *The Wake of War: Encounters with the People of Iraq and Afghanistan.* Boston: Beacon Press, 2005.

Nixon, Rob. "Of Land Mines and Cluster Bombs." *Cultural Critique* 67, no. 3 (Fall 2007): 160-74.

O'Donovan, Oliver. *The Just War Revisited.* Cambridge: Cambridge University Press, 2003.

Orend, Brian. "*Jus Post Bellum.*" *Journal of Social Philosophy* 31, no. 1 (Spring 2000): 117-37.

———. "*Jus Post Bellum*: A Just War Theory Perspective." In *Jus Post Bellum: Towards a Law of Transition from Conflict to Peace.* Edited by Carsten Stahn and Jann K. Kleffner, 31-52. The Hague: TMC Asser Press, 2008.

———. "Justice after War." *Ethics and International Affairs* 61, no. 1 (2002): 43-57.

———. "Kant's Just War Theory." *Journal of the History of Philosophy* 37, no. 2 (1999): 323-53.

———. *The Morality of War.* Peterborough, Ontario: Broadview Press, 2006.

———. *War and International Justice: A Kantian Perspective.* Waterloo, Ontario: Wilfred Laurier University Press, 2000.

Pabst, Adrian. "Can There Be a Just War without a Just Peace?" *New Blackfriars* 88, no. 1018 (November 2007): 722-38.

Pontifical Council for Justice and Peace. *Compendium of the Social Doctrine of the Church.* Washington, DC: United States Conference of Catholic Bishops, 2004.

Portier, William L. "Are We Really Serious When We Ask God to Deliver Us from War? The Catechism and the Challenge of Pope John Paul II." *Communio* 23, no. 1 (Spring 1996): 47-63.

Ramsey, Paul. *The Just War: Force and Political Responsibility.* New York: Charles Scribner's Sons, 1968.

———. *Speak Up for Just War or Pacifism: A Critique of the United Methodist Bishops' Letter "In Defense of Creation."* University Park: Pennsylvania State University Press, 1988.

Recchia, Stefano. "Just and Unjust Postwar Reconstruction: How Much External Interference Can Be Justified?" *Ethics and International Affairs* 23, no. 2 (Summer 2009): 165-87.

Rigby, Andrew. "Forgiveness and Reconciliation in *Jus Post Bellum.*" In *Just War Theory: A Reappraisal.* Edited by Mark Evans, 177-200. New York: Palgrave/Macmillan, 2005.

Russell, Fredrick H. *The Just War in the Middle Ages.* Cambridge: Cambridge University Press, 1975, 1977.

Schuck, Michael. "When the Shooting Stops: Missing Elements in Just War Theory." *Christian Century* 111, no. 30 (October 26, 1994): 982-83.

Sharma, Serena K. "Reconsidering the Jus ad Bellum/Jus in Bello Distinction." In *Jus Post Bellum: Towards a Law of Transition from Conflict to Peace*. Edited by Carsten Stahn and Jann K. Kleffner, 9-30. The Hague: TMC Asser Press, 2008.

Stahn, Carsten. "The Future of Jus Post Bellum." In *Jus Post Bellum: Towards a Law of Transition from Conflict to Peace*. Edited by Carsten Stahn and Jann K. Kleffner, 231-38. The Hague: TMC Asser Press, 2008.

———. "Jus Post Bellum: Mapping the Discipline(s)." In *Jus Post Bellum: Towards a Law of Transition from Conflict to Peace*. Edited by Carsten Stahn and Jann K. Kleffner, 93-114. The Hague: TMC Asser Press, 2008.

———, and Jann K. Kleffner, eds. *Jus Post Bellum: Towards a Law of Transition from Conflict to Peace*. The Hague: TMC Asser Press, 2008.

Stassen, Glen, ed. *Just Peacemaking: The New Paradigm for the Ethics of Peace and War*. New ed. Cleveland: Pilgrim Press, 2008.

Tan, Kok-Chor. "National Responsibility, Reparations and Distributive Justice." *Critical Review of International Social and Political Philosophy* 11, no. 4 (December 2008): 449-64.

Verdeja, Ernesto. "A Normative Theory of Reparations in Transitional Democracies." In *Genocide's Aftermath: Responsibility and Repair*. Edited by Claudia Card and Armen T. Marsoobian, 166-85. Malden, MA: Blackwell, 2007.

Walzer, Michael. *Arguing about War*. New Haven: Yale University Press, 2004.

———. *Just and Unjust Wars: A Moral Argument with Historical Illustrations*. 3rd ed. New York: Basic Books, 2000.

Wenski, Thomas G. "Toward a Responsible Transition in Iraq." United States Catholic Conference of Bishops. January 12, 2006. http://www.usccb.org/comm/archives/2006/06-006.shtml.

Wiebe, Virgil. "Footprints of Death: Cluster Bombs as Indiscriminate Weapons under International Humanitarian Law." *Michigan Journal of International Law* 22, no. 1 (2000): 85-168.

Wink, Walter. *Engaging the Powers: Discernment and Resistance in a World of Domination*. Minneapolis: Fortress Press, 1992.

———. *When the Powers Fall: Reconciliation in the Healing of Nations*. Minneapolis: Fortress Press, 1998.

Winright, Tobias. "The Challenge of Policing: An Analysis in Christian Social Ethics." PhD diss., University of Notre Dame, 2002.

———. "Community Policing as a Paradigm for International Relations." In *Just Policing, Not War: An Alternative Response to World Violence*. Edited by Gerald Schlabach, 130-52. Collegeville, MN: Liturgical Press, 2007.

———. "Compunction over Cluster Bombs." *The Cresset* 70, no. 1 (September 2006): 45-47.

———. "Just Cause and Preemptive Strikes in the War on Terrorism: Insights from a Just-Policing Perspective." *Journal of the Society of Christian Ethics* 26, no. 2 (Fall/Winter 2006): 157-81.

———. "The Liturgy as a Basis for Catholic Identity, Just War Theory, and the Presumption against War." In *Catholic Identity and the Laity*, College Theology Society Annual Volume 54. Edited by Tim Muldoon, 134-51. Maryknoll, NY: Orbis Books, 2009.

———. "The Morality of Cluster Munitions." *Studies in Christian Ethics* 22, no. 3 (August 2009): 357-81.

———. "Pacifism in Roman Catholicism." In *The Encyclopedia of Religion and War*. Edited by Gabriel Palmer-Fernandez, 379-84. New York: Berkshire/Routledge, 2004.

Yoder, John H. "How Many Ways Are There to Think Morally about War?" *Journal of Law and Religion* 11, no. 1 (1994-95): 83-107.

———. "Just-War Tradition: Is It Credible?" *Christian Century* 108, no. 9 (March 13, 1991): 295-98.

———. *Nevertheless: The Varieties and Shortcomings of Religious Pacifism.* Scottdale, PA: Herald Press, 1971.

———. *The Original Revolution: Essays on Christian Pacifism.* Scottdale, PA: Herald Press, 1971.

———. *When War Is Unjust: Being Honest in Just-War Thinking.* 2nd ed. Maryknoll, NY: Orbis Books, 1996.

INDEX